# garden photography

## a professional guide

Tony Cooper

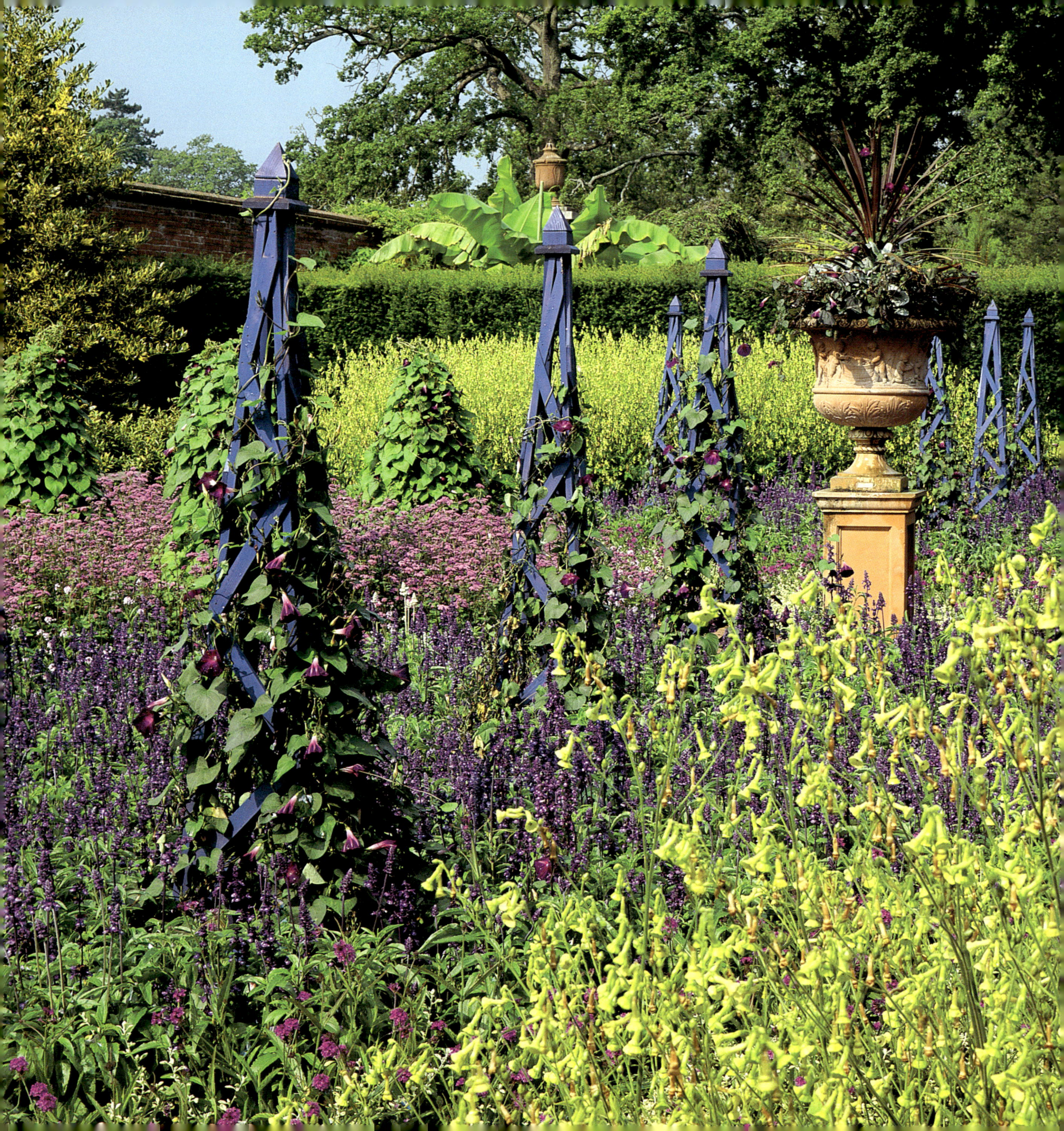

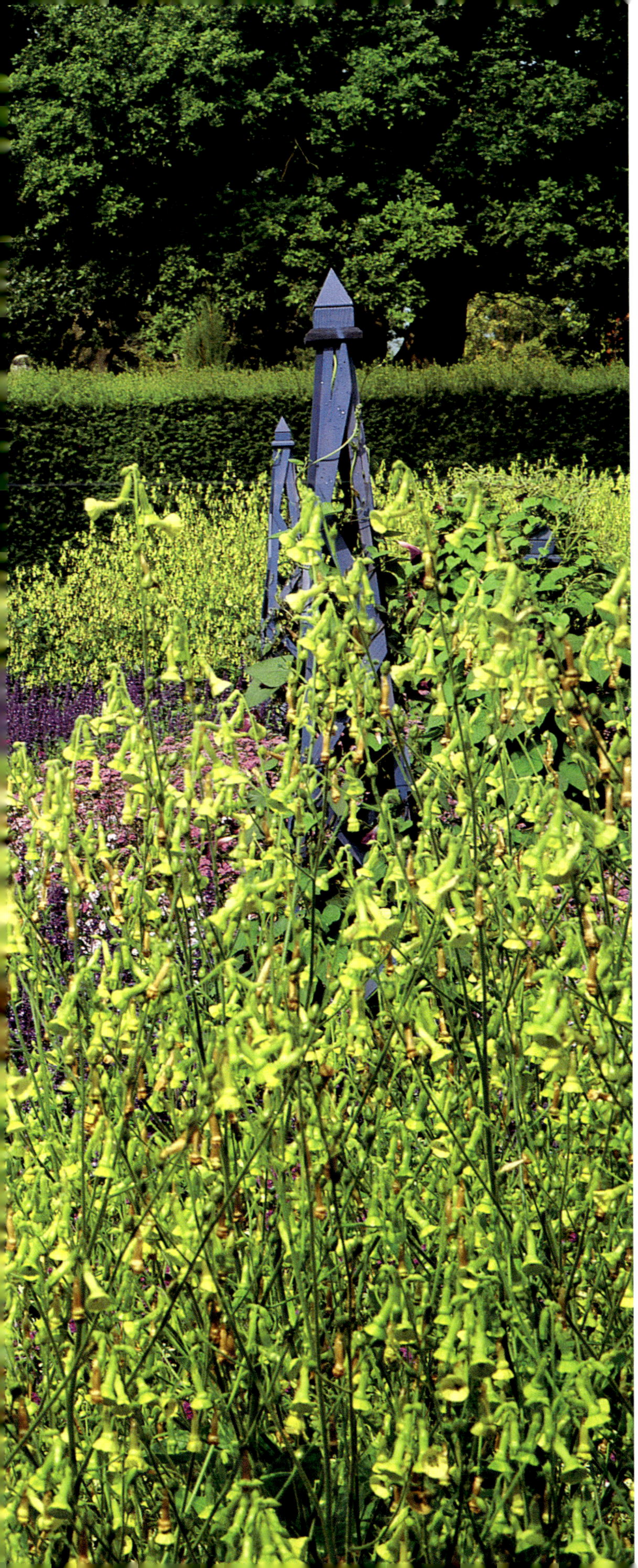

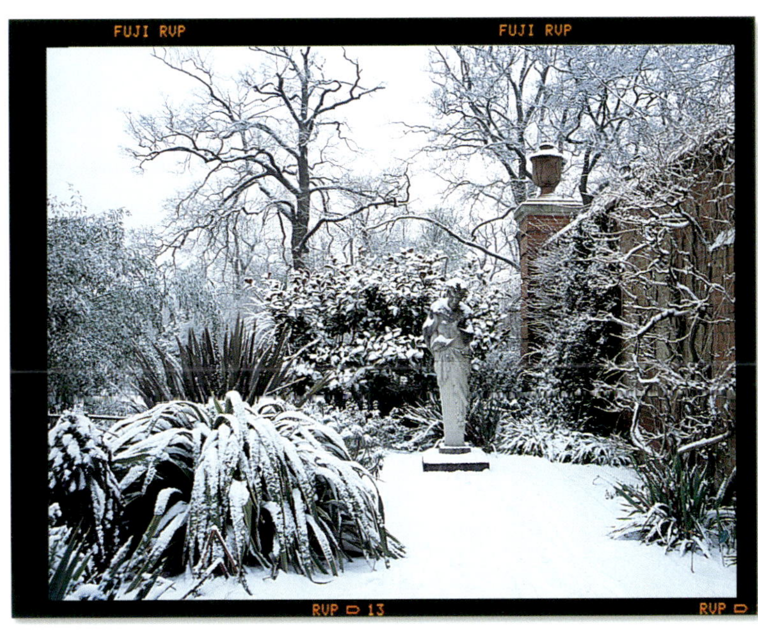


# garden photography

## a professional guide

**Tony Cooper**

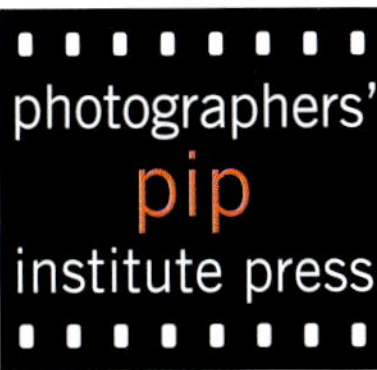

First published 2004 by
Photographers' Institute Press/PIP,
an imprint of The Guild of Master Craftsman Publications Ltd,
166 High Street, Lewes,
East Sussex BN7 1XU



ISBN 1 86108 392 0
A catalogue record of this book is available from the British Library.



Publisher: Paul Richardson
Art Director: Ian Smith
Production Manager: Stuart Poole
Managing Editor: Gerrie Purcell
Commissioning Editor: April McCroskie
Editor: James Evans
Art Editor: Gilda Pacitti

Typefaces: Helvetica and Palatino

Colour origination: Icon Reproduction, London, England
Printed and bound: Kyodo Printing Co. Pte Ltd, Singapore

**To Hazel, my wife**

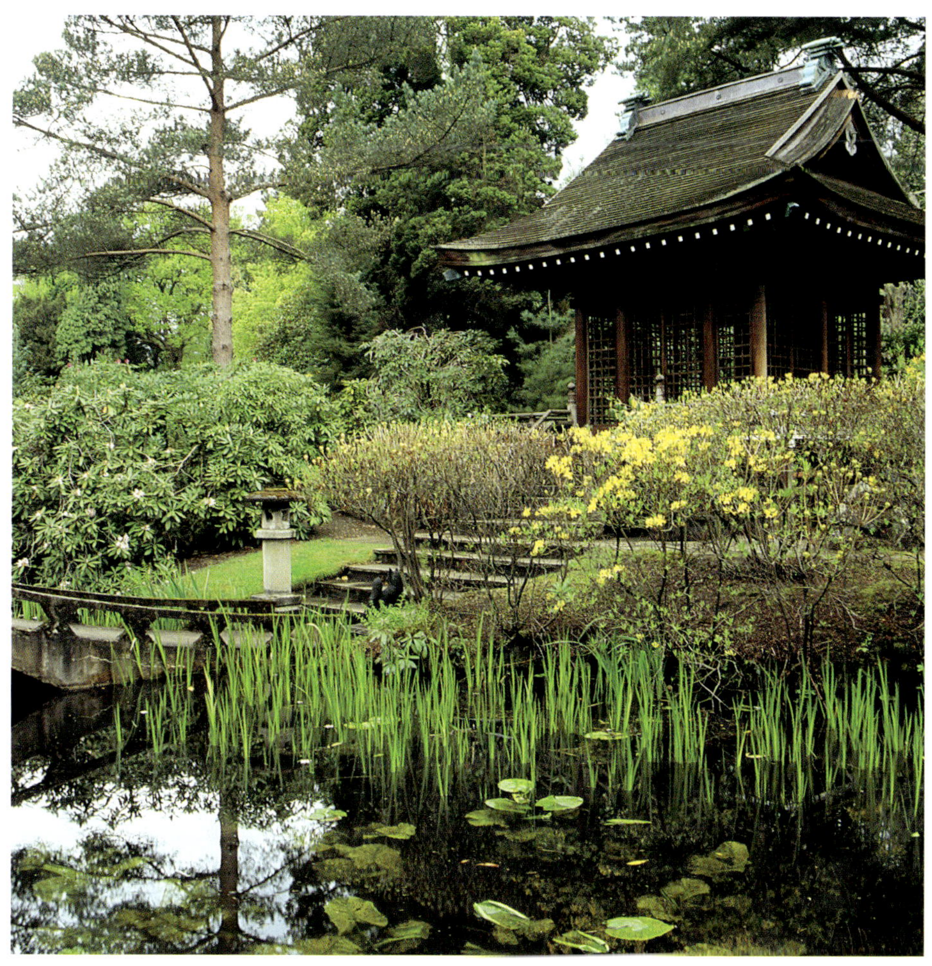

# Contents



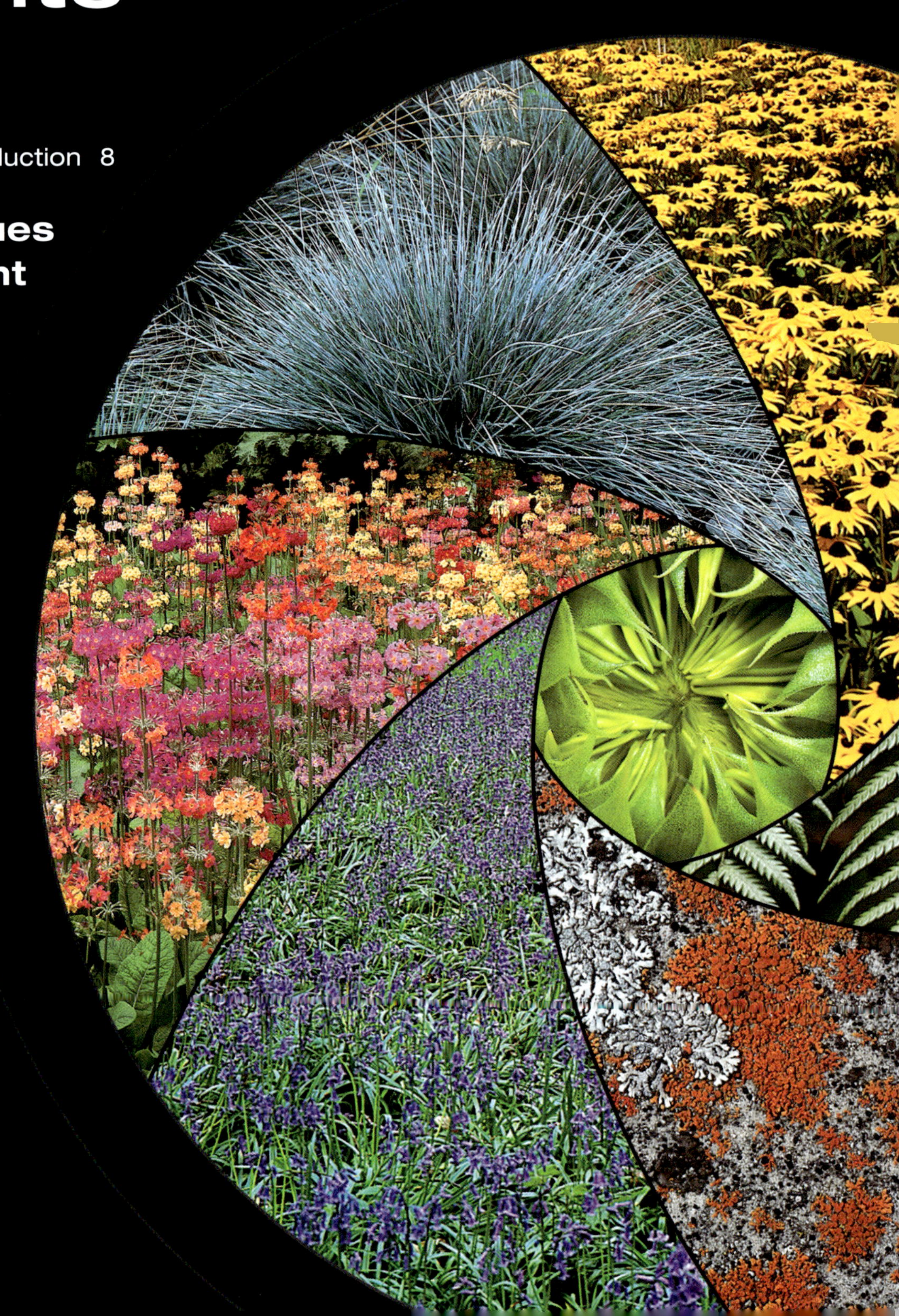

## Part two: **In the Garden**

**This book aims to provide some answers to the what, why, when, where and how of garden photography in colour. It has been written for those who have a knowledge of photography and wish to improve their skills to a level at which saleable results are the norm; where their photography becomes 'professional'.**

The book deals mainly with gardens and the plants cultivated in them, but it should not be forgotten that gardens, lovely as they can be, are anything but natural. It is often refreshing to go out and see how nature organizes matters in the wild, and for me this enhances my appreciation of the art and skill of the dedicated gardener. Think of the centuries-old tradition of the Japanese garden and the comparatively recent introduction of the naturalistic prairie and flowering-meadow style of ecological gardening. Both of these are inspired by the natural landscape and attempt to distil it into garden form.

## Starting Out

We all have our own particular reasons for taking pictures of plants and gardens. One of these is almost certainly to remind ourselves of beautiful scenes, and another is probably to capture the fleeting beauty of individual blooms. I recently came across some black-and-white prints that I took as a boy, and they confirmed that these must have partly been my own reasons. A particular flag iris had just opened its first flower; I must have been aware of its perfection and tried to record it using a simple snapshot camera with black-and-white film. I was pleased to see that the iris looked fairly sharp, but the less said about the rest of the picture, with an old towel used as partial background to the bloom, the better.

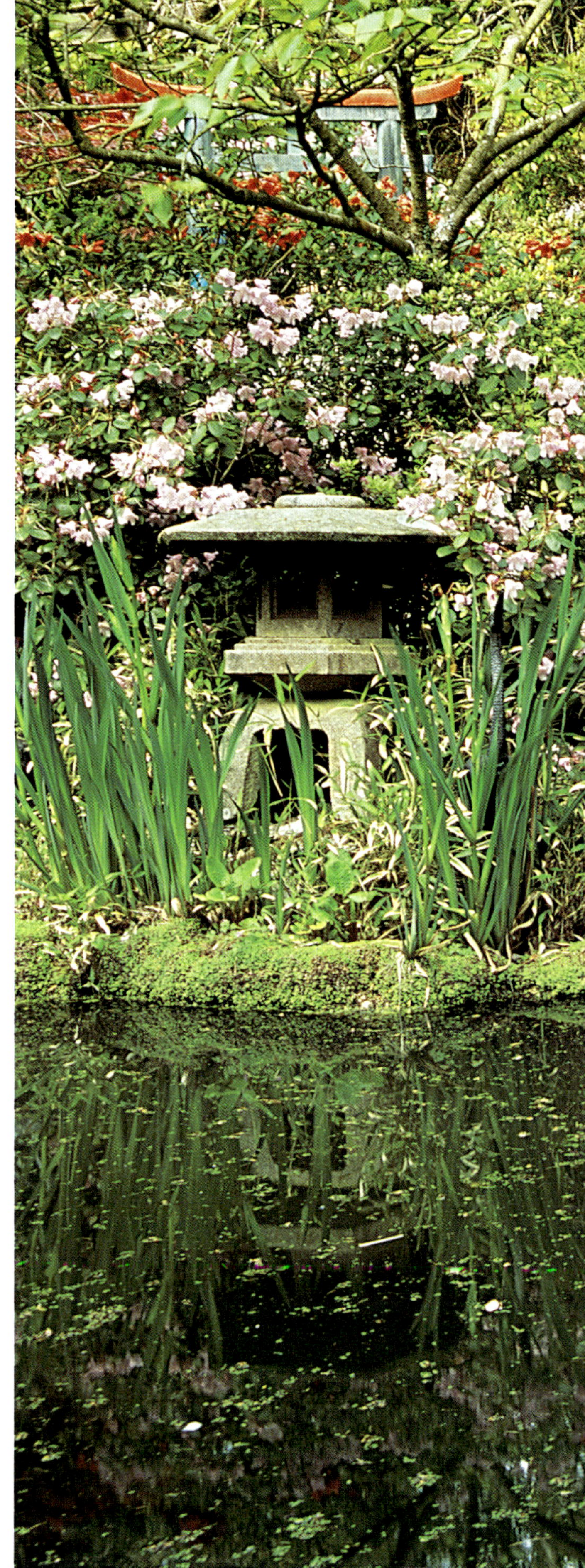

An orange-red bridge in the Japanese garden at Compton Acres in Dorset. The bridge, a miniature drum bridge, is painted the same colour as the tea house, from which this picture was taken.

**Minolta Dynax 7, 28–135mm lens, 81B filter, tripod. 1/4sec at f/16 on Provia 100F**

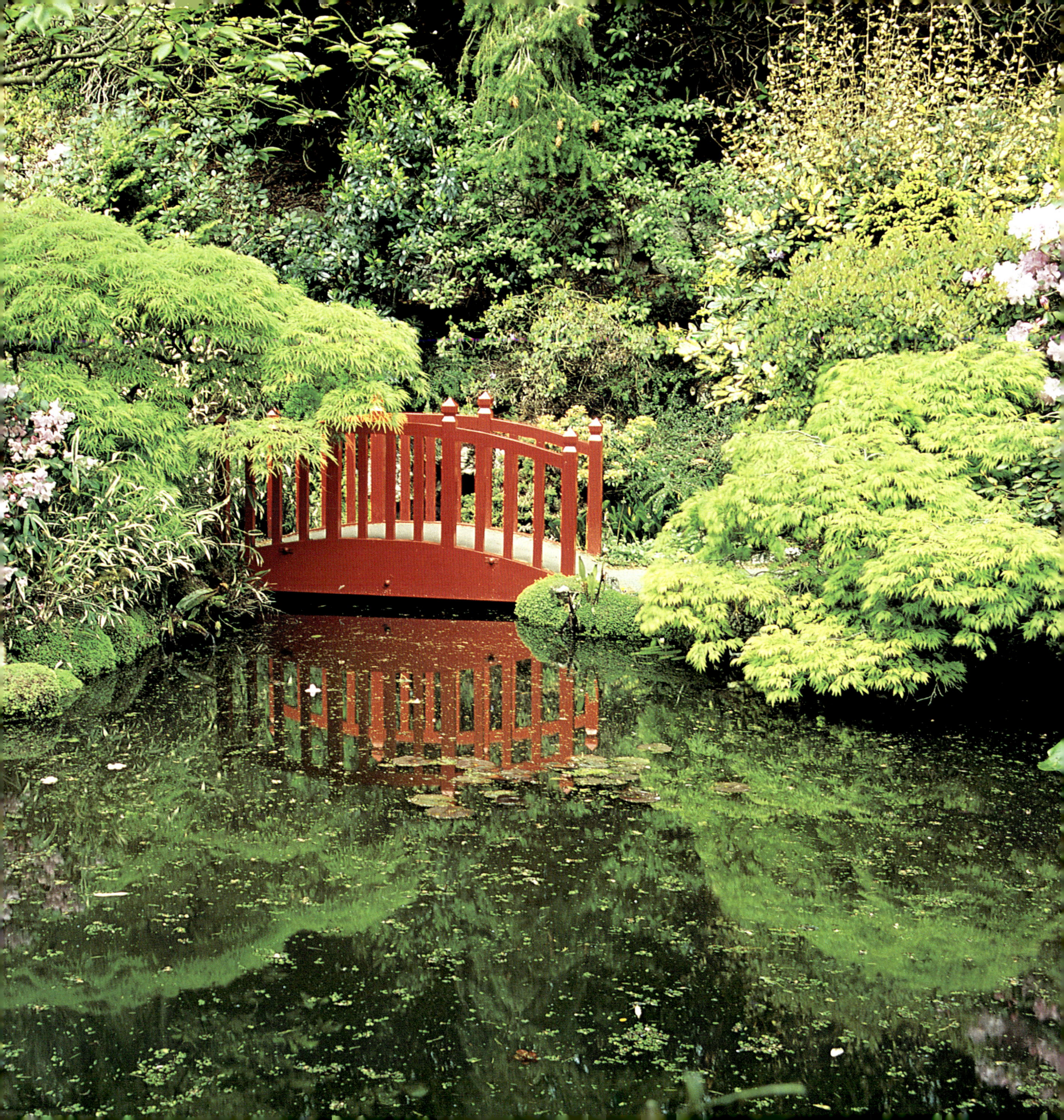

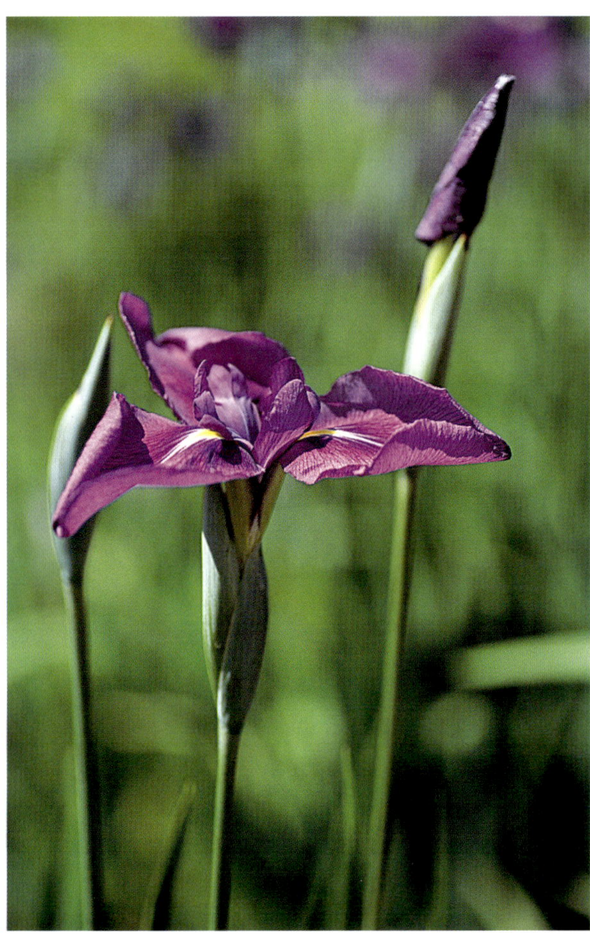

A more recent attempt at capturing the beauty of irises. Here a cultivar of *Iris ensata* – at Wakehurst Place in West Sussex – displays perfection of form.

**Minolta Dynax 7000i, 90mm macro lens, 81A filter, tripod. f/4 on Provia 100F**

## Turning 'Pro'

I renewed my interest in taking photographs, as opposed to family snapshots, in the early 1970s with the purchase of a Praktica SLR, and some years later I started contributing to a picture library holding images of natural-history subjects. Now, apart from on family occasions, I always have an eye on possible publication while taking photographs. When I look through the viewfinder I consider whether the image would be suitable for the marketplace, and if it is not I hesitate to trip the shutter and look instead for an improved angle.

Although over the years I have found my own markets, the substantial majority of the sales of my pictures have emanated from picture libraries. Four picture libraries (specializing in the environment, horticulture and natural history) currently file my work, and in Chapter 10 I have included some advice on choosing one should you wish to add this string to your bow.

## Recording the Natural World

The enjoyment to be derived from garden photography must be emphasized, for there is immense pleasure to be obtained in photographing the plant world. It is both interesting and stimulating, and for the most part is carried out in the fresh air in a fascinating and normally lovely environment. Also, I think most photographers would agree that the thrill of anticipation when photographs arrive back from processing never fades. Now, a similar excitement can be found when viewing downloaded digital images on a workstation monitor.

Everyone sees things in their own way and this is certainly true for garden photography. Put a group of photographers together in a garden and I am certain

Right: The wild flowers of yesteryear are now becoming increasingly scarce. This joyous spectacle of early summer shows a sweep of cornfield annuals at RHS Hyde Hall, Essex. Five species were sown: cornflower, corn marigold, field poppy, corn chamomile and corn cockle.

**Fuji GW670III, 81B filter, tripod. 1/8sec at f/27 on Velvia**

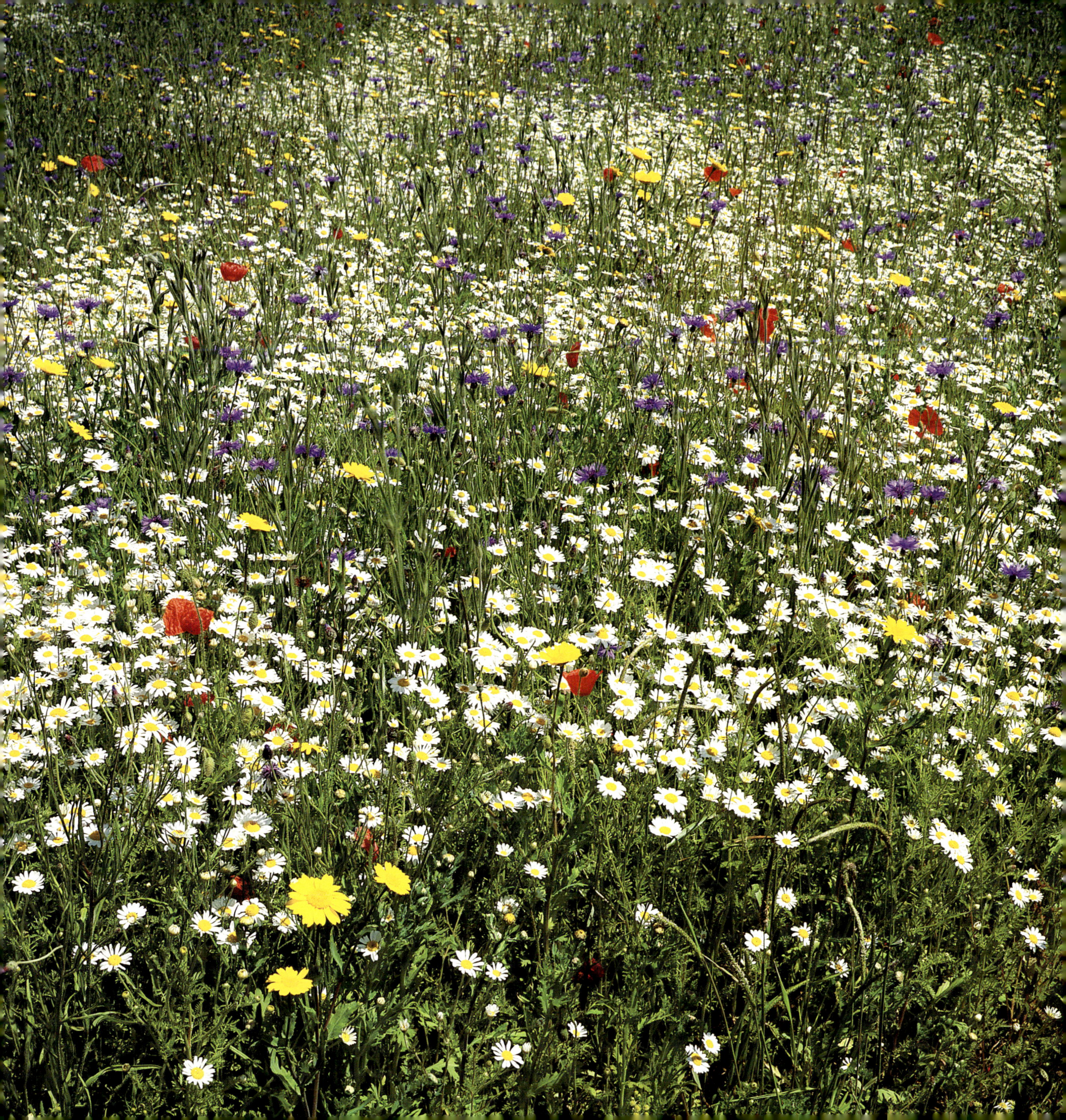

that the subjects chosen and their interpretations of them would vary widely from photographer to photographer. There is not necessarily a 'correct' way to take garden photos, although some ways are preferable to others and I will try to indicate some of the better ones in this book.

### At Home and On Location

Many of the pictures shown here have been taken in my own garden, which I designed to some extent to provide an outdoor studio for plant photography. Largely constructed by me from a builder's bare plot, it is now in its sixth year. As a studio it has been reasonably successful; many pictures taken in it have already been published in books and magazines, a national newspaper and a calendar. However, the majority of the pictures in this book have been taken in public gardens, the addresses of which are shown in the Appendix (see page 140), along with telephone numbers and website and email addresses where appropriate. All the photographs were taken during normal visiting hours. These do vary from garden to garden, and it is recommended that you check them by telephone or on the Internet before travelling.

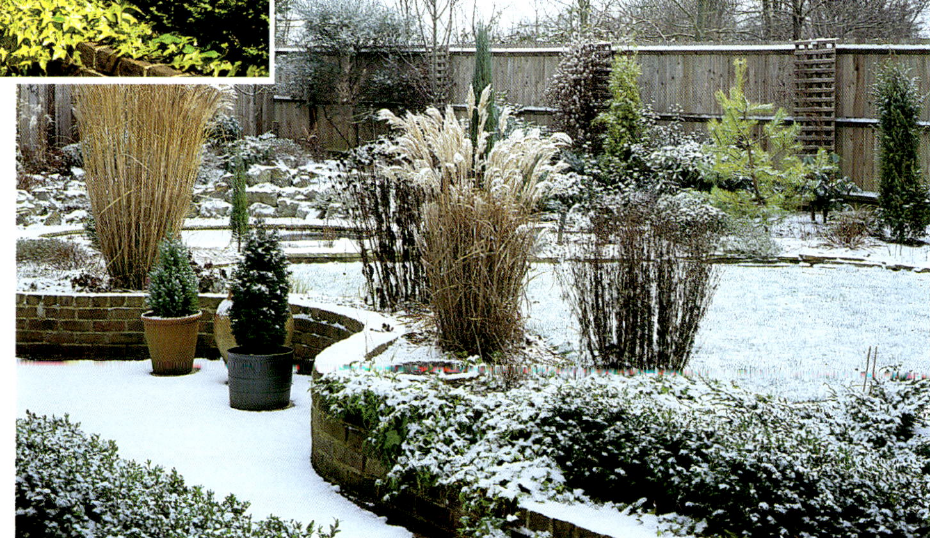

My own garden in South-east England. The great thing about having a garden on hand is that pictures can be taken in ideal conditions for photography. Each subject can be captured in its prime, and one can carry out any necessary 'gardening' – the removal of unsightly dead blooms, weeds and so on – not possible in gardens open to the public.

**Both shots: Fuji GW670iii, tripod. 1/8sec at f/27 and 1sec at f/32 (respectively) on Velvia**

An indication of location is generally given in the caption to each picture. Where this is omitted, the picture will have been taken in my own garden.

### A Note on Exposure Details

In photographic books and magazines it is customary to show exposure details against each photograph. Personally, I often feel these are of academic interest only. Light levels are apt to vary and, except where I have happened to record these details at the time, I have only an approximate idea of the shutter speed (although a much firmer idea of the aperture). Apart from in breezy conditions or when photographing waterfalls, for example, shutter speeds are normally of marginal significance in garden photography. Pictures will therefore be annotated with exact exposure data only where these are known.

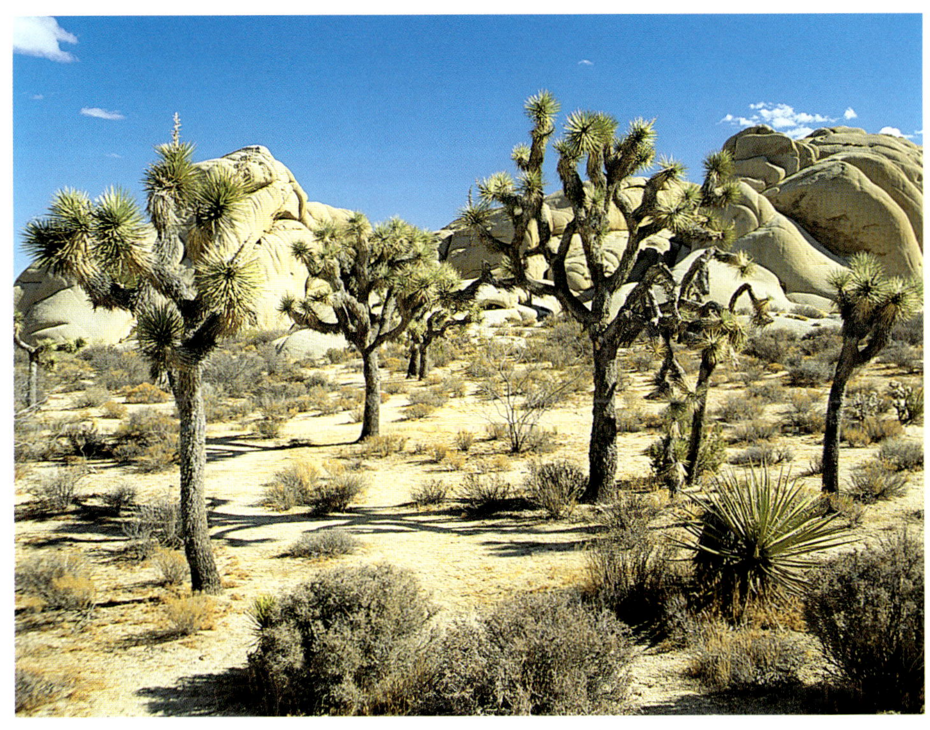

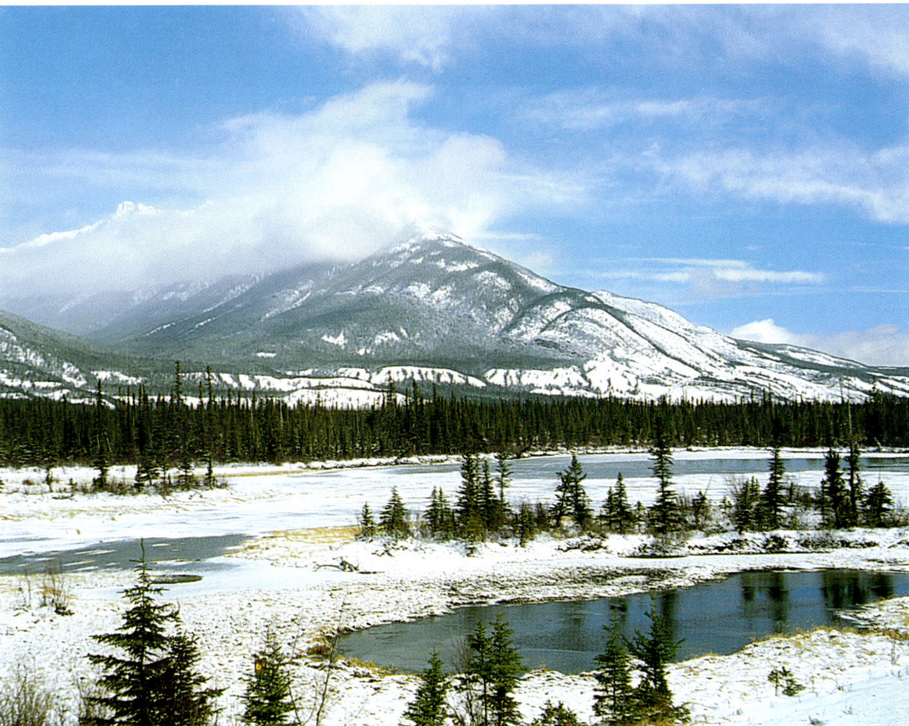

Above: Joshua trees *(Yucca brevifolia)* in Joshua Tree National Park, California, growing naturally in the high Mojave Desert.

**Minolta Dynax 7, 28–135mm lens, 81A and polarizing filters, tripod. f/16 on Velvia**

Left: Subalpine firs *(Abies lasiocarpa)* in spring in the Athabasca River valley, north of Jasper, Canada. Although not strictly a garden photograph, it is useful to study how nature organizes matters. I relied on Velvia film (see page 18) to produce the strong colours – it was too cold to fiddle about with filters!

**Minolta Dynax 7, 28–135mm lens, tripod. f/16 on Velvia**

# Part one: **Techniques and Equipment**

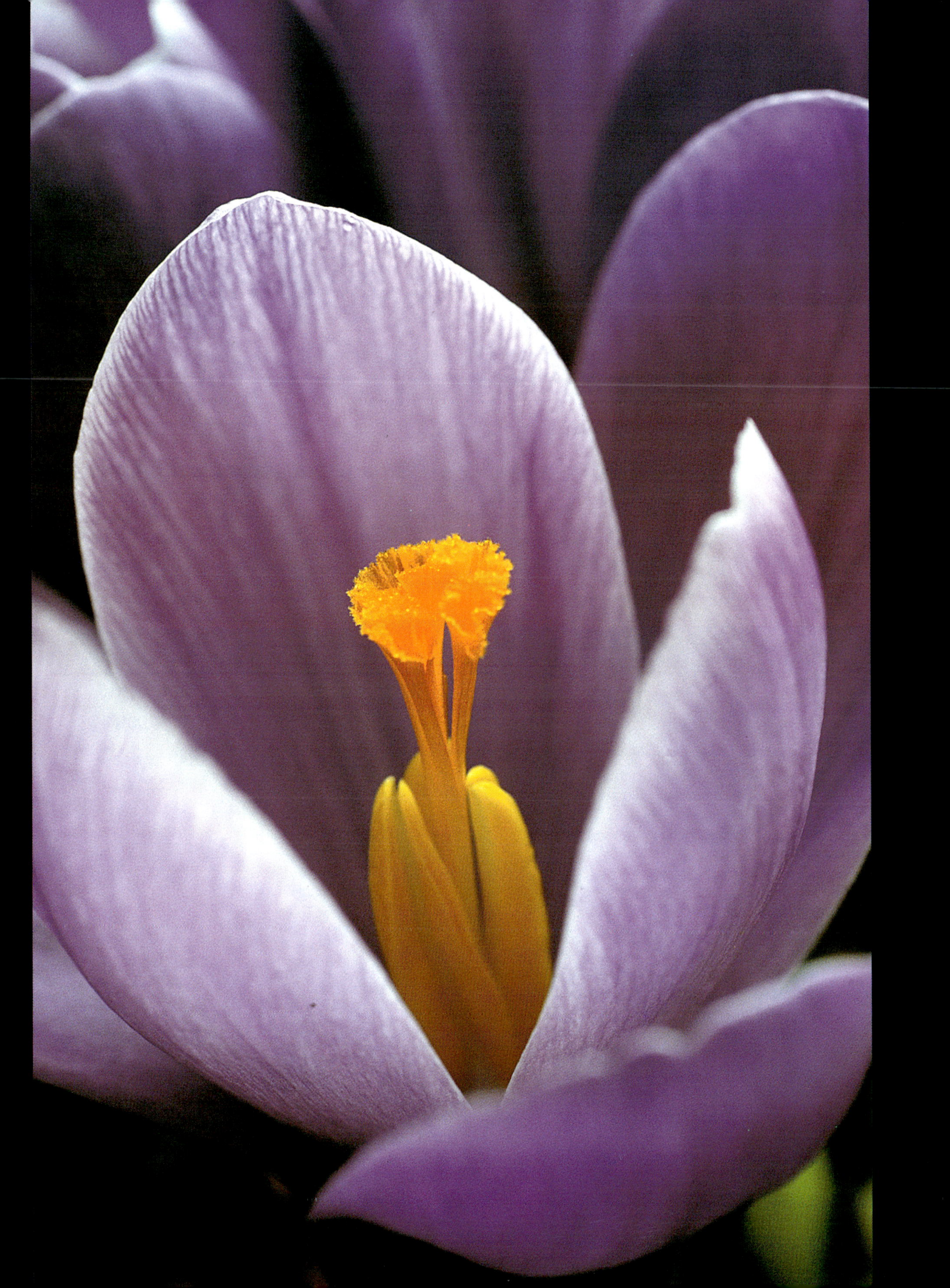

1

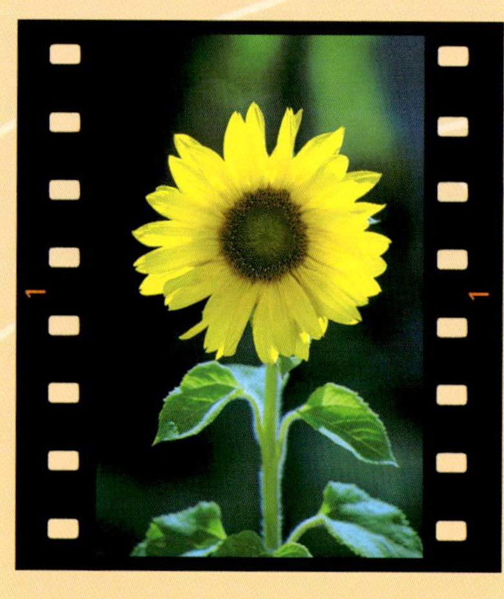

# **Equipment** and **Film**

**The range and sophistication of photographic equipment available is such that it is tempting to invest immediately in the full 'kit', but successful garden photography can be undertaken on a modest budget and equipment added as required and, most importantly, as experience is gained.**

The range of film-based still cameras on the market (digital cameras are considered in the following chapter) is huge, and many types – SLRs, Rangefinder cameras and so on – will produce good pictures of the majority of subjects covered in this book. However, for anyone wishing to take pictures suitable for publication, consideration of film format and size is important. To achieve acceptable image quality, this should be 35mm or larger. The cameras used for taking the film-based pictures in this book range from 35mm SLRs to medium-format cameras producing images on roll film of 6x4.5cm, 6x6cm and 6x7cm. The lenses used range in focal length from 28mm through to 300mm.

## Equipment: **Large Format**

Large-format cameras taking individual sheets of film yield transparencies of unbeatable quality, but few photographers use large format for garden work, the cameras being rather heavy and slow to operate. Additionally, the film they use is expensive.

## Film

It might seem surprising in this digital age that many publishers and picture libraries still work with film or, increasingly, film-originated digital files (i.e. scanned film), but this is so. A glance through the *Writers' and Artists' Yearbook* or *The Freelance Photographer's Market Handbook* (see Bibliography, page 150), both annual publications, reveals the phrase 'Digital media accepted' against the entries for many publishers of gardening books and magazines. This normally denotes scans or digitally captured files (i.e. images taken with a digital camera) of sufficient size. To meet what the market demands – always a golden rule – it is therefore necessary to submit either transparencies or digital files of acceptable size, but not prints, which are only occasionally suitable. Note that some photo libraries prefer to carry out their own scanning of transparencies (for more, see page 132).

It should be emphasized that the market is changing rapidly and no doubt at some point in the future digitally originated pictures will be preferred by publishers and photo libraries to film-based images. The signs are, however, that film and digital will coexist happily for some time yet.

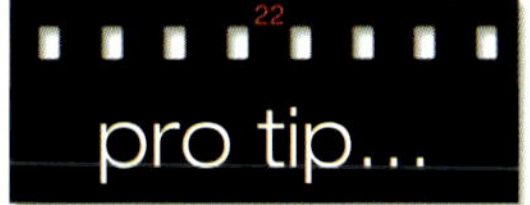


**Go slow**

Slow films have finer grain, which equates to sharper enlargement and better reproduction. My advice is not to use film with an ISO of over 100.

## Transparency Film

The quality of transparency film is very high, but it is crucial to select a film with a slow ISO speed. At the start of the 1990s, most professionals used Kodachrome, either Kodachrome 64 or Kodachrome 25. However, since the launch of Fujichrome Velvia (50 ISO), many professionals have switched to this fine-grained E6 processed film. Velvia colours are 'punchy' and saturated, and the definition excellent, the film performing well in both bright and dull light. Velvia can, if necessary, be 'pushed' to 100 ISO with minimal loss of quality. In garden photography up-rating film is not often necessary, but it's reassuring to know it can be called upon if required.

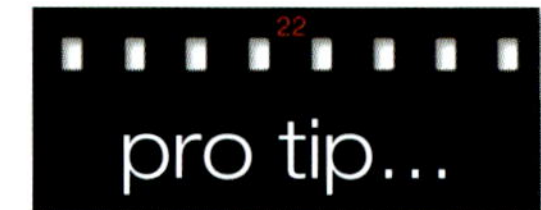


**Film processing**

When possible, I have had film processed abroad during a trip. Besides ensuring that a proportion of output is secure from X-ray fogging, it is also a useful check against camera malfunction.

Fuji also manufactures other films of value to the garden photographer. One that I use frequently is the one-stop faster Provia 100F, which is fine grained and capable of being pushed to 200 ISO with very little loss in quality. Fujifilm have also released a 100 ISO version of Velvia, called Velvia 100F Professional. Unfortunately, the timing of its UK launch meant that not many images using this film could appear here, but one example – a shot of the trumpet-like *Brugmansia* x *insignis* – is shown on page 105.

As well as Kodachrome 64 (Kodachrome 25 no longer being available), Kodak manufactures an extensive range of fine-grained E6 processed films of 100 ISO, and I have used the professional Ektachromes

## Equipment: **Film Formats**

All things being equal, the larger film size of 120 roll film results in improved quality, but in my opinion the difference is fairly marginal and should not be exaggerated. The quality obtained from 35mm film is very high and many professionals use it for much of their output; good technique is a far more important factor in obtaining accomplished images suitable for publication.

Reproduced life-size, these four pictures show the camera/film formats most used by professional garden photographers. One that is not shown, but shouldn't be overlooked, is the panoramic format obtainable from cameras like the Hasselblad XPan.

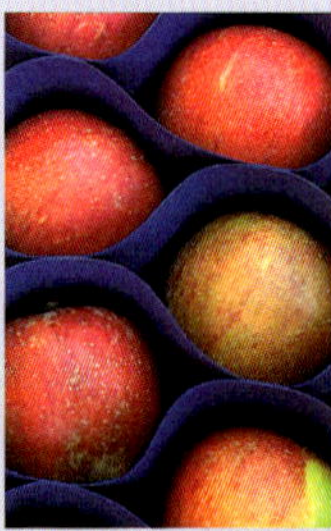

35mm: Fuji Velvia (50 ISO)

**Minolta XG-M SLR, 90mm macro lens, gold reflector, tripod. f/22**

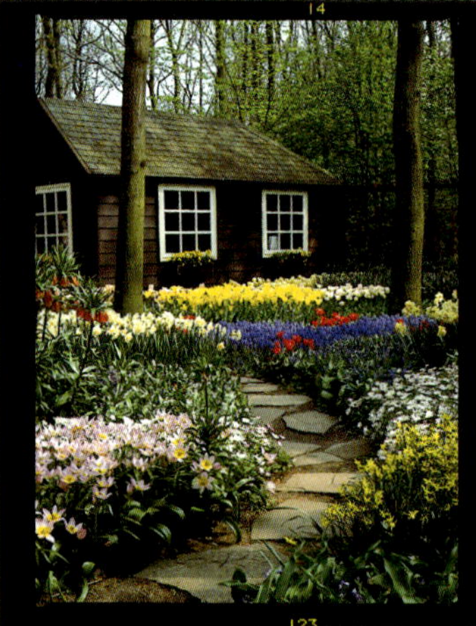

6x4.5cm: Fujichrome 100P

**Mamiya 645 Super, 80mm lens, tripod. f/22**

100VS and E100G for several of the pictures in this book. Literature on their films is available on request from Kodak, Fuji, and from Agfa. (Some pictures taken with Agfachrome RSX II Professional film are also included in the book.)

### Looking after Film

From the moment it is coated onto the film, the emulsion is affected by radiation, heat and humidity. Manufacturers store 'professional' film in an ideal environment, free from radiation, and it is released for sale at the optimum time for use. Once purchased, film should be stored in a refrigerator or (in a plastic bag) in a freezer; the instructions on the box indicate

### Film Buying and Care

-  It is cheaper to buy film in bulk, but don't buy more than you think you will realistically use over a period of two or three months
- ✓ Check the use-by dates before buying any film and before using film from your stock
- 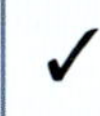 'Professional' film should always be stored in a refrigerator or in a plastic bag in the freezer. Allow time for it to come back to room temperature before using
-  If possible, don't allow film to go through a security X-ray machine; carry it separately and have it hand-checked at the airport
- ✓ Have film processed as soon as possible after exposure

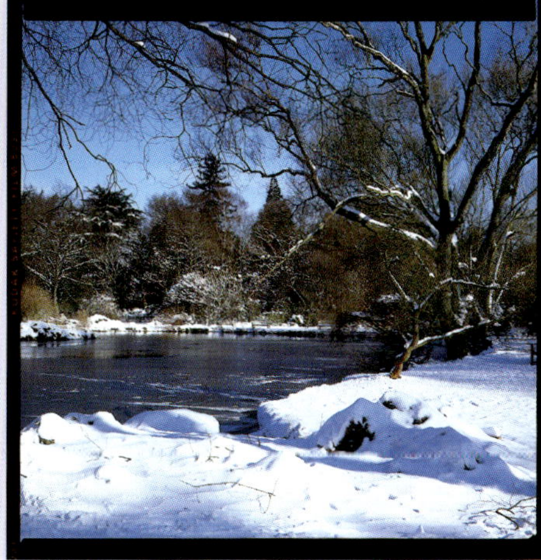

6x6cm: Kodak Ektachrome 64

**Mamiya C330f, 80mm lens, tripod. f/32**

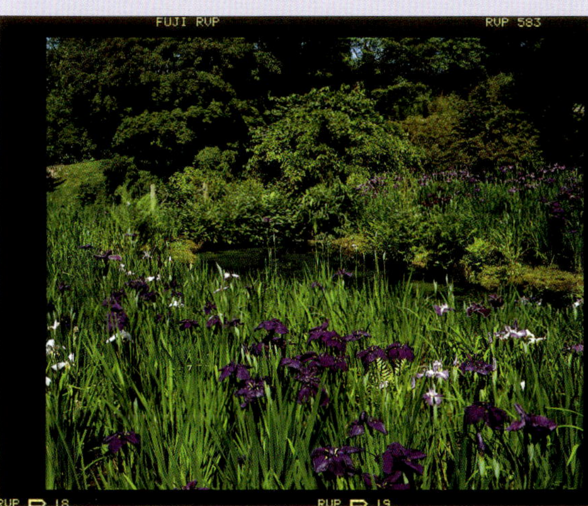


6x7cm: Fuji Velvia (50 ISO)

**Fuji GW670III, fixed 90mm lens, 81B filter, tripod. f/32**

## Technique: **'Pushing' or 'Up-rating' Film**

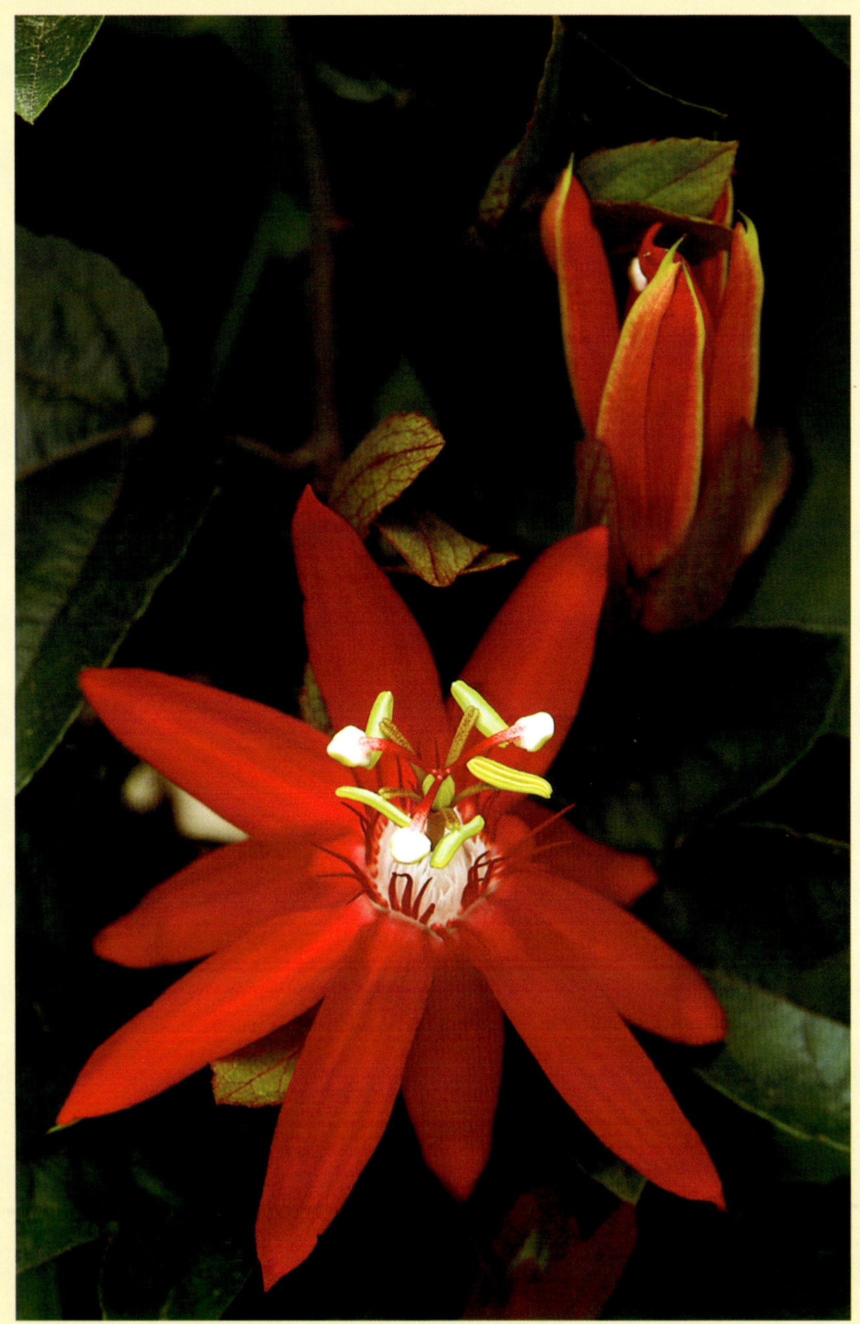

It can be advantageous to use film at a higher (faster) ISO number than it is rated at – i.e. to give the film less exposure to light. For example, if moderate light levels combined with a breeze would result in blurred images, 50 ISO film can be exposed at 100 ISO (or 100 ISO film at 200 ISO). There are, however, two provisos: the entire film must be exposed at the revised ISO speed, and the processing lab must be informed of the revision. In the examples given, the film is said to have been 'pushed' one stop.

Film can also be treated in the opposite way. For example, a 100 ISO film exposed at 50 ISO would have been 'pulled' one stop – i.e. it would have been given one-stop extra exposure. In practice this might be employed (perhaps in conjunction with an ND filter) in photographing a waterfall, where a white blurring effect is sought by setting a long shutter speed.

*Passiflora phoenicea* x *quadrangularis* was flowering in the shade at Quail Botanical Gardens in Southern California and a breeze was blowing. I therefore up-rated Provia 100F by one stop to ensure that I obtained a sharp image with sufficient depth of field.

---

**Minolta Dynax 700si, 180mm macro lens, 81A filter, tripod. f/16 on Provia 100F exposed at 200 ISO**

maximum storage temperature to ensure that any deterioration is kept to a minimum. It is essential to allow film taken from the freezer to come up to ambient temperature gradually over several hours, thus avoiding condensation and brittleness. It is also a good idea to allow film from the fridge an hour or so to come up to room temperature.

The selection of a laboratory for the processing of exposed film requires care. There is variation in quality and good results are not necessarily linked to high cost. The obvious solution is to shop around until one is satisfied on both counts. Have film processed as soon as possible after exposure.

One further point to make about film concerns possible X-ray damage at airports. The perceived wisdom used to be that no damage or discernible deterioration should occur to film stored in hand luggage, especially if 'slow' film is involved.

Developments in security X-ray machine technology have, however, thrown all this out of the window. Some new machines are far more powerful and a single pass can fog all film, regardless of its speed. It would seem that the only satisfactory procedure is to carry film by hand and have it hand-checked. Finally, never put film in checked-in luggage destined for the hold.

## Equipment

**Tripods** The number of garden photographs I take in the course of a year without using a tripod is minimal. This is simply part of the way I work and increases the success rate, eliminating rejects caused by camera shake. However, even if you wish to dispense with the use of a tripod for general garden views (and I don't recommend that you do), one will be essential for close-ups.

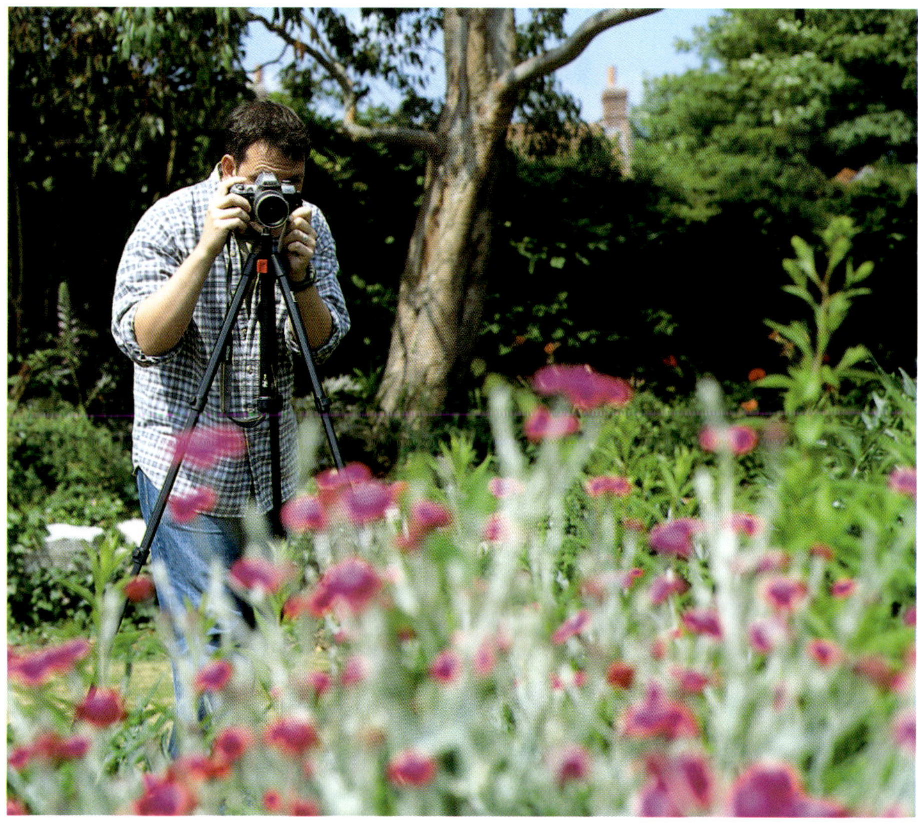

Besides providing stability, a tripod enables the possibilities of a subject to be explored in an objective fashion, and can improve the composition and balance of your photos.

Using a tripod as a matter of course brings many advantages. It can help to gauge the effect of varying the aperture and allows a reflector or diffuser to be placed exactly as required. Furthermore, on breezy days it is simply a matter of waiting for a lull knowing that the essentials of set-up have been taken care of.

It's often said that a flimsy tripod is worse than useless. That may well be true, but it underlines the important point that a dependable tripod needs to be stoutly constructed and not something that could generally be referred to as 'light'. Ideally, a tripod should be used all the time, so my advice is to ensure you do not burden yourself with one that is too heavy, while at the same time enduring some weight inconvenience in the cause of better pictures. I have two Manfrotto tripods: a substantial one with a 'pan

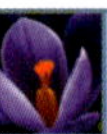

### A Dependable Tripod...

- ✓ should be light but stoutly constructed
- ✓ extends to around eye level
- ✓ is easy to use close to the ground
- ✓ has legs that can be extended and locked independently.

and tilt' head for forays into the garden or when travelling by car, and a lighter one for carrying around for much of the day and for use abroad. On a practical level, a tripod should be able to extend to around eye level, preferably without extending the centre column, as well as being usable at a level close to the ground. When working on uneven ground it is sometimes useful to have the facility of extending the angle of the legs outwards independently of each other, locking them in position. Finally, a tripod should be used in conjunction with a remote shutter release, as it is possible to cause camera shake by clumsily tripping the shutter by hand.

## Filters

In the belief that colours should be kept as natural as possible, there was a time when I did not use any filters other than a polarizer and a skylight over the lens as protection against minor scratches and debris. This resulted in many pictures being reasonably good, but sometimes missing that something extra, notably warmth, if only to counteract the cool colour temperature of an overall blue sky. Filters should be employed, but with discretion. The trick is to enhance the result without making it obvious that a filter has been used. Of course, care should also be taken to ensure that flower colours are not adversely affected.

The variety of filters on the market is huge, but for garden photography I suggest consideration is given to warm-ups (particularly 81A, B and C), polarizers and neutral-density graduated filters.

**Warm-up filters** The 81A amber warm-up filter can be used frequently; indeed most of the time it can be left attached to a lens to protect the front element against dust and scratches. On dull, grey days, or those bright ones with sunshine from a cloudless blue sky, film can take on a bluish cast, especially in the shadows, and a warm-up filter will help to counteract this. The bluish cast is caused because daylight-

*Continued on page 26*

## Equipment: **Tripod Heads**

Tripod heads can be divided into 'pan and tilt' and 'ball and socket', and as much consideration should be given to the choice of a tripod head as to the tripod itself. Try both – photographers often swear by one sort or the other. Well worth consideration is Manfrotto's 'Grip Action Ball Head', which I have on my lighter tripod. Basically it's a clever version of a ball and socket head. Adjustment is made by squeezing a hand lever that, on release, securely clamps the camera in position. I have found it quick to use and more than adequate for lenses up to 200mm.

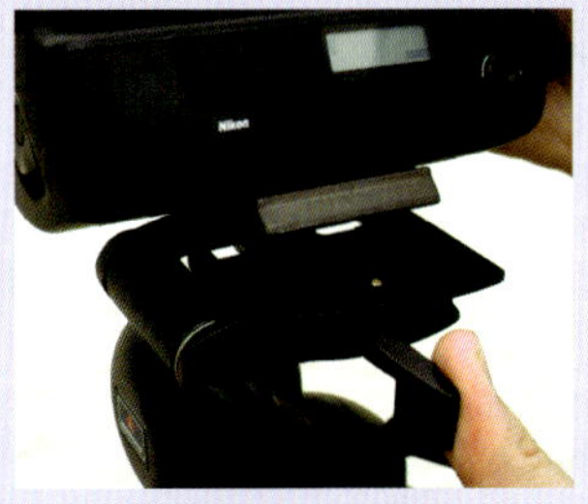


A quick-release plate attached to the camera enables it to be fastened to and released from the tripod with a minimum of delay, which can be extremely useful.

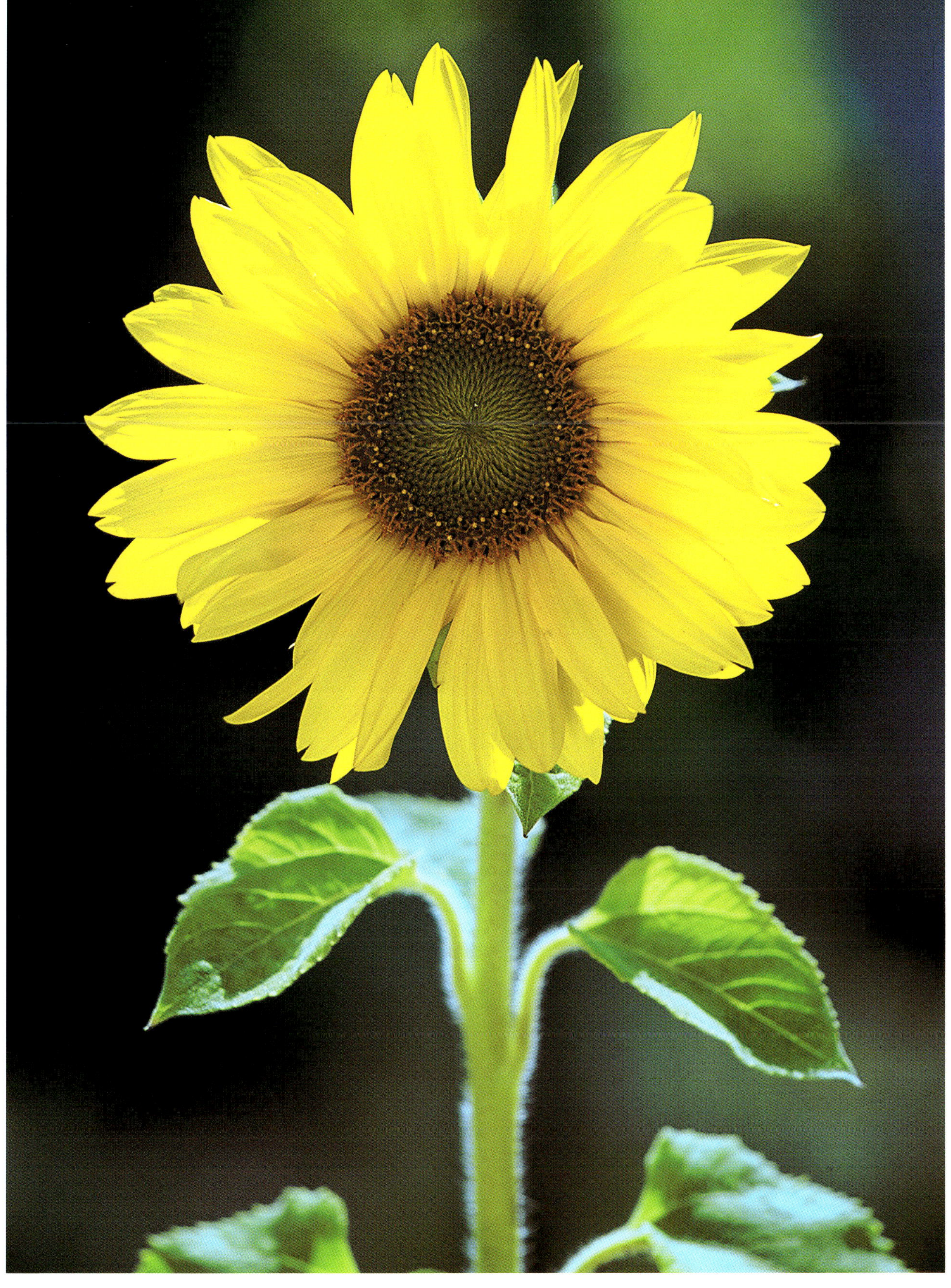

pro tip…

**Warm vs. cool**

It is worth mentioning that if an art director has the choice of two similar images, one cool and the other warm, the warm one is more likely to be selected: readers seem to prefer warmer pictures.

A gold reflector was used to throw some warm light onto the face of this sunflower backlit by sunlight.

**Minolta Dynax 700si, 180mm macro lens, gold reflector, tripod. f/5.6 on Velvia**

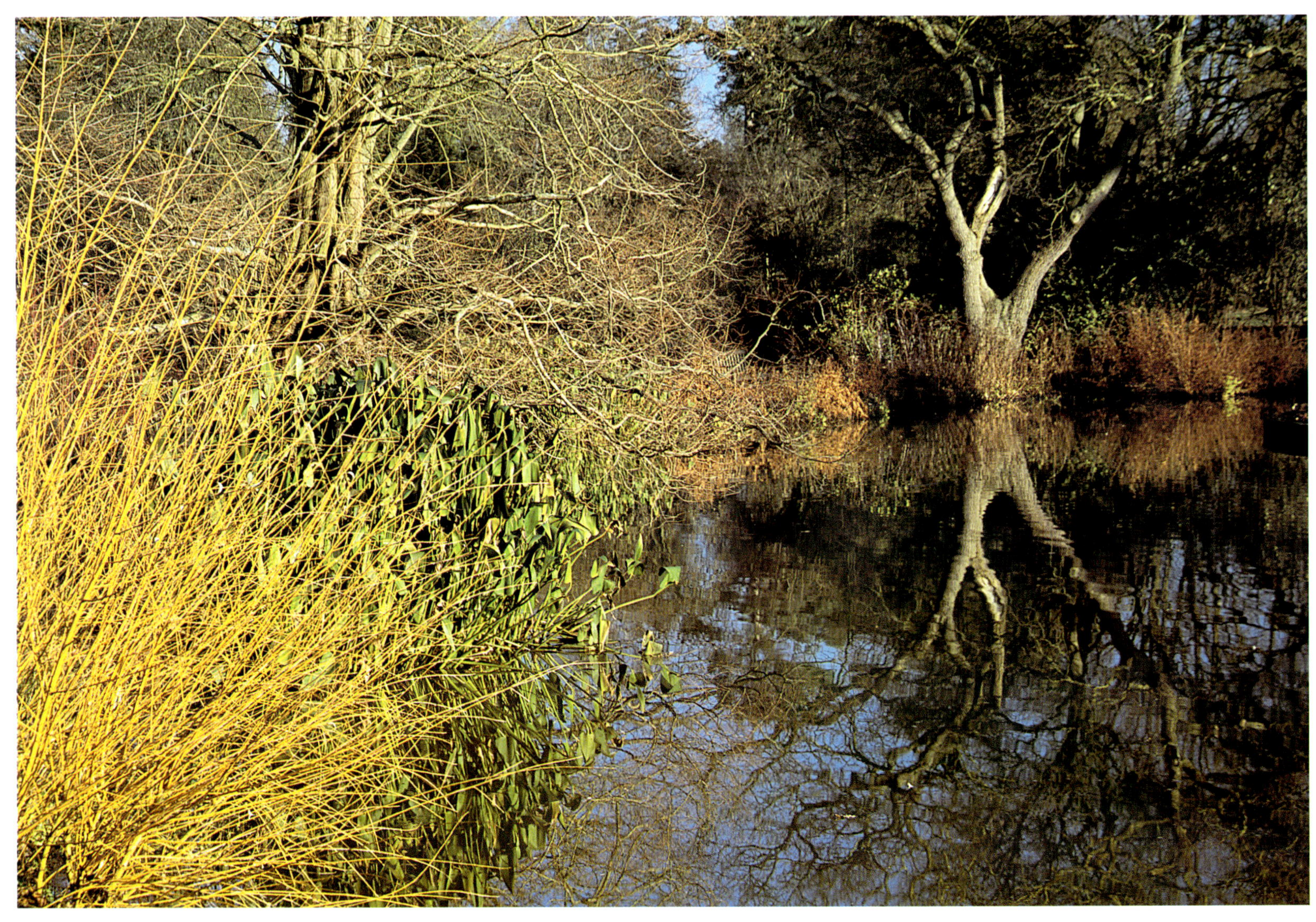

81A (warm-up) and polarizing filters have emphasized the colourful stems of *Salix alba* 'Golden Ness' in this winter scene taken with a zoom lens at a focal length of 70mm. RHS Wisley in Surrey.

**Minolta Dynax 700si, 28–135mm lens, 81A and polarizing filters, tripod. 1/8sec at f/13, Provia 100F**

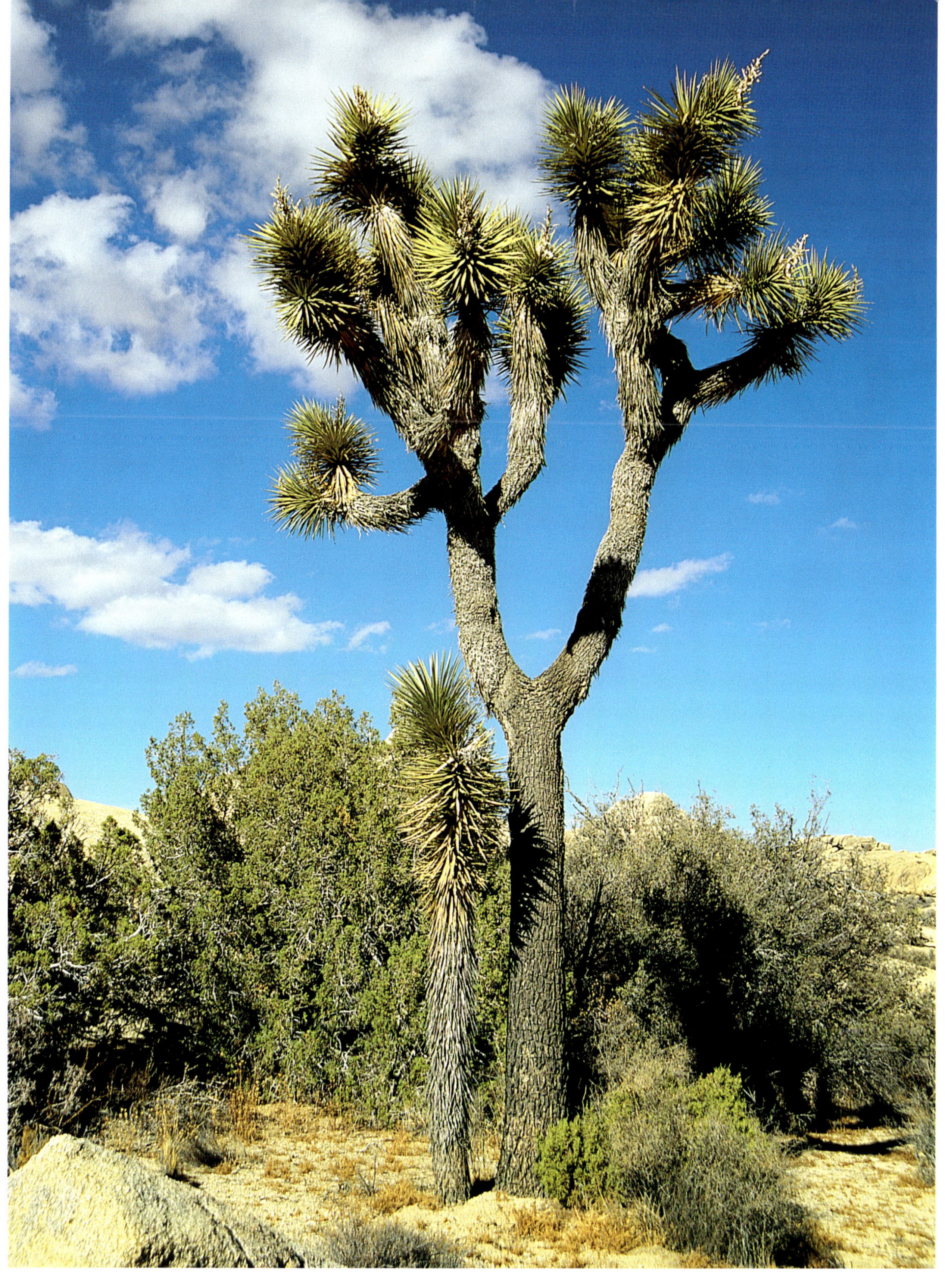

81A and polarizing filters were used for this image of a Joshua Tree *Yucca brevifolia* in the Mojave Desert ecosystem in California.

**Minolta Dynax 7, 28–135mm lens, 81A and polarizing filters, tripod. f/11 on Velvia**

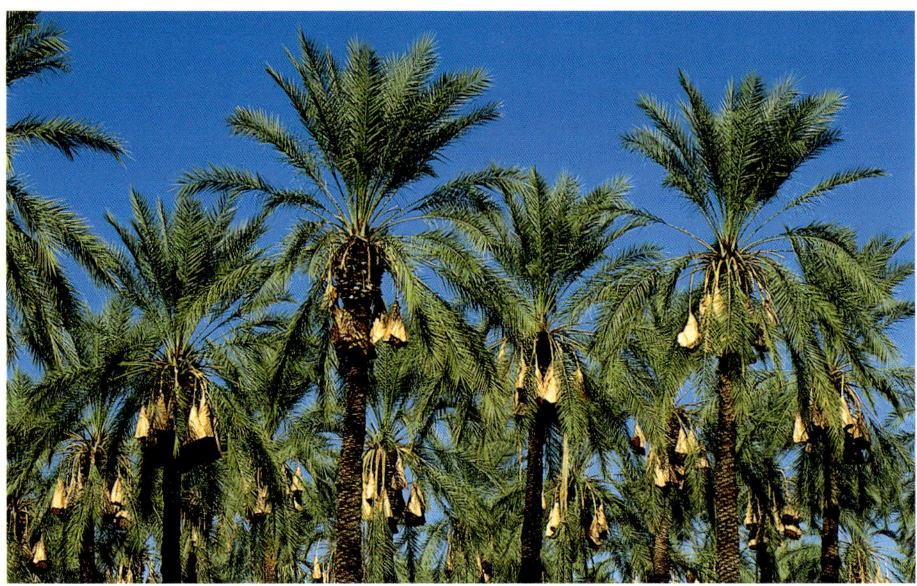

The fruit on these date palms in Southern California is protected from rain by special sleeves. The polarizing filter was adjusted to give just a small degree of polarization.

**Minolta Dynax 700si, 35–90mm lens, polarizing filter, tripod. f/11 on Velvia**

balanced film is manufactured to deliver accurate colours in a hypothetical standard of midday sunlight having a colour temperature of 5500 degrees Kelvin. An overcast day, or one with bright sunshine from a cloudless summer sky, has a colour temperature higher than standard. (For more, see page 72.)

**Polarizing filters** Polarizing filters are available as 'linear' or 'circular'. Each has a similar effect, but circular polarizers are essential for use with autofocus cameras if the focusing is to function properly. Polarizers deepen colours, enhancing those of border plants and garden views when the effect is most marked if the filter is used at right angles to the sun. Views with blue sky and white clouds can be improved significantly. Equally important, polarizers can be employed to remove sheen from grass and leaves in order to give more saturated colours. Surface sheen is also removed from water. The use of polarizers need not be limited to sunny days; try them on dull days to improve leaf colours.

The level of polarization can be gauged by looking through the filter at the scene: these filters are simple to use on an SLR, when the degree of polarization can be clearly seen through the viewfinder. It is worth making the point that it is often not desirable to use the filter fully polarized. If this is done with Velvia, a blue Californian sky can come out on film almost black! A drawback with polarizers is a loss of up to two stops of light. TTL metering will of course make the necessary adjustment automatically.

**Neutral-density graduated filters** Neutral-density graduated filters (or ND grads) are available in various strengths, reducing light by up to three stops. Much used by landscape photographers, they bring the relative brightness of sky and the relative darkness of land to within a range at which film can record detail in both satisfactorily. If, for example, the exposure reading for the sky of a scene is two stops brighter than that for the land, the appropriate grad (in this instance 0.6, which reduces the light by two stops) is positioned in the holder so that the sky portion of the scene coincides with the gradation on the filter. In other words, the sky is darkened without affecting the exposure for the land. ND grads can also be used to even out exposure where the foreground needs more exposure than a brighter background.

In regard to exposure, I think it best to set the exposure manually for the land before fitting the filter, rather than fitting the filter and letting the camera's meter sort out the exposure automatically. ND grads are obtainable either with a 'hard' or 'soft' gradation. Those with a soft gradation are more useful for garden photography than those with a hard edge because the horizon is normally uneven, with the outlines of trees and so on breaking up the skyline.

**Cool-down filters** There is an occasional call in garden photography for pale blue filters. These will cool a late evening scene so that flower colours are more correctly rendered (see page 100 for more details). A snow scene can be given a distinctly cold feel by using these filters, which can also be used to counteract the warmth of a film such as Velvia.

## Reflectors and Diffusers

Reflectors are useful out of all proportion to their low cost. A reflector can be as simple as a white sheet of paper or card, or some aluminium foil crumpled up and then spread out and affixed to a piece of cardboard. As their name suggests, reflectors are used to reflect light into the side of a subject in shadow. A simple diffuser can be made from white muslin, which is held between the light source and the subject in order to reduce contrast.

The most convenient portable reflectors and diffusers for use outdoors are manufactured ones made of material stretched over custom-made hoops. These pack down easily into small circular pouches, and are usually available with white on one side and silver or gold on the other side.

### Technique: **Using a Reflector to Balance the Light**

In many situations a reflector – generally either gold, silver or white – can be employed as an alternative to fill-in flash (see page 75), with the advantage that the exact effect can be seen in advance. A gold reflector gives a pleasant warming effect and a silver one a slightly cool effect, while a white one is more neutral.

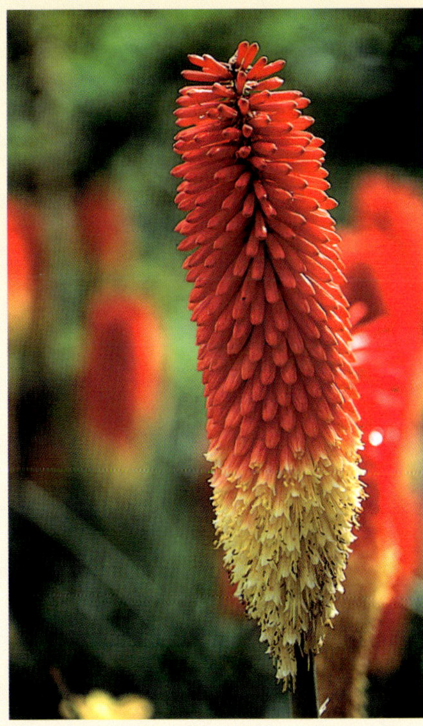

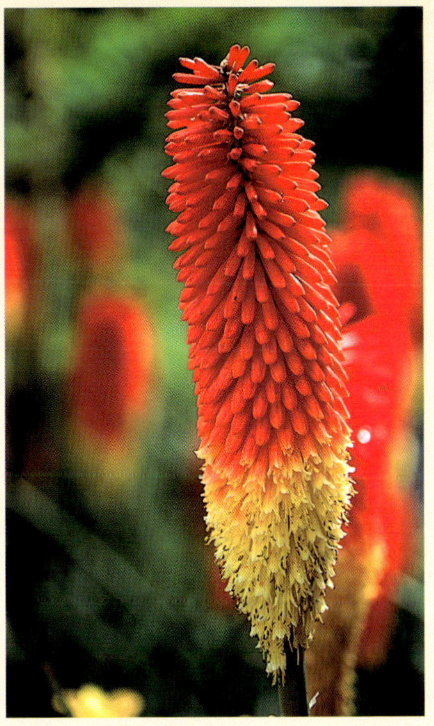

Right: The side of a spike of *Kniphofia* 'Red Admiral' away from the light photographed without a reflector. Far right: With a gold reflector throwing back light onto the bloom. RHS Wisley.

**Both pictures: Minolta Dynax 700si, 90mm macro lens, 81A filter, tripod. f/4 on Velvia**

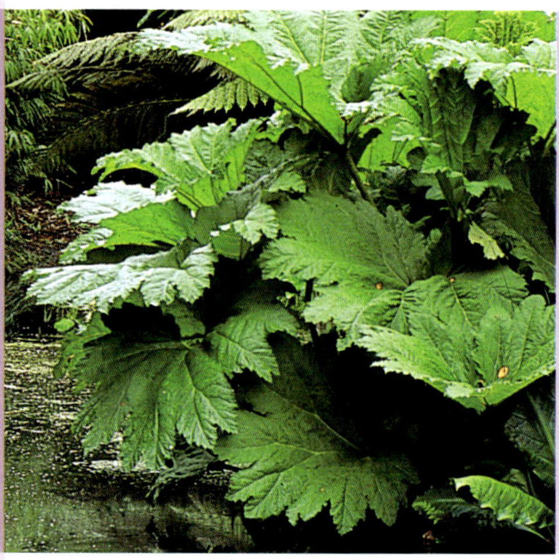

# Conservation Projects

**Conservation of the environment is becoming ever more important, and so should not be overlooked by professional garden photographers. It is reassuring to note that the 'fun' element is not being lost in the seriousness of the situation, and in horticulture the emphasis is often on the sharing of information and on general enjoyment. These qualities have deliberately been highlighted in the photographs shown here.**

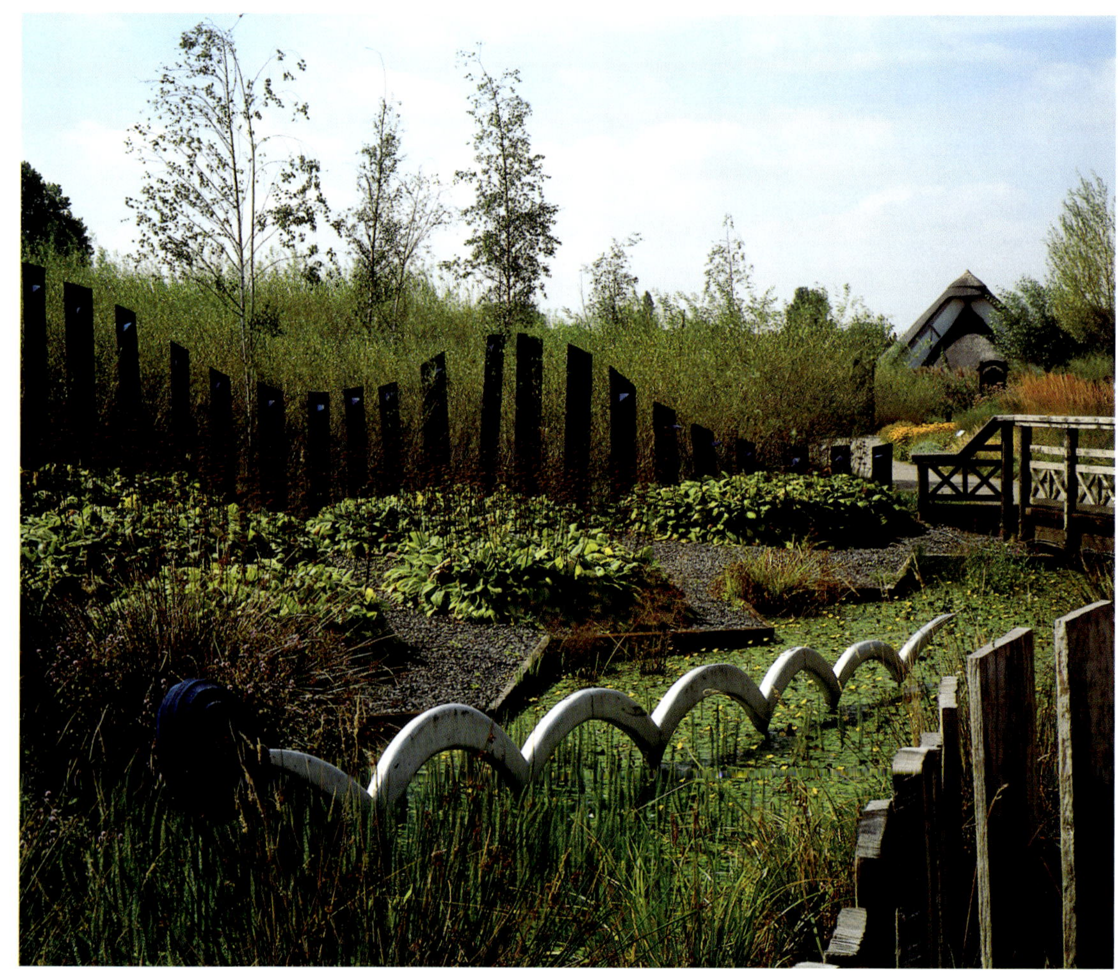

The sustainable garden at the Wetland Centre, Wildfowl and Wetlands Trust, Barnes, London. The bouncing-egg sculpture in this modern garden, a part of which is shown in this view, is designed to appeal to children. Many aspects of water conservation are featured in the garden, but the designers, Cleeve West and Johnny Woodford, have not lost sight of the 'fun' element in getting their message across.

**Fuji GW670III, 81B filter, tripod. f/32 on Velvia**

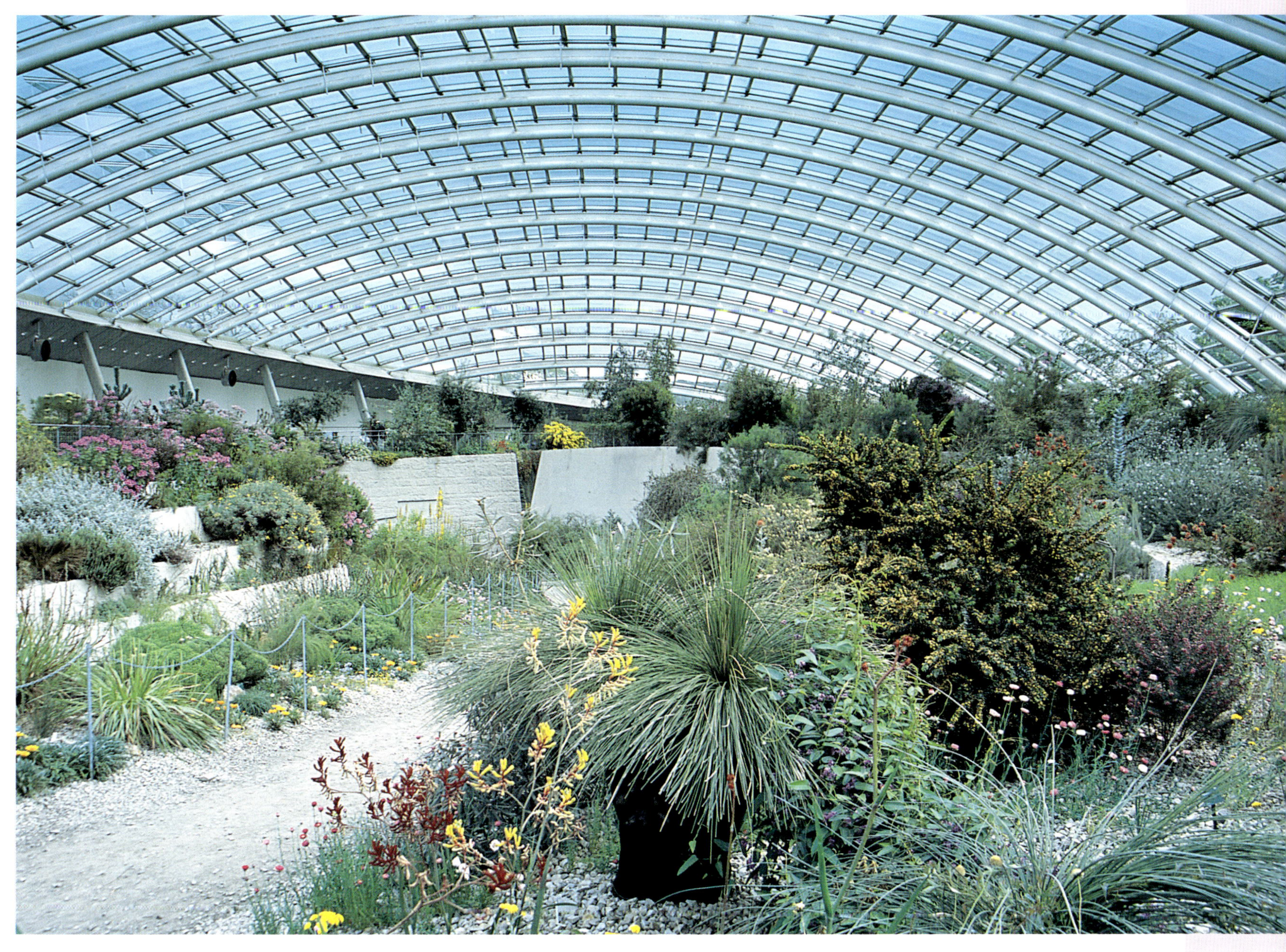

The National Botanic Garden of Wales at Llanarthne, Carmarthenshire is the first one to be created in the UK for nearly 200 years. The garden, which will be under continual development for many years to come, already boasts a wide variety of features and this photograph shows a view inside the Great Glasshouse, designed by Norman Foster and Partners. This energy-efficient structure houses plants of Mediterranean climates and is, according to the guidebook, 'an elliptical torus 95m long and 55m wide, tilted seven degrees on its axis for maximum sunlight'. It is the world's largest single-span glasshouse.

**Minolta Dynax 700si, 28–135mm lens, two-stop ND filter with soft graduation, tripod. 1/10sec at f/11 on Provia 100F**

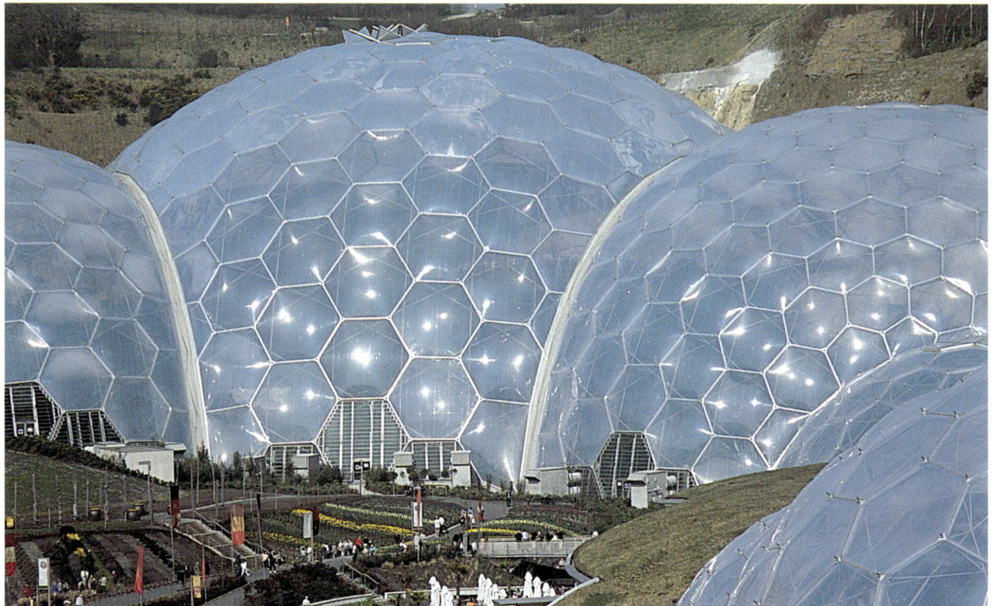

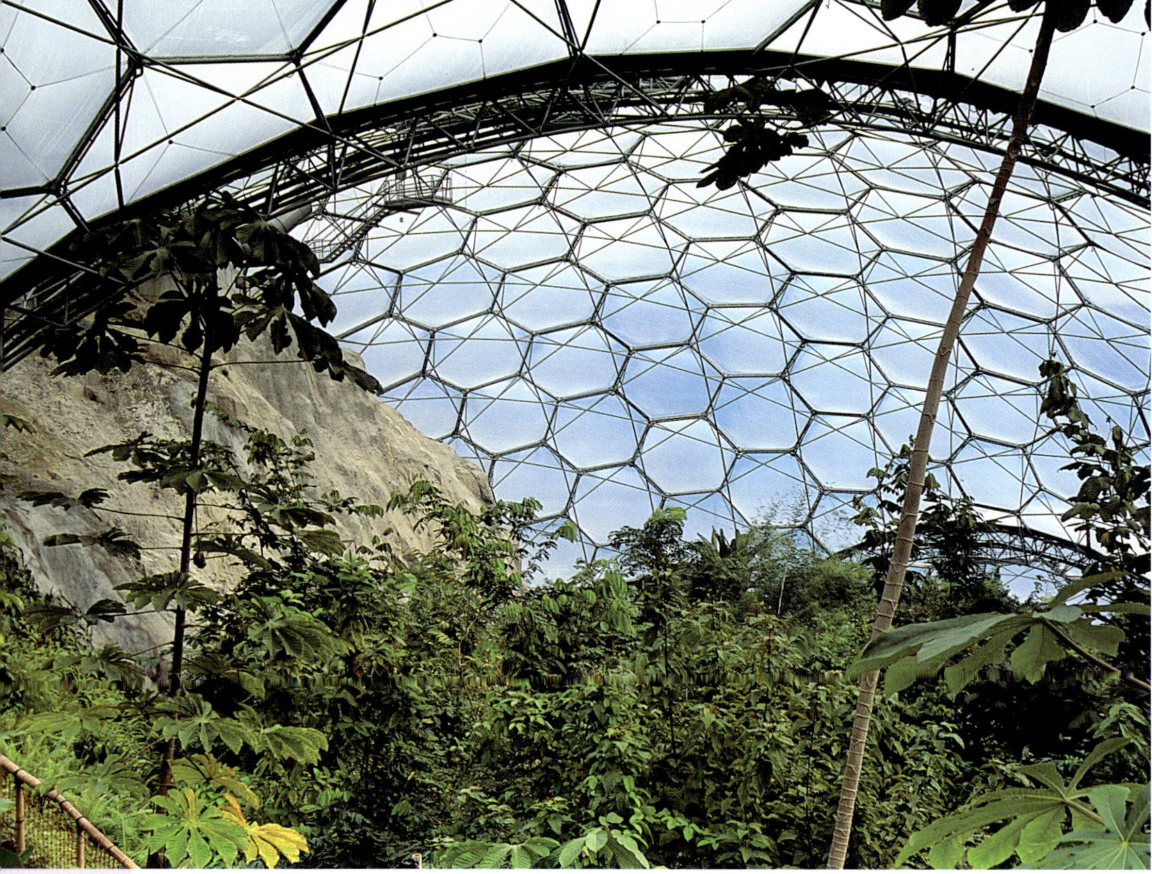

The Tropical Biome at the Eden Project, St Austell, Cornwall. The project, which is situated in an enormous exhausted china-clay pit, is a series of geodesic domes called biomes, and it has been described as one of the wonders of the modern world. The biomes are not glasshouses; the material covering them is Teflon foil, which is very thin but also very strong.

Eden has been a success from the day of its opening in March 2001. In fact, it was a major attraction even before that, with over half a million visitors turning up just to view building progress. I was one of them and my lasting memory of that first visit is of a giant earth-moving machine, seen through a gap in the hexagon panels, looking just like a toy, so dwarfed was it by its surroundings.

Aimed at showing the relationship between plants and humans, Eden is a scientific and educational resource combined with a very enjoyable day out. Tim Smit (of the Lost Gardens of Heligan, see opposite) was the visionary behind the project.

---

**Top: Minolta Dynax 7, 28–135mm lens, 81A filter, tripod. f/13 on Provia 100F**

**Bottom: Minolta Dynax 700si, 28–135mm lens, two-stop ND filter with soft graduation, tripod. f/8 on Velvia**

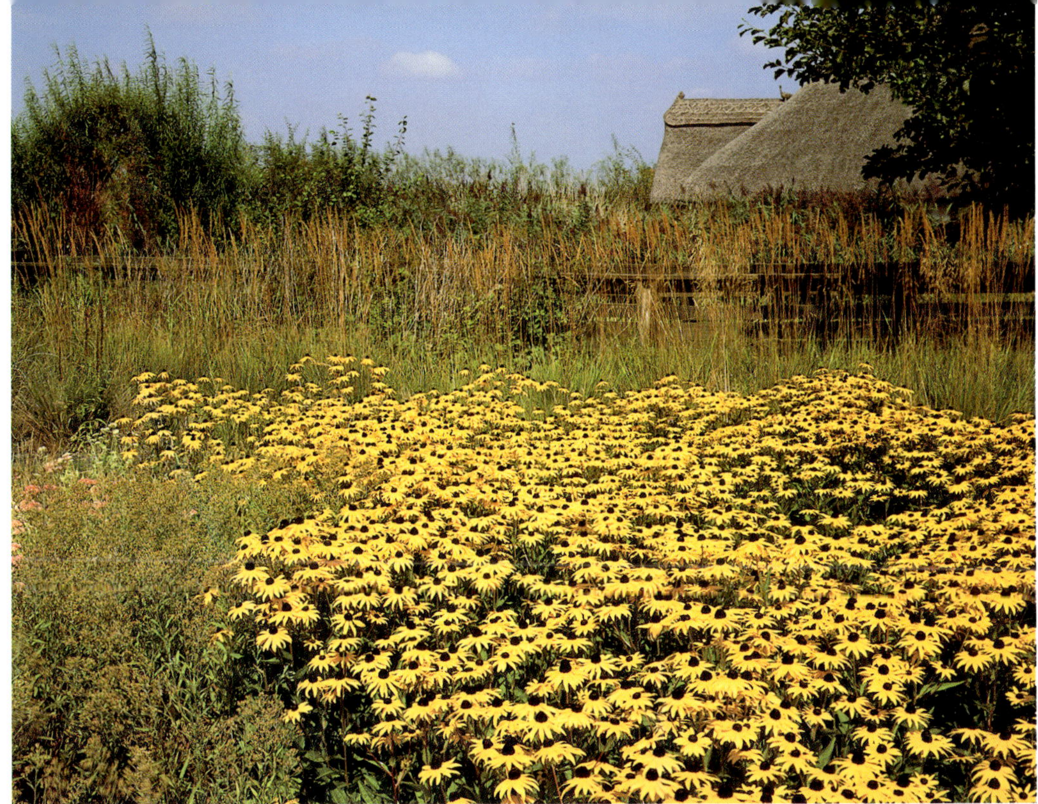

Left: The Wetland Centre at Barnes in south-west London has a sustainable garden designed by Land Art in the naturalistic style. This photo shows an arresting sheet of golden yellow from *Rudbeckia fulgida* var. *sullivantii* 'Goldsturm'.

**Fuji GW670III, 81B filter, tripod. f/22 on Velvia**

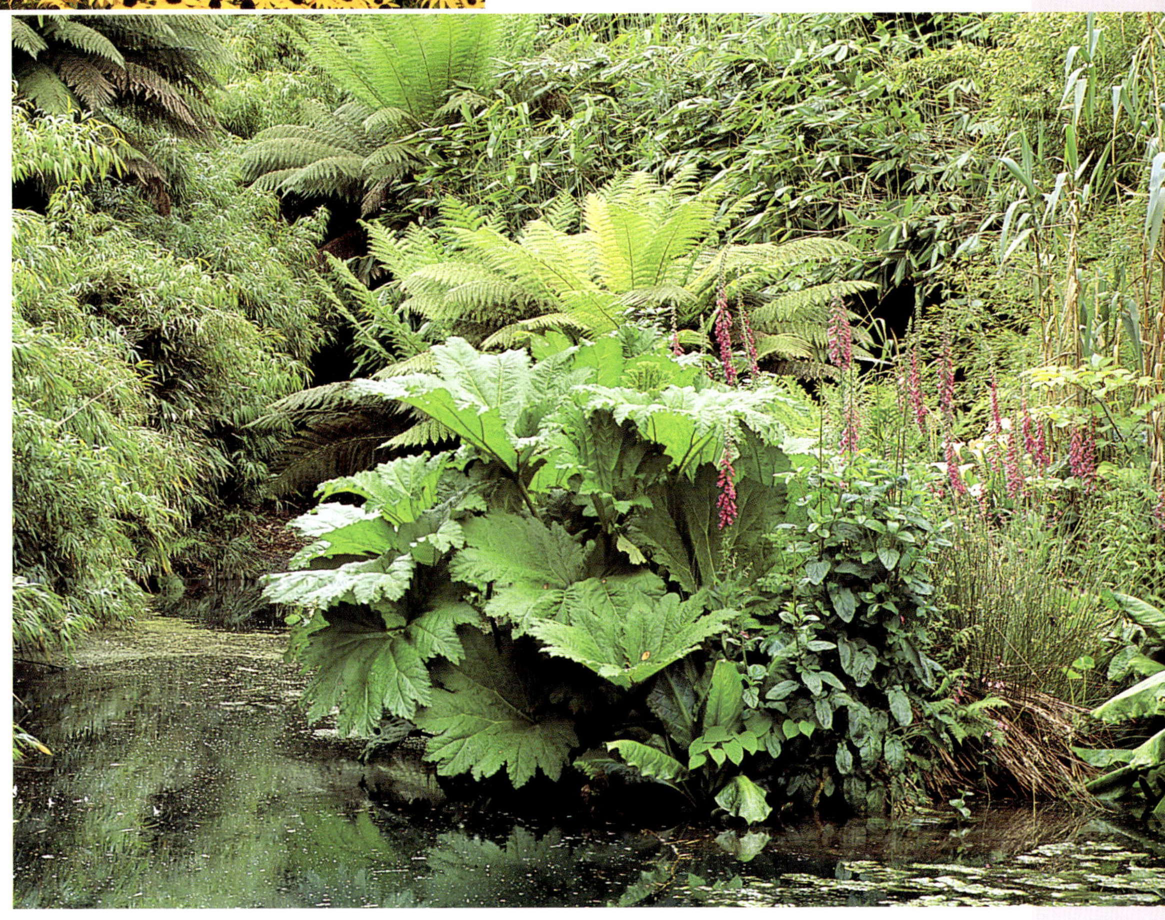

Right: The Lost Gardens of Heligan, near Mevagissey, Cornwall, had suffered years of neglect until in 1991 Tim Smit and John Nelson decided to bring them back to life. They and their helpers had their work cut out: everything had disappeared under brambles and undergrowth up to 15ft (4.5m) high. There is a superb walled kitchen garden, an Italian garden, a grotto, herbaceous borders, an old potting shed and a pineapple pit, and (as shown right) a lush sub-tropical valley with tree ferns, giant gunneras, bamboos and rhododendrons of tree-like proportions. It's an exciting and romantic place; no wonder so many visitors are enchanted by it.

**Minolta Dynax 700si, 90mm macro lens, 81A filter, tripod. f/16 on Velvia**

# 2

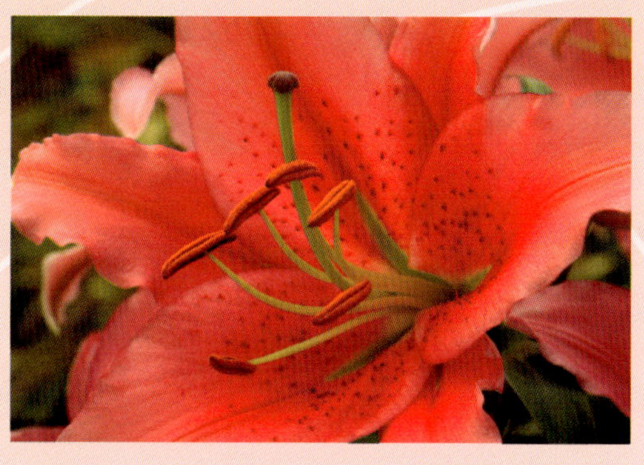

# **Digital** Photography

**Digital photography is here to stay, so why not switch to it right away? The answer is that it is too soon to write off all the capital tied up in film-based equipment and that a complete swap to digital is inappropriate at present.**

The quality of images taken with the latest generation of digital cameras does not clearly surpass film-based images for reproduction, and some experts assert that roll-film transparencies still have the edge over digital.

Market readiness to deal with online digital data for picture research and sales has meant that digital picture files are being requested, and preferred, where formerly they were not. Three libraries that hold many of my transparencies have confirmed this to me. My interpretation of the situation is that the libraries' expertise in digital matters (and that of their clients) is always increasing, and the convenience of digital files has swept away any lingering objections. In this context, three plusses for digital have been crucial:

- the speed of transmitting images
- an absence of complications and cost arising from loss, delay or damage in the post
- no hassle obtaining insurance cover.

Printing standards are also continually improving, helping matters considerably. The arrival of this situation thus jump-started the libraries' willingness to consider accommodating image files from digital cameras, as expensive scanning time is eliminated when the photographer presents digital data on CD. Transparencies are still sometimes requested by clients, but the ability to view low-resolution images and then make a choice is still an advantage.

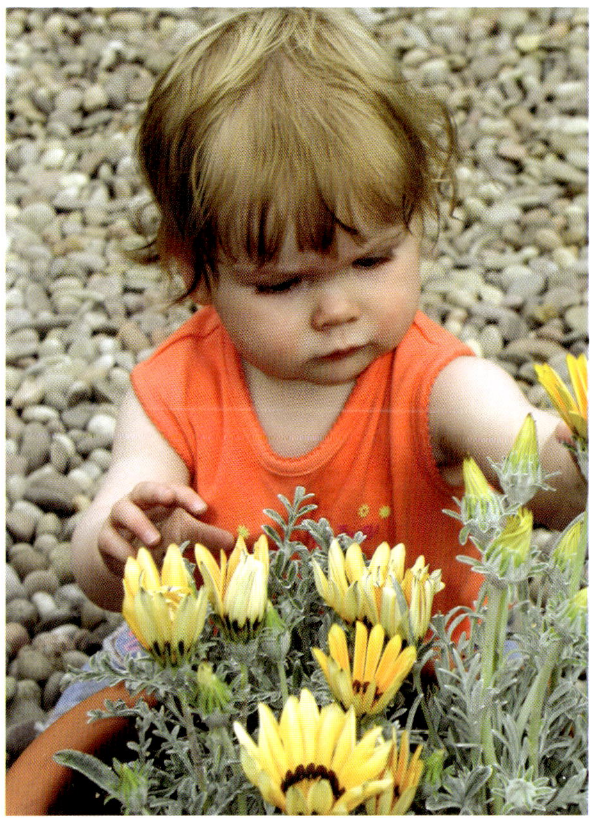

Right: One-year-old Charlotte intent on gazanias in a pot, in this shot taken with a digital compact camera.

**Olympus Camedia C-4040 Zoom, fill-in flash, tripod. ISO sensitivity 100, JPEG 1.9MB**

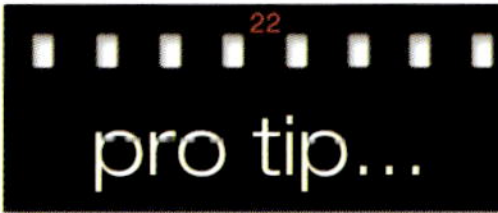


**Submitting digital work**

Most publishers and horticultural photo libraries are now happy to receive digital image data in large files (around 50MB) scanned on quality equipment from transparencies, or in digitally originated (i.e. camera-produced) files of sufficient size (around 18MB).

## Starting Out with Digital

Digital capture has a steep learning curve and a digital compact camera, although it is less likely to produce images good enough for reproduction, offers a cheaper starting point than a digital SLR. Three of the images shown in this chapter were taken with the four megapixel (4MP) compact camera I purchased in order to familiarize myself with the new technology.

The Olympus Camedia C-4040 Zoom camera produces a TIFF image of 2272x1704 pixels. Publishers require a digital image of 300 dots per inch (dpi) to obtain a picture on the printed page that is the same quality as film. To find out what size an image can be printed at and still compete with film in terms of quality, it is therefore necessary to divide the number of pixels by the dpi figure.

The image reproduced below was taken with the Olympus Camedia C-4040 Zoom camera that I bought to familiarize myself with digital photography. The picture is from a TIFF file of over 11MB and the maximum size of reproduction is, in theory, 7.57x5.68in (19.23x14.43cm).

A shot of Heale House, in Wiltshire, using a compact digital camera.The enlargement comparison here is the theoretical maximum reproduction size.

**Olympus Camedia C-4040, tripod. f/10, TIFF 11MB**

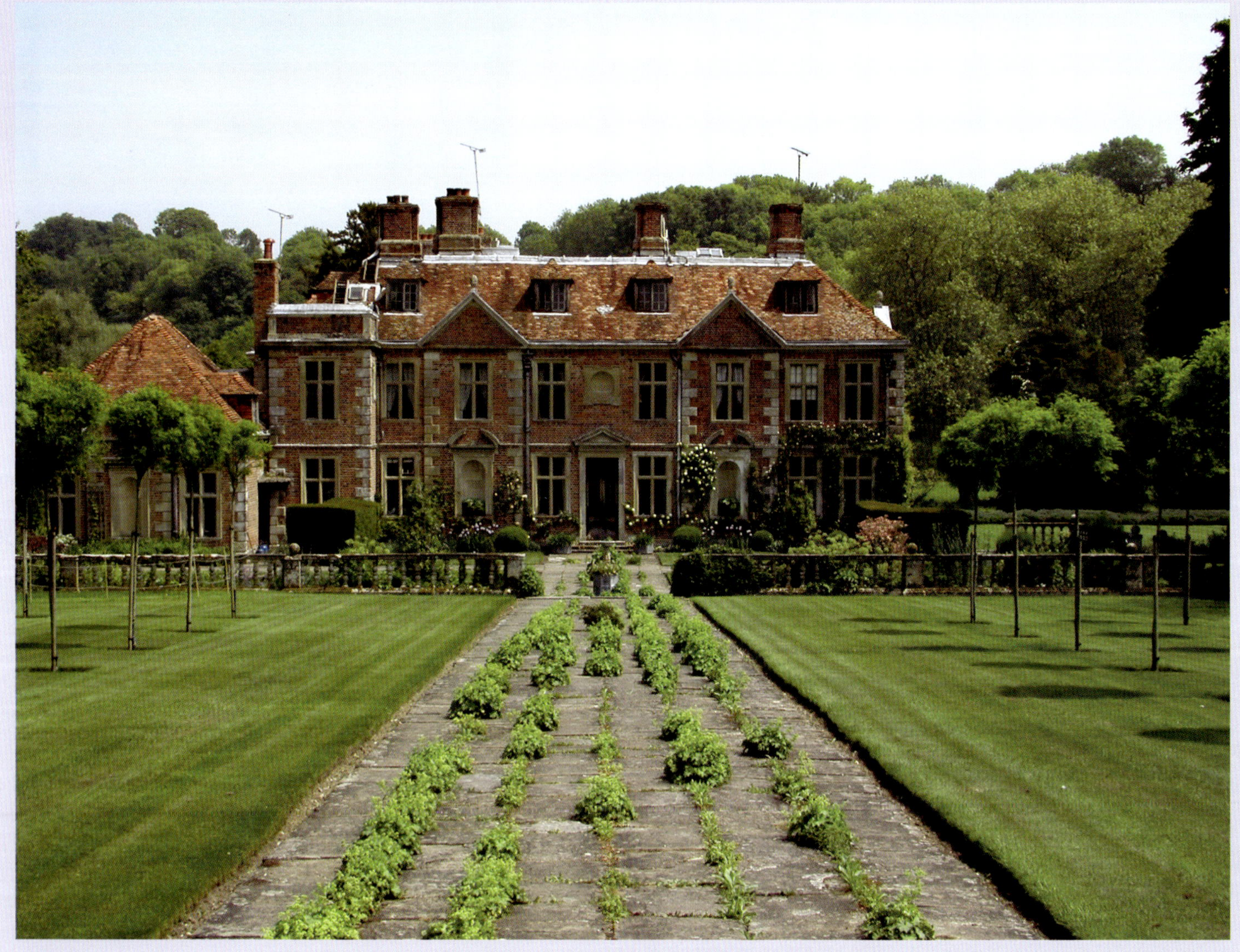

Below is an equivalent transparency image taken at the same time on 35mm film of 100 ISO, the ISO value selected on the digital camera. Using these parameters digital has compared well, but the small reproduction size makes a 4MP camera of limited use professionally.

The same scene, taken on conventional 35mm film and reproduced to the same size.

**Minolta Dynax 7, 28–135mm lens, tripod. 1/40 sec at f/16 on Ektachrome 100G**

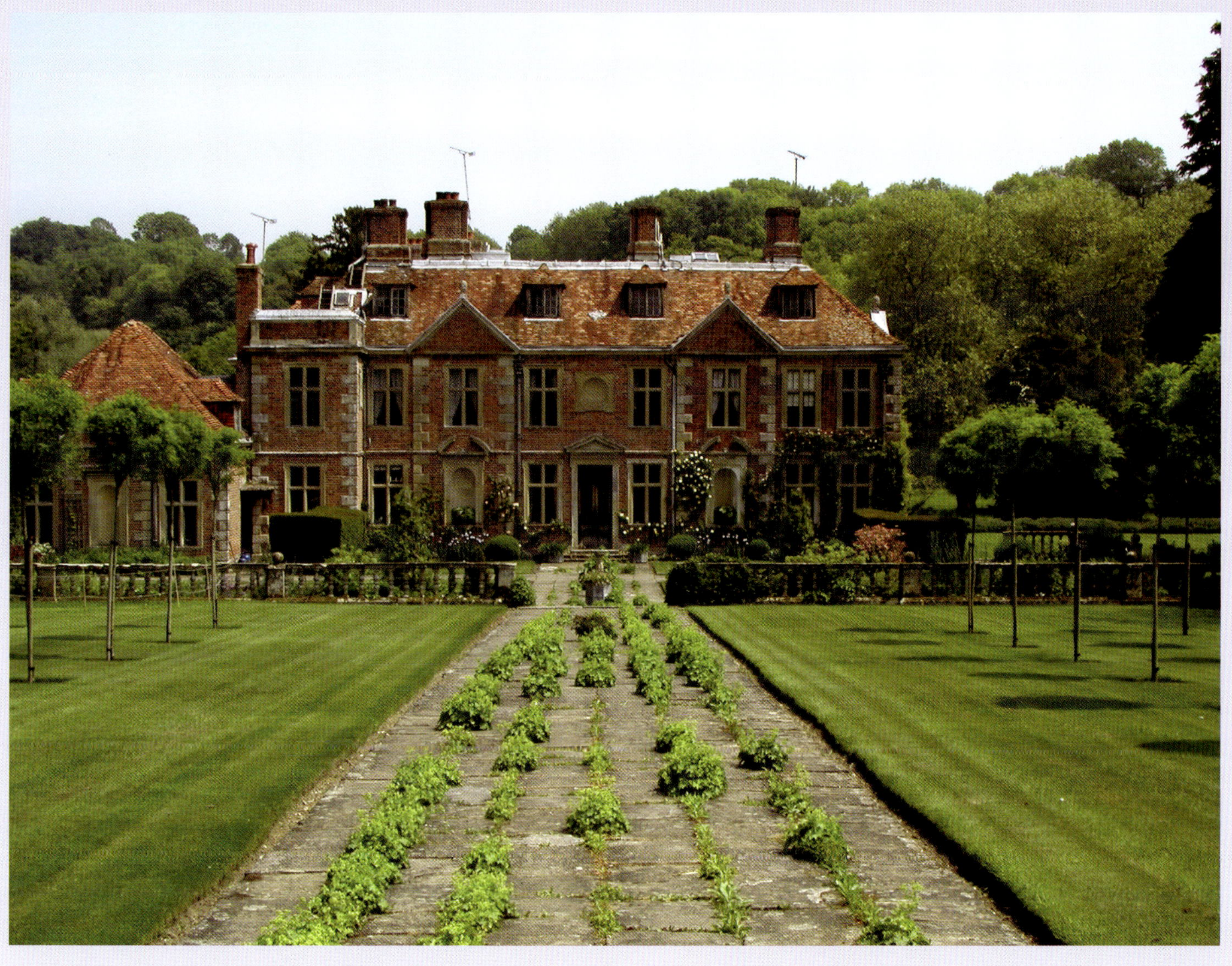

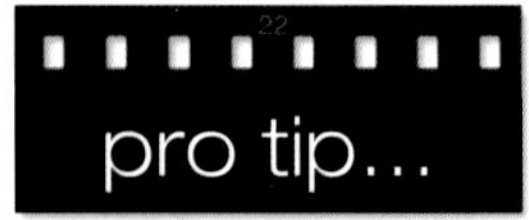


**Storing files**

CompactFlash cards soon become full if you shoot high-resolution TIFFs, and a regime of ruthless in-camera editing coupled with file storage on CD, rather than on the computer's hard drive, is necessary.

## Digital SLR Cameras

Three of the photographs shown in this chapter were taken with a digital SLR, which produces a choice of TIFF images. I normally opt for a TIFF image of 3024x2016 pixels (a file of 17.5MB). The camera will produce one of 4256x2848 pixels (nearly 35MB), but only 14 of these can be contained on one of the 512MB CompactFlash memory cards I use. Lack of memory space when out in the field could be solved by a battery-powered portable storage device, but another option is to opt for the least-compressed JPEG file available, known as 'Fine' on the S2. A JPEG image of 4256x2848 pixels produces a file of around 4.7MB, allowing room for around 108 images on the card. The difference in reproduction quality is said to be marginal, and the two pictures reproduced on page 39 bear this out, although full TIFF files are required in the marketplace.

## The LCD Screen

It is useful to be able to view the image that has just been captured on the camera's LCD, but the screen shouldn't be relied on too much. Slight camera shake or incorrect exposure might not show up on the LCD, unless the camera has the facility to display histograms indicating exposure accuracy or an on-screen zooming facility for checking focusing. Underexposure of reasonable proportions can be rectified on a computer, but overexposure, where detail is lost, cannot. In all instances the screen is extremely useful for gauging composition, and obvious duds should be erased straightaway. This allows test shots to be made without the constraints imposed by film costs.

## Image Sensor

Because the dimensions of the image sensor on most digital SLRs are smaller than those of the 35mm frame, any 35mm lens used on these digital SLRs has its focal length increased by a factor of about x1.5. For example, a 28mm lens when used on most digital SLRs becomes a 42mm lens, a 50mm lens has an equivalent focal length of 75mm, and so on. Although bad news for wide-angle photography in gardens, this is good news for macro work. The reason for this is that depth of field at any given magnification of, for instance, a 90mm macro lens, remains the same when the lens, now equivalent to a 135mm macro, is used digitally. In other words, the lens's focal length increases, but the depth of field remains the same.

Dust can be a major problem when it comes into contact with a digital camera's image sensor, something that can occur when changing lenses. The S2 has a Nikon F lens mount and I have just the one lens (a Nikkor 28–105mm zoom), all my 35mm lenses having the Minolta lens mount. I therefore have no need to change lenses on the camera, but the risk of dust being attracted onto the sensor is still present, giving rise to random black spots on images. The problem can be dealt with to some extent at home, but the chances are that the camera will require professional cleaning at regular intervals. Olympus has addressed the problem on its E-1 by fitting a protective filter, which vibrates at high frequency when the camera is switched on. No doubt in time all the digital-camera manufacturers will introduce their own solution to this problem.

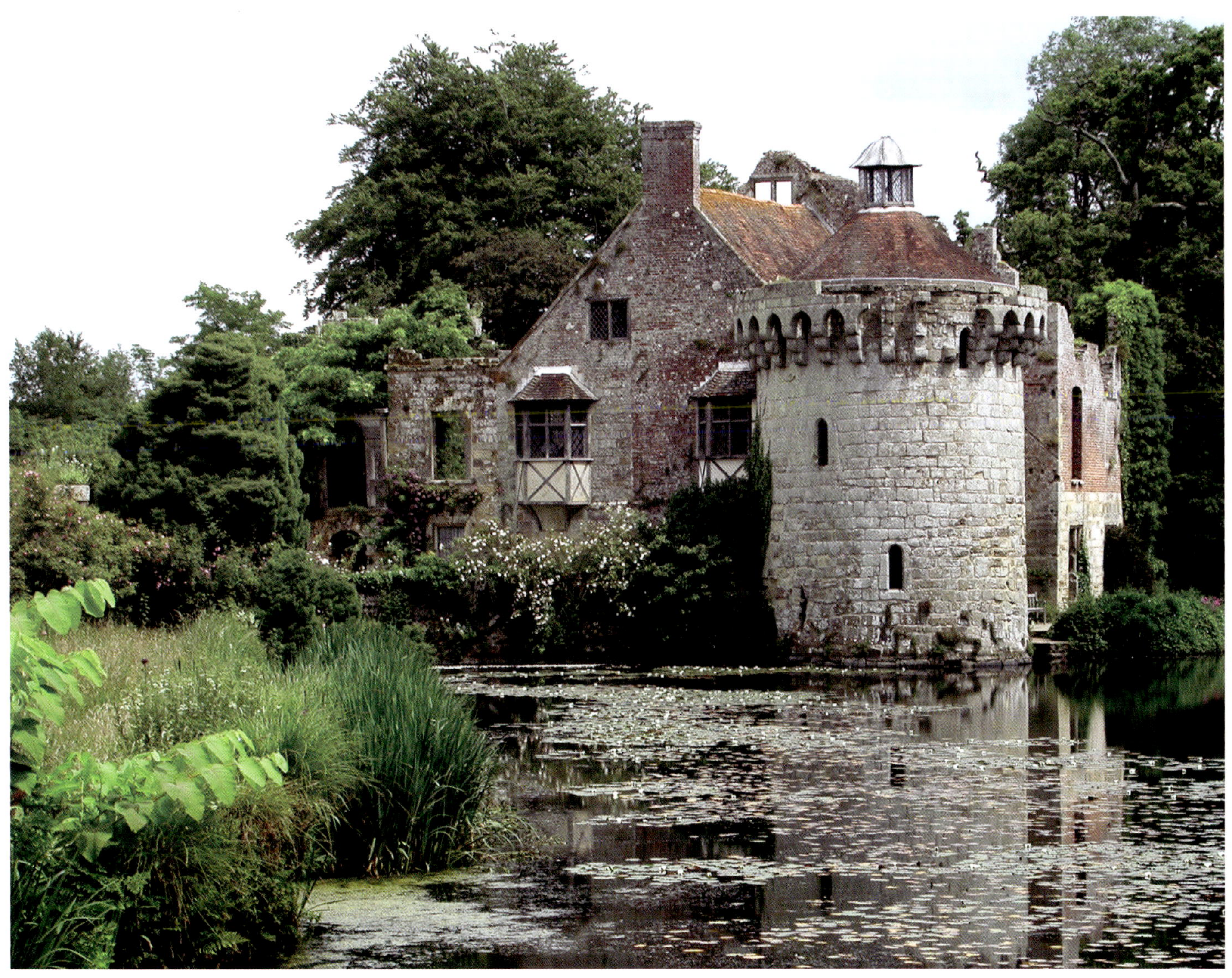

The detail in this scene at Scotney Castle, Kent, is well resolved by the digital technology of a four-megapixel CCD when reproduced at this size.

**Olympus Camedia C-4040, tripod. TIFF 11MB**

## Technique: **Adjusting the White Balance**

In digital cameras, colour temperature is determined using the 'white balance' feature, which allows the camera to adjust the colour balance to suit the colour of the ambient light. This can be set automatically, although some digital SLRs also enable the user to adjust the white balance manually to suit specific light sources (as shown right). It is worth noting that filters still have an effect on an image regardless of the camera's white-balance function. Therefore, if a warmer feel is required it can be added by using a warm-up filter or by setting the white balance to, for example, 'Shade' for a sunny scene. Alternatively, the image can be altered later on a computer, although my preference is to do everything possible 'in-camera'.

| **Common Settings:** | **Symbol:** | **Colour Temperature (°K):** |
|---|---|---|
| Auto White Balance | AWB | 3000–7000 |
| Daylight Sunny | 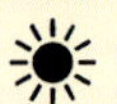 | 5200 |
| Daylight Shade | 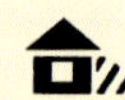 | 7000 |
| Daylight Cloudy/Hazy |  | 6000 |
| Flash |  | 6000 |
| Indoor Fluorescent Light | 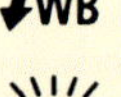 | 4000 |
| Indoor Tungsten | 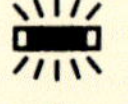 | 3200 |
| Colour Temperature | 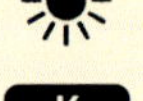 | 2800–10,000 |
| Custom WB | 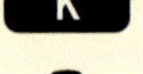 | 2000–10,000 |

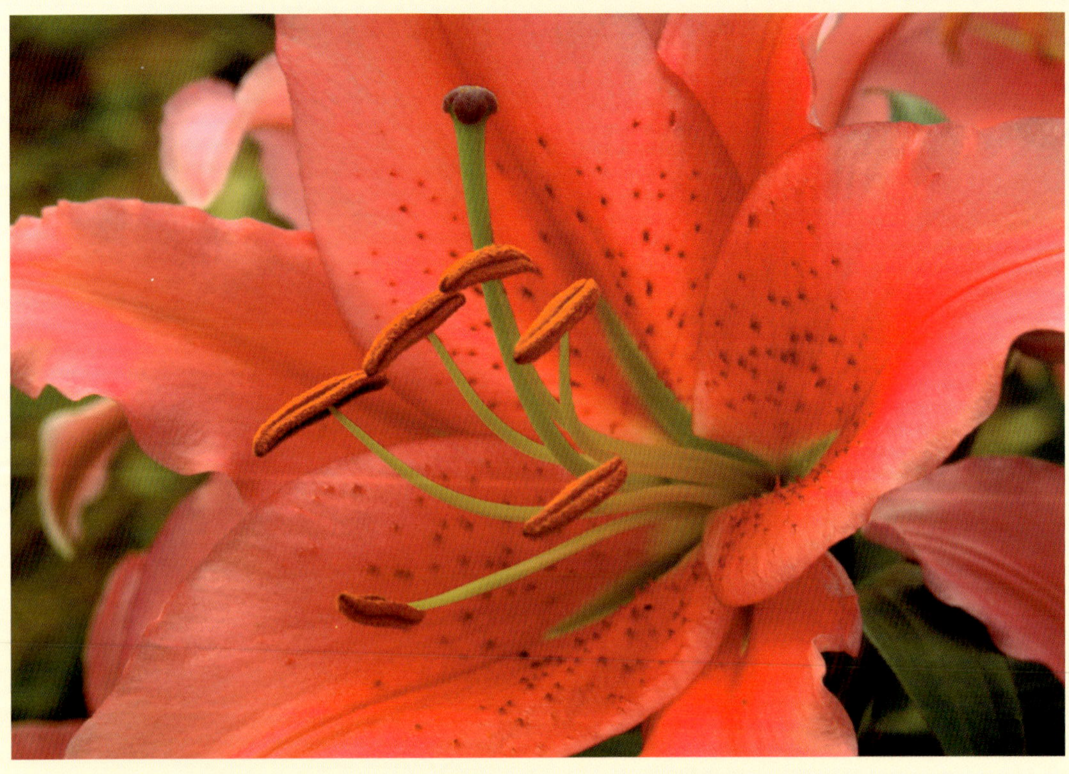

This image of *Lilium* 'Acapulco' was taken shortly after dawn, before the sun caused any problems with contrast and while conditions were still calm. I used a gold reflector to provide even illumination on the flower. This had a warming effect on the picture, which was fine in this instance, but in other circumstances use of the camera's white-balance settings could have provided an alternative solution.

**FinePix S2 Pro, 28–105mm lens, tripod. f/22 at ISO sensitivity 100, TIFF 17.5MB**

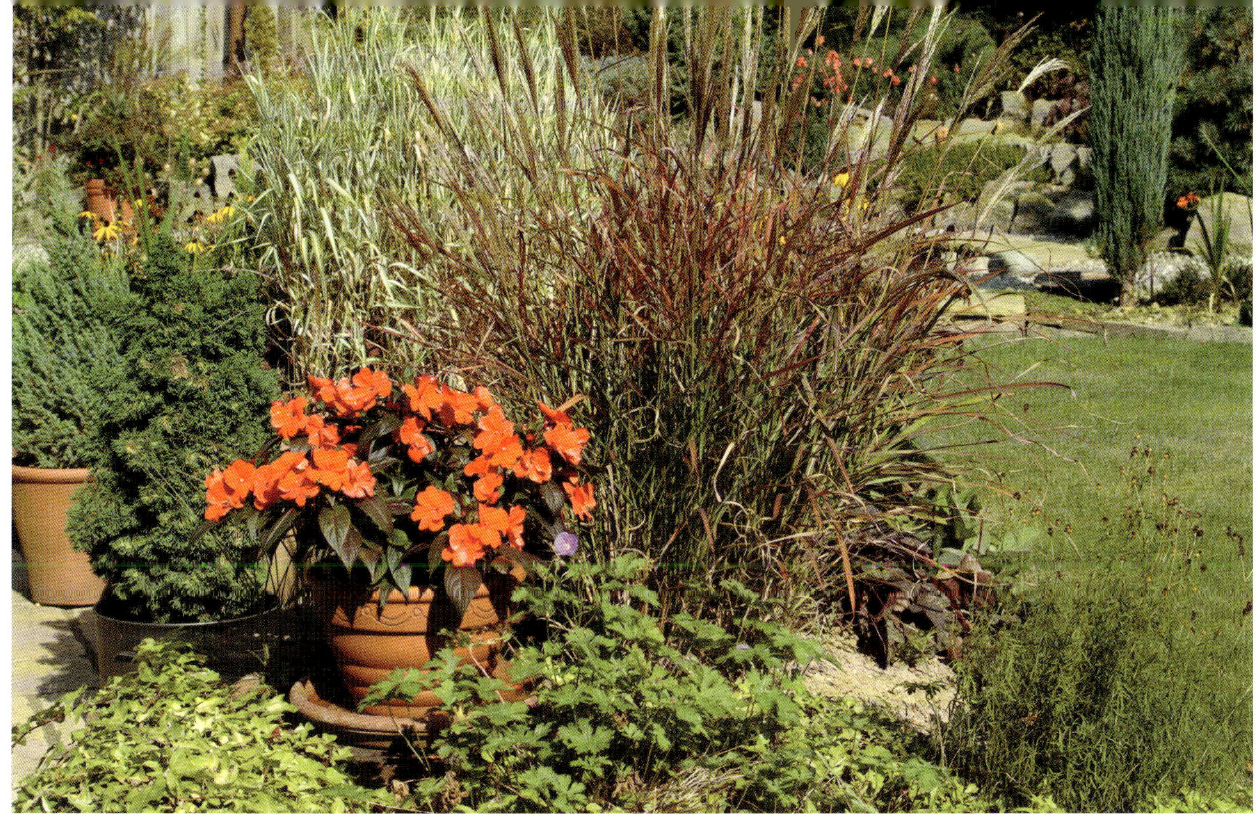

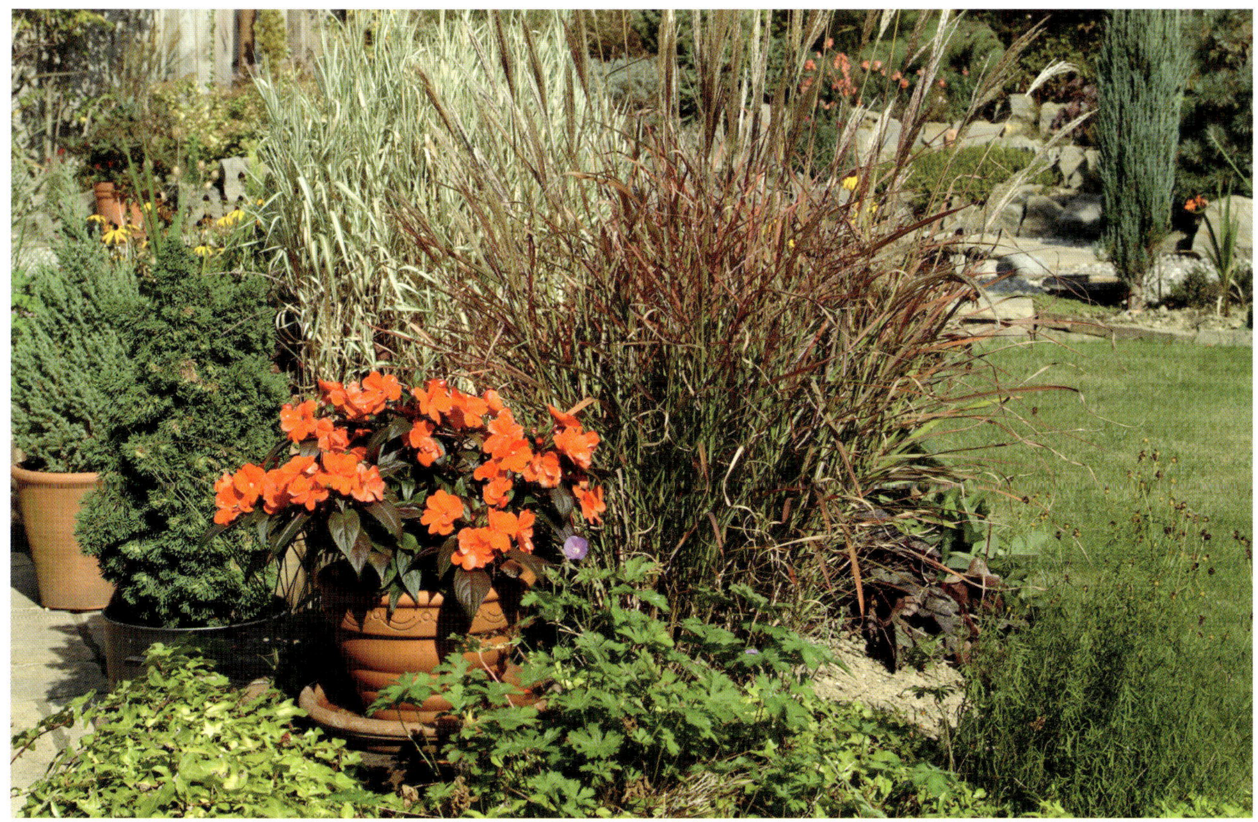

Can you spot the difference? The top image of an early autumn scene in my garden is reproduced from a 'Fine' JPEG file of 4.7MB, whereas the lower one is from a TIFF file of 17.5MB.

**Both pictures: FinePix S2 Pro, 28–105mm lens, tripod. f/8 at ISO sensitivity 100**

pro tip...

### ISO settings

The facility to alter the ISO speed, known as ISO sensitivity, between frames is a useful option offered by digital cameras. I normally set this at 100 ISO, but in changing light conditions it can be increased to 160, 200 or beyond. However, the difference in image quality between 100 and 200 is minimal.

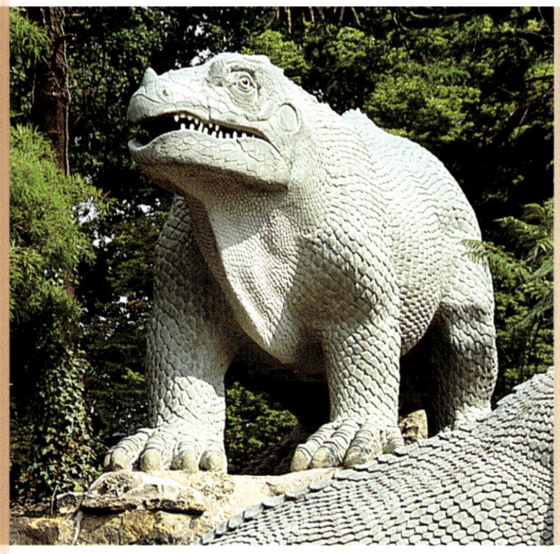

# Themed Gardens

**Gardens with themes are always particularly fascinating, and can present a difficult challenge for the professional garden photographer. Although the themes adopted by the gardens shown here are by no means unique, they all have a strong identity and carry off their dedication to an ideal magnificently. Careful consideration must be given to how this can best be conveyed in a single photograph.**

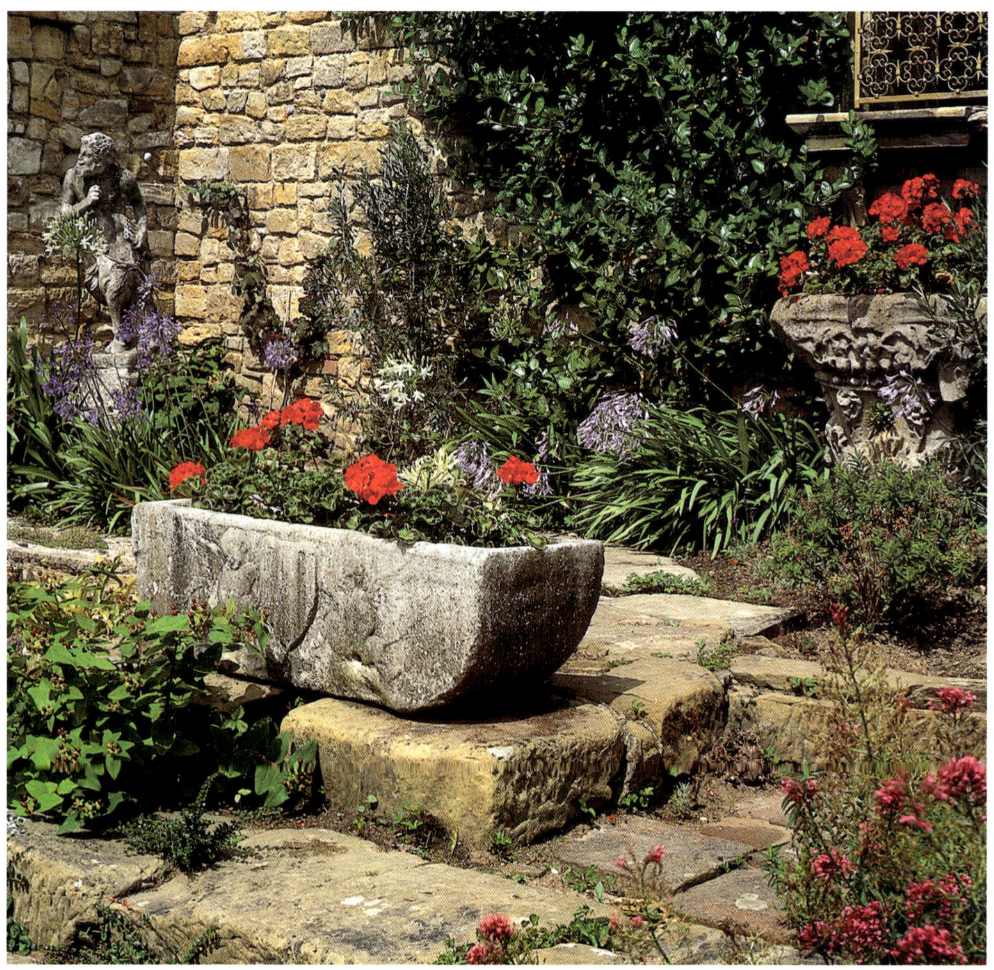

Hever Castle in Kent is indelibly linked with Henry VIII's second wife, Anne Boleyn, whose childhood home it was. The castle was restored by William Waldorf Astor, who bought the property in 1903 and laid out the magnificent gardens in 1904–8.

This photograph shows a section of the Pompeiian Wall in the Italian-style garden. The wall on the north side of the four-acre garden is adorned along its length with classical statuary and sculpture acquired by Astor when he was American Minister in Rome.

---

**Mamiya 645 Super, 80mm lens, 81B filter, tripod. 1/15sec at f/22 on Velvia**

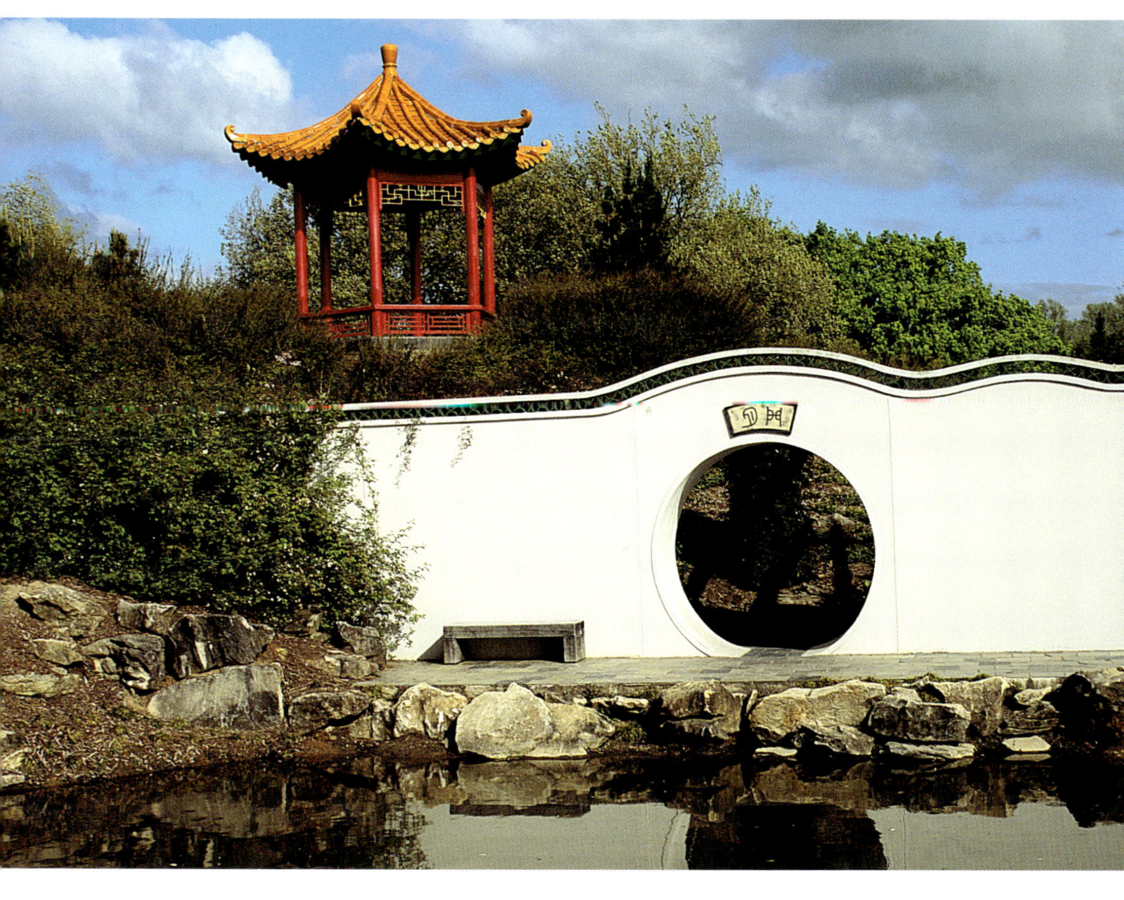

Below: A simple slab bridge over a 'riverbed' in the Japanese garden at the National Botanic Garden of Wales.

**Minolta Dynax 7, 90mm macro lens, 81A filter, tripod. f/16 on Ektachrome 100S**

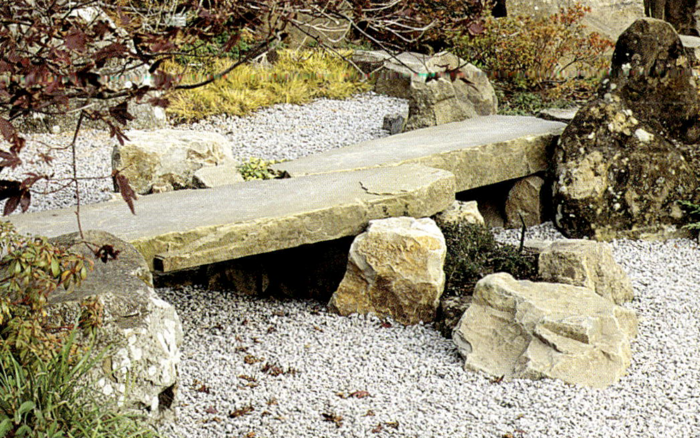

Above: This beautifully constructed garden, known as 'The Chinese Scholar's Garden', can be found tucked into a corner of Hamilton Gardens on the North Island of New Zealand. It is largely based on a traditional Chinese garden from the Sung Dynasty (960–1279AD). Scholars' gardens were places of allegory, mystery and fantasy, where symbolism played a large role. The picture above shows a moon gate and, beyond the wall, the roof of the Golden Pavilion.

**Minolta 7000i, 35–90mm lens, tripod. f/22 on Velvia**

Right: Bamboo gate in a Japanese garden designed by Maseo Fukuhara. This garden was exhibited at the Chelsea Flower Show in 2001, winning a gold medal. It was subsequently moved to its present location at the National Botanic Garden of Wales.

**Minolta Dynax 7, 28–135mm lens, 81B filter, tripod. 1/15sec on Agfachrome RSXII**

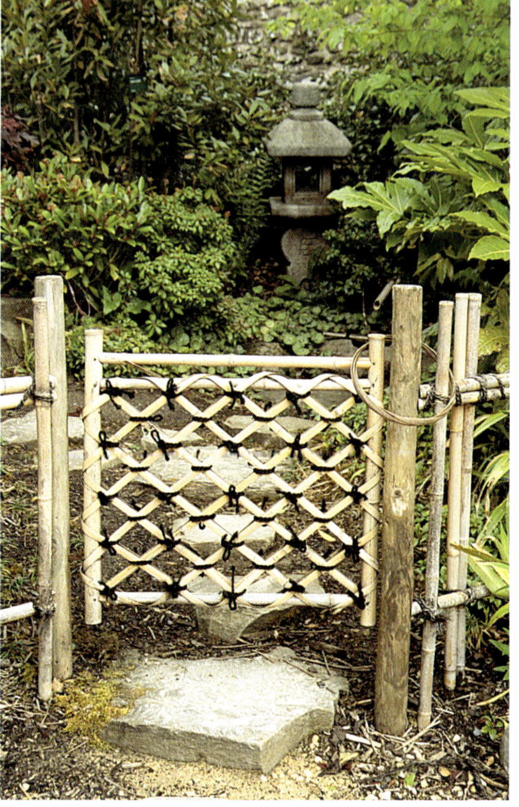

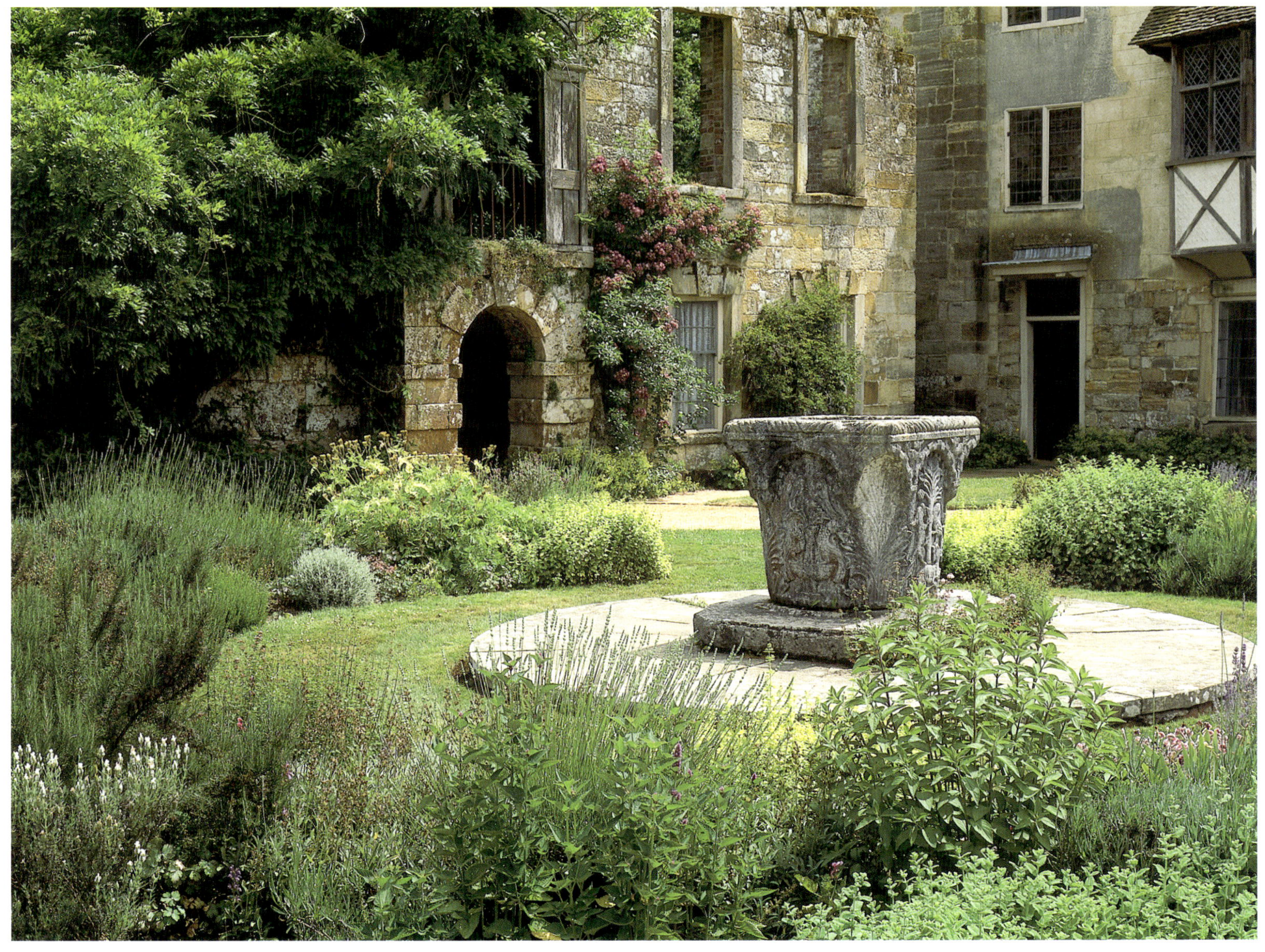

Tucked beside the ruins of Scotney Castle Garden at Lamberhurst, Kent, this little courtyard herb garden brings a touch of formality to the romantic ambience of the fourteenth-century round tower. Herb gardening has been practised through the ages and herb gardens remain popular to this day. Although this one is a modern addition and is somewhat modest in size, for me it scores highly because the medieval context seems just right.

**Mamiya 645 Super, 80mm lens, 81B filter, tripod. 1/4sec at f/22 on Velvia**

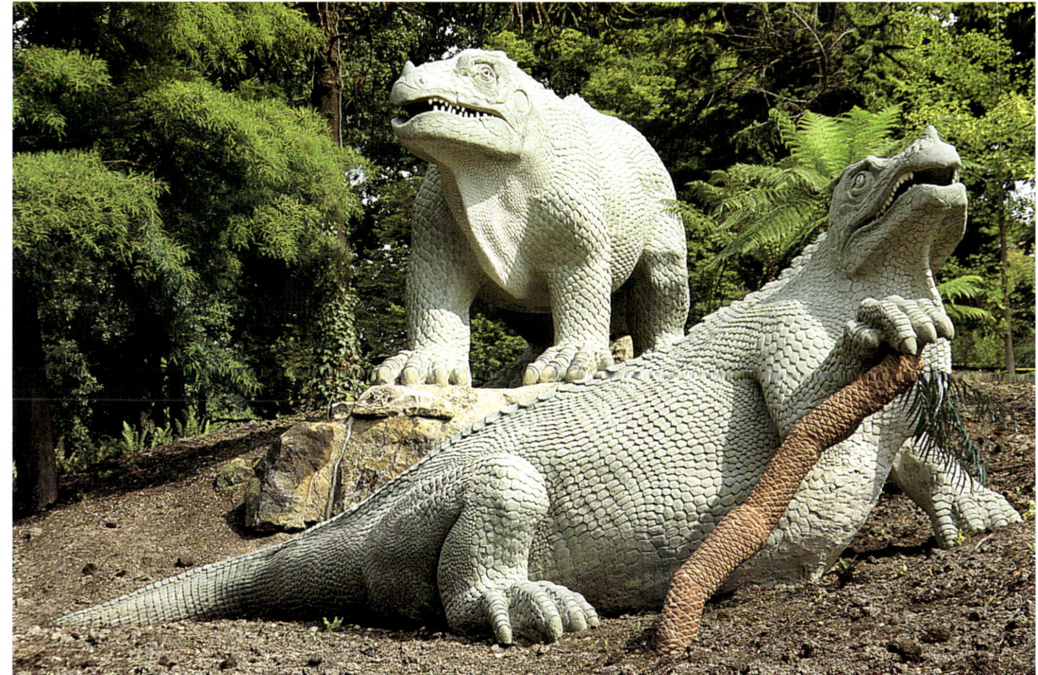

Left: Designed by the nineteenth-century palaeontologist, Professor Richard Owen, the dinosaurs in the park at Crystal Palace are life-size reconstructions. They were sculpted by Waterhouse Hawkins, and the park, opened in 1854, was a world first. The ravages of time had taken their toll of the 29 models, but an extensive programme of renovation, funded by Bromley Council and the Heritage Lottery Fund, has recently been completed.

**Minolta Dynax 7, 28–135mm lens, 81A filter, tripod. 1/30sec at f/11 on Velvia**

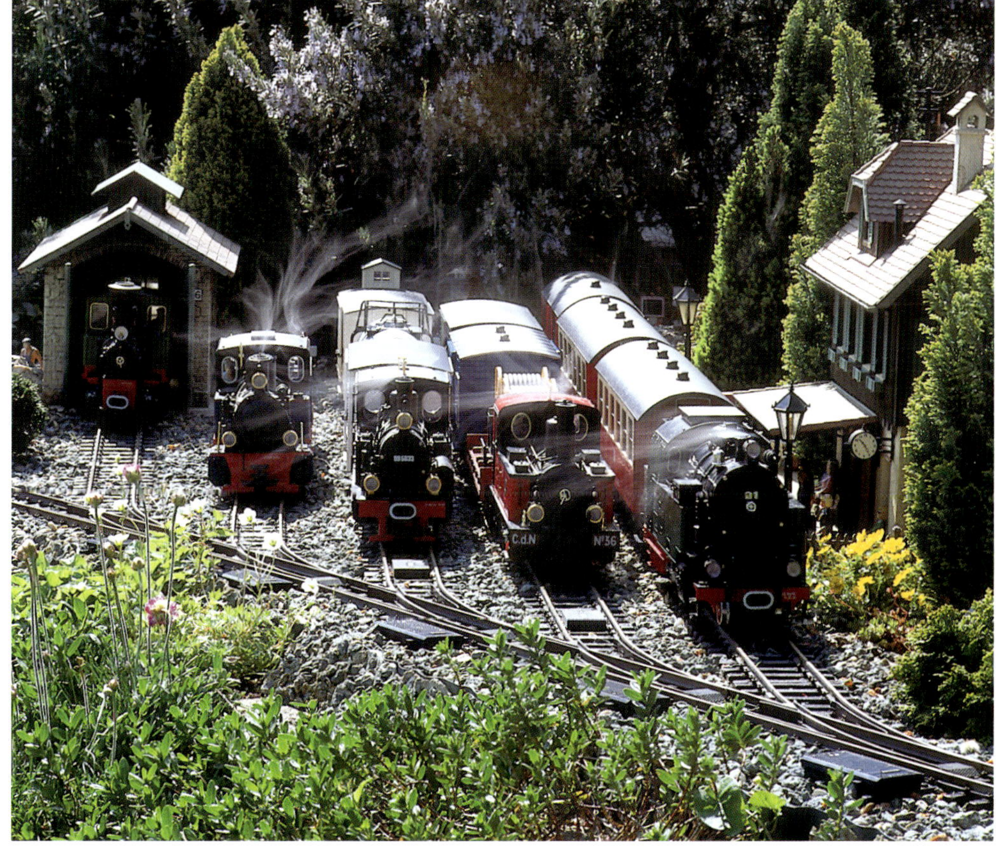

Right: Some properties have extraordinary surprises lurking in the back garden. This example belongs to a friend who has turned a portion of his garden into a train-addict's wonderland, complete with dwarf trees in scale. Smoke issues from locomotives, carriages light up at dusk, and hoots and hisses mingle with real-time birdsong. For those interested, the gauge is 'G scale' and the trains are manufactured by LGB of Nuremberg in Germany.

**Mamiya C330f, 180mm lens, tripod. f/32 on Velvia**

3

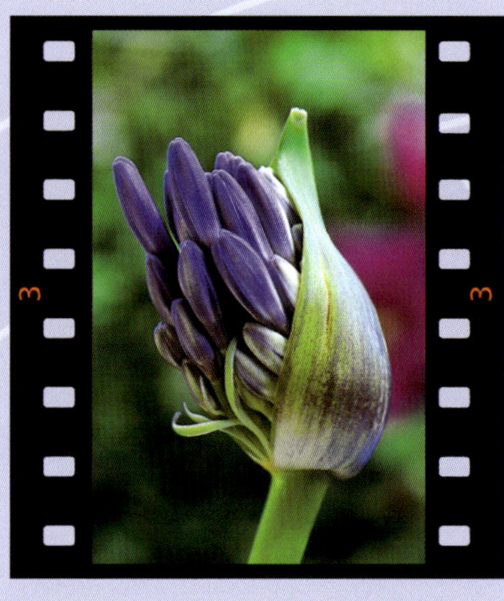

# Composing the Picture

**Composition sounds rather esoteric and perhaps a trifle mysterious, but at its basic level it is simple - just arranging the elements of a scene into a visually pleasing picture.**

Apart from the proportions the elements occupy in the frame, their tones and colours are crucial to the overall balance of the picture. Red, orange and yellow leap out of the picture, bright red especially, and their placement within the frame requires care. Composition applies to close-ups as well as to garden views. Often it is a case of the simpler the picture and the fewer the elements (and colours), the better. Finally, don't overlook the option of turning the camera on its side to use the 'portrait' format.

Quality of light apart, the choice of viewpoint and the exact position in which the camera is placed are the all-important factors in this selection process. The alteration of the camera's position, even by a metre or less, and the height at which it is placed can make a big difference to the look of a picture. With close-ups this difference can be made by an alteration of as little as half an inch (1cm).

### Arranging Elements within the Frame

Facility in the art of composition is largely intuitive, although thankfully it can be learned through experience. As stated earlier, the elements of a picture

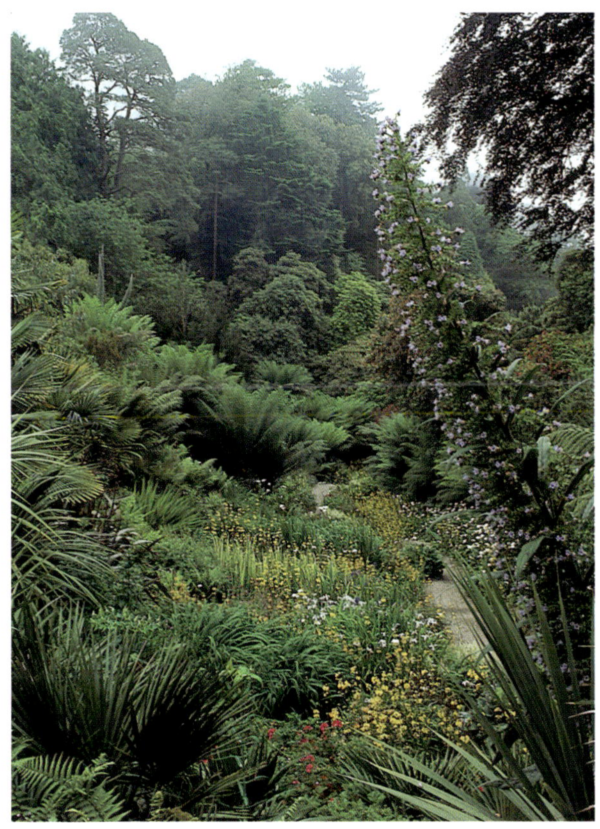

A great spike of *Echium pininana* frames and gives depth to this scene in the wild and wonderful garden at Trebah, in the mild climate of the southern coast of Cornwall.

**Minolta Dynax 7000i, 35–90mm lens, tripod. f/16 on Velvia**

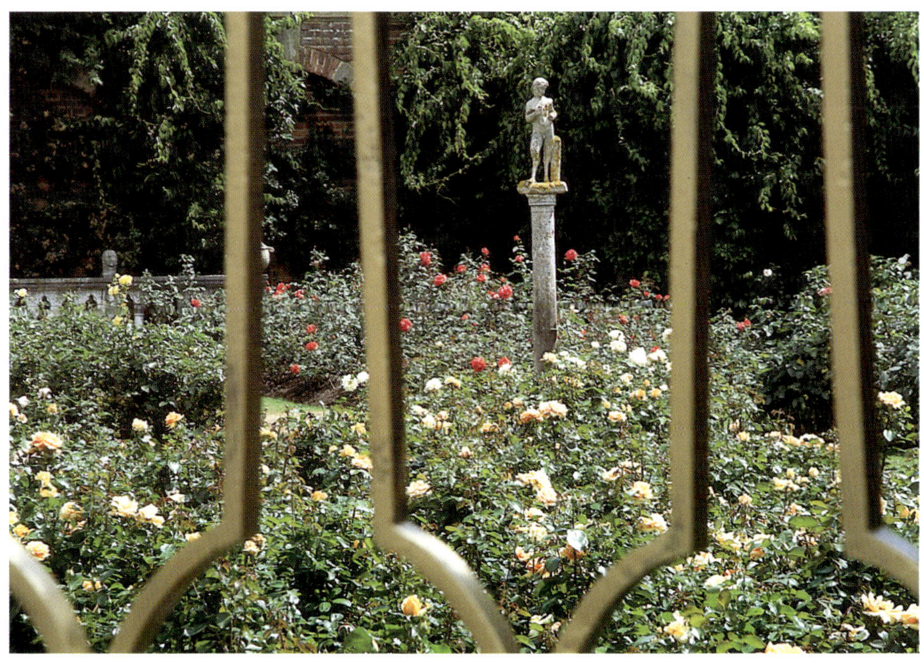

This statue in the Rose garden at Hever is positioned to give balance to the image, while the gold-painted fencing provides foreground interest.

**Minolta Dynax 7, 28–135mm lens, tripod. 1/10sec at f/22 on Velvia**

## Equipment: **Focal Length and Composition**

Lens selection has a crucial impact on the final photo. Lenses ranging between wide angle (around 28mm) and medium telephoto (around 200mm) will be sufficient to cover more than 95% of situations for garden and plant photography; 28mm to around 100mm will cover perhaps 90%.

Variation in the images obtained from these focal lengths can be great. The differences shown in these three pictures of the walled garden at RHS Wisley are relatively subtle. All three were taken from the same position with a zoom lens set at 28mm, 40mm and 70mm respectively. All have a tranquil feeling, with the left half of each picture balanced by a roughly mirror image in the right half. I prefer the middle image, obtained at 40mm, which I think encapsulates the enclosed feeling of the garden most successfully.

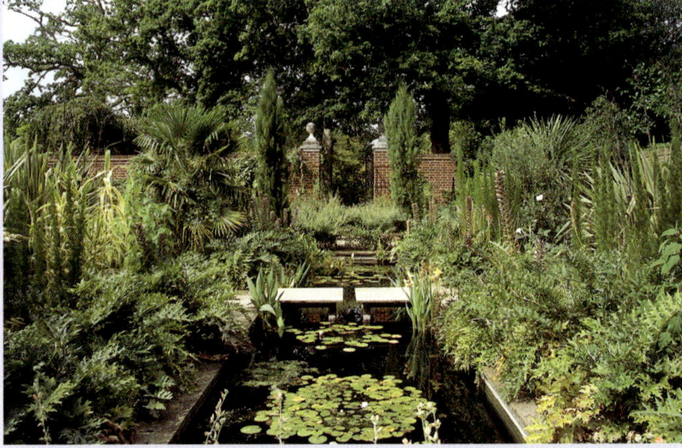

Zoom lens set at 28mm

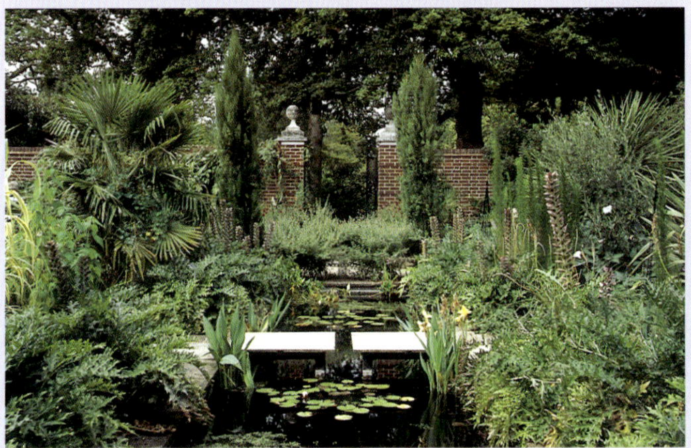

Lens set at 40mm

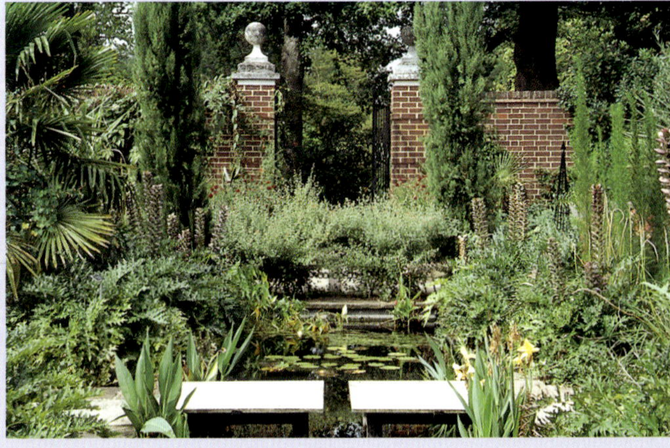

Lens set at 70mm

**All three shots: Minolta Dynax 700si, 28–135mm lens, 81A filter, tripod. f/22 on Ektachrome 100G**

need to be marshalled so that the result is pleasing to the eye and the 'balance' is right.

Composition is too subjective to be tightly defined by rules, but one that is normally effective is known as the 'Rule of Thirds'. This can be applied to the rectangular formats of 35mm, 6x4.5cm and 6x7cm cameras. The 'thirds' in question can be explained as follows. Mark off in your mind the four edges of an image rectangle into three equal divisions and then join up each point with the corresponding point on its opposite side, so that you are left with an imaginary grid. The intersection of the lines creates the 'thirds' in the rule, which states that the composition of an image will look right if the point of interest is placed on any one of the four points of intersection.

It is not normally a good idea to divide a picture in half by having, say, the sky in the top half and the land in the bottom half, but this is only a guideline. A picture that is bisected in this way by the shoreline of a lake could look stunning if most of the bottom half of the picture contains reflections in the water from trees or plants in the top half.

## Diagonal Elements

A diagonal element can bring a sense of dynamism to a picture. This effect works best if the picture is not divided into two equal triangles: the diagonal, if it reaches the edges of the frame, is best positioned somewhere along an edge, but not plumb in the corner.

## Backgrounds

An important attribute for the photography of plants is the ability to throw backgrounds out of focus. This will draw attention to the main subject and prevent fussy backgrounds spoiling the picture. There are degrees to which this can be accomplished, depending

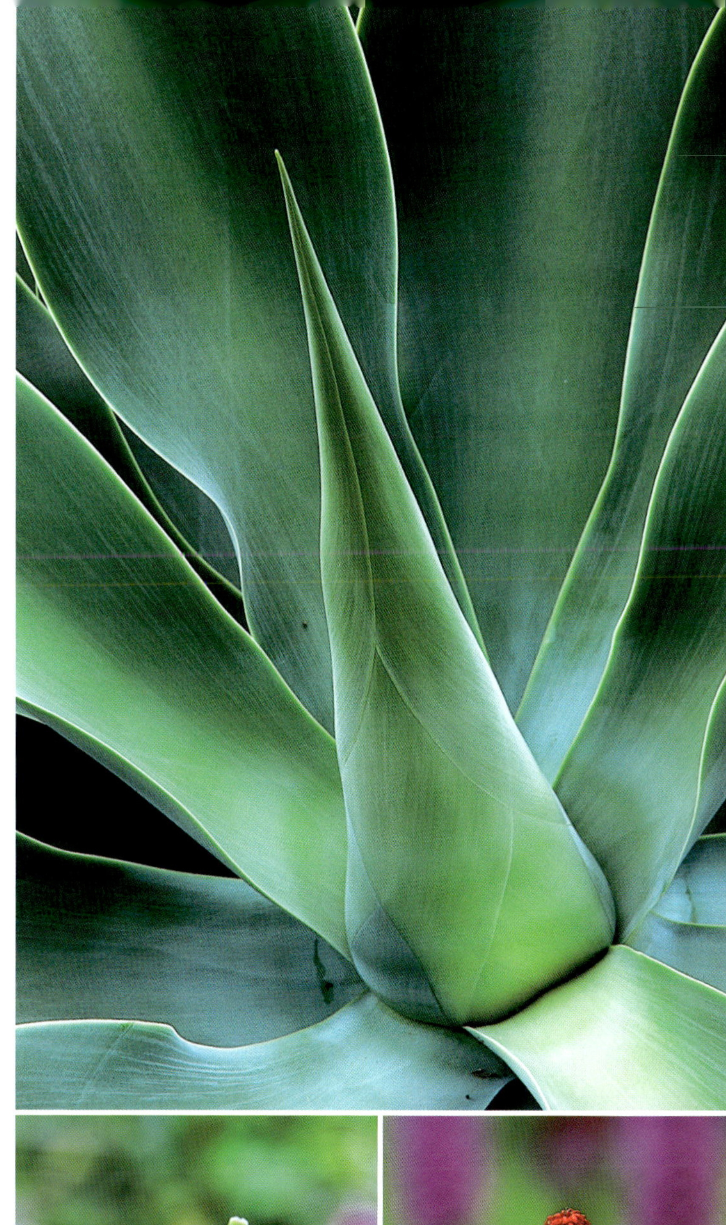

Right: Placing the growing shoot of *Agave attenuata* diagonally in the frame provides interest and balance to this close-up, which was taken in the glasshouse at Wisley.

**Minolta Dynax 7000i, 28–135mm lens, tripod. f/22 on Velvia exposed at 100 ISO**

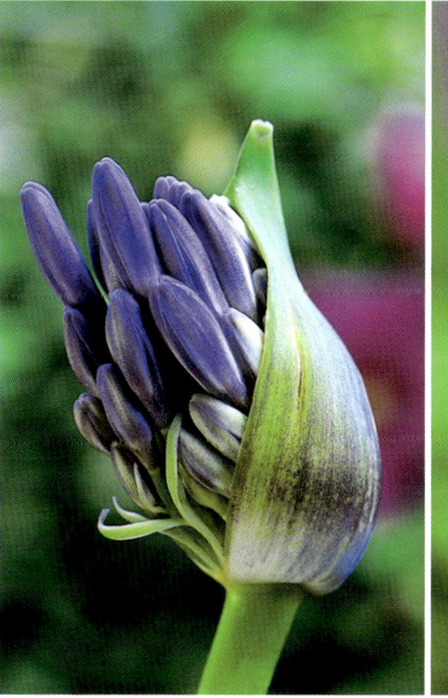

Below right: Differential focusing was used to emphasize the opening bud of *Agapanthus* 'Loch Hope' at Wisley. The large aperture allowed a faster shutter speed necessary in the gentle breeze.

**Minolta Dynax 7, 90mm macro lens, tripod. f/4 on Velvia**

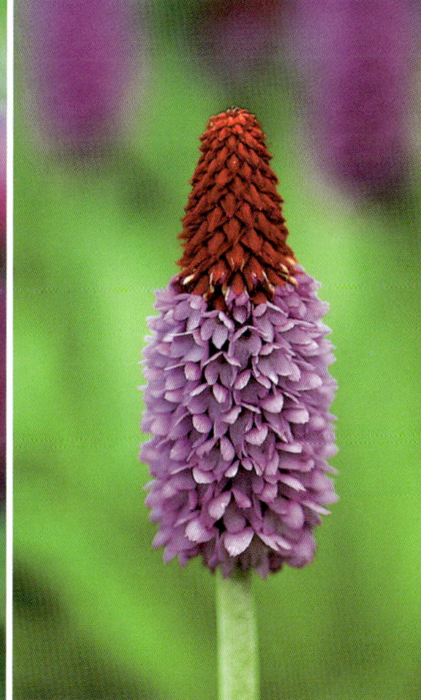

Far right: Here differential focus gives this close-up of *Primula vialii* a bit of a twist.

**Minolta Dynax 7000i, 90mm macro lens, tripod. f/3.5 on Velvia**

## Technique: **Controlling the Background with Depth of Field**

To control the effect that the background has on the main subject of your photographs, you can adjust the depth of field by enlarging or reducing the aperture of your lens. A plant or garden ornament about a third of the way into the picture, which stands out as the focal point of a general scene, can be selected and focused upon. The lens can then be 'stopped down' to widen the depth of field – i.e. to increase the zone of acceptable sharpness in the picture so that it includes objects both nearer to and farther away from the camera.These three figures in a sculpture exhibition at RHS Wisley illustrate depth of field.

**All three shots: Minolta Dynax 700si, 90mm macro lens, 81A filter, tripod. Ektachrome 100G**

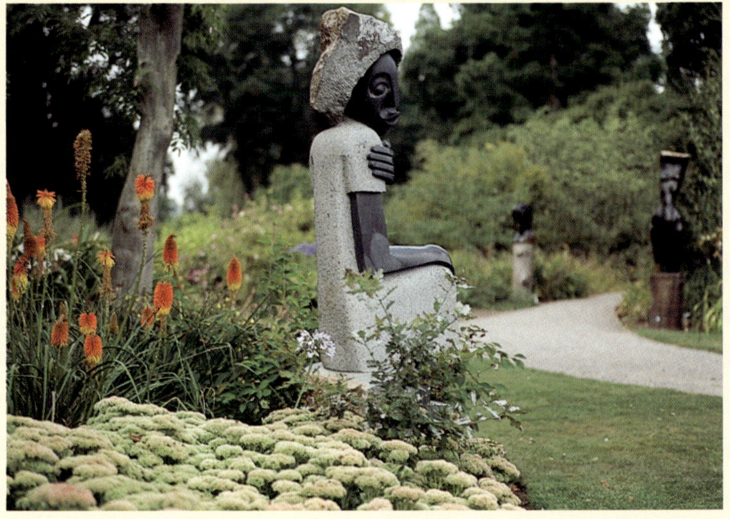

At f/2.8: In this image the lens was focused on the nearest figure and set at f/2.8. Little else is in focus, except for the spikes of *Kniphofia* 'Nobilis', which is in the same plane of focus as the figure.

on the distance between subject and camera, and on the widest aperture of the lens employed (lenses with large apertures work best).

Another way of throwing backgrounds out of focus, particularly useful when using a lens that doesn't have a large aperture, is to use a teleconverter (see page 74) or extension tubes (see page 102). The technique of applying focus in this way is known as 'differential focus'. Focus itself is usually a straightforward action of focusing on the subject.

Where a garden view of some depth is being photographed, however, there is a choice of two methods of focusing. You can either 'stop down' the lens to widen the depth of field (see box above) or use a method known as 'hyperfocal focusing'. This can be employed when using lenses with a clear depth-of-field scale marked on their barrel. It is a quick and easy method of focusing that involves choosing a suitable aperture and turning the lens's infinity mark to coincide with the mark on the lens barrel of the chosen aperture. The distance shown between the nearest distance indicated for that aperture and infinity will then be acceptably sharp in the picture.

It should be added, however, that the second method will not work with zoom lenses or with the many lenses manufactured now that do not have

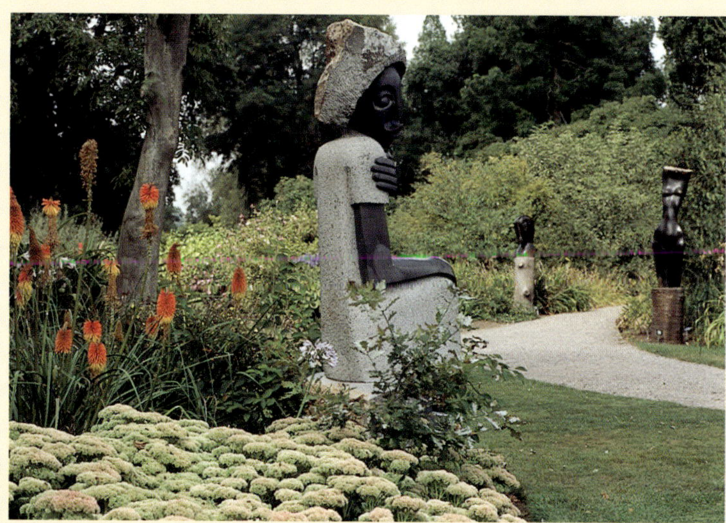

At f/8: With the lens stopped down to f/8, but still focused on the nearest figure, the depth of field has been increased considerably.

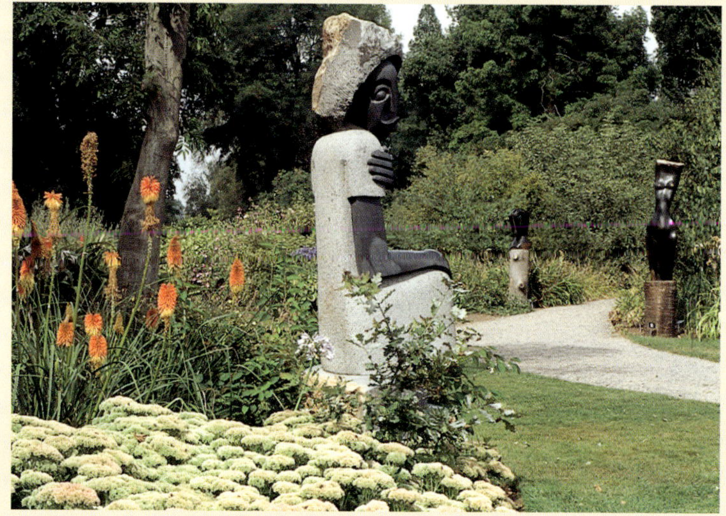

At f/32: With the aperture at f/32 even the farthest sculpture is sharp. In practice it would be preferable to focus manually just beyond the nearest figure and use an aperture of f/16 or f/22 to have everything in focus and take advantage of a faster shutter speed.

apertures and comprehensive distance scales marked on them. In the majority of cases, therefore, the first method will have to be used. Alternatively, depth of field can be checked using a depth-of-field preview button, if one is fitted.

### A Note on Autofocus

Autofocus has proved to be a major asset in many branches of photography, and although it is a nice option to have, it is not really essential for many of the subjects covered by garden photography. It is best not used for close-up photography, for example, where it is easier to focus manually on the part of a flower that needs to be really sharp. Autofocus can be of help in poor light conditions, when it is a useful check on visual focus.

### Patterns and Abstract Shots

Searching out patterns in plants and successfully committing them to film is an enjoyably challenging facet of garden photography. There are, of course, patterns everywhere: in plants, leaves, flowers, seeds and barks. Many of these pictures will be close-ups and, as ever, lighting has to be carefully considered (see Chapter 5, page 68, for more information on light in garden photography).

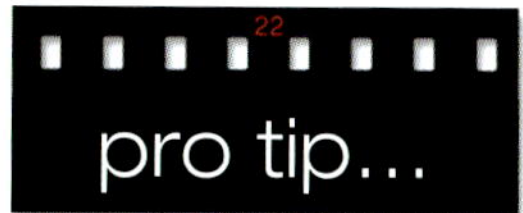


**Attention to detail**

An ever-present bugbear in gardens open to the public is the presence of plant labels and out-of-focus highlights from them. Check every area of the frame carefully before taking a photo.

Case study 1:

# WAKEHURST PLACE, SOUTH-EAST ENGLAND

**When taking pictures for a commission, perhaps with a tight deadline, often the best has to be made of conditions that are not ideal for photography. In this case the light was harsh and, as a result, I had to rule out most general overviews of this attractive water garden.**

Left: Minolta Dynax 700si, 28–135mm lens, 81B filter, tripod. f/22 on Ektachrome 100VS

Below: Minolta Dynax 700si, 28–135mm lens, 81B filter, tripod. f/22 on Ektachrome 100VS

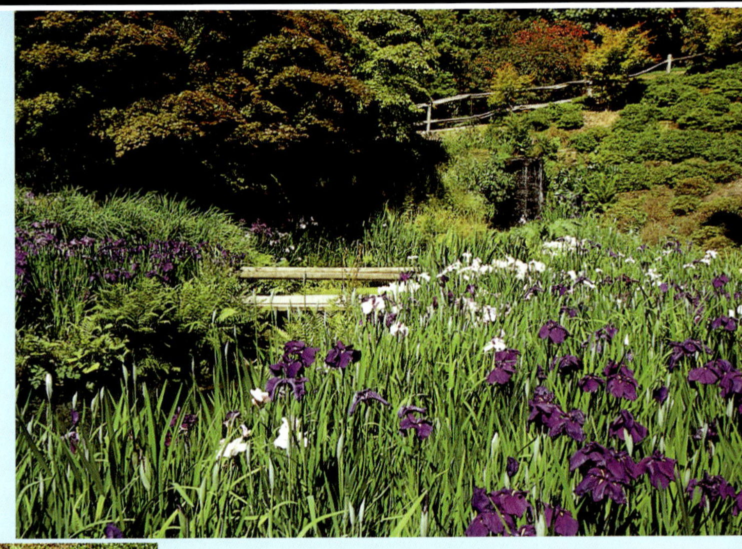

Camera: Minolta Dynax 700si

Film: Ektachrome 100VS

Lens: 28–135mm zoom

Filters: 81A–C warm-ups

Notes: Harsh, early summer light a problem to overcome

The problem was how to treat this scene of the Iris Dell at Wakehurst Place, which was full of *Iris ensata* in early summer. The afternoon sunshine gave unacceptablly harsh shadows in the middle distance, so several potentially attractive views had to be ruled out.

I decided to concentrate on the waterfall, where shadows were not a problem and where the field of view was unobstructed by the large number of visitors the weather had attracted to the garden. A small aperture has given a wide depth of field and slowed the shutter speed to emphasize the falling water lit by the afternoon sun. A fast shutter speed `freezes' falling water, while a slow speed produces a curtain effect. A very slow speed gives a white blur that can look effective.

## Equipment: **Close-ups**

A macro lens focusing right down to a 1:1 ratio, possibly used with a teleconverter, is ideal for abstracts because most will be close-ups. Two cheaper alternatives to a macro lens are close-up lenses or extension tubes. Using a bellows unit is another possibility, though an expensive one.

Abstracts are another branch of the patterns and shapes genre of garden photography. The abstract can vary from the immediately recognizable to 'What's this of?' and, as with patterns, seeking out abstract subjects is both challenging and ultimately satisfying.

### Additional Considerations

On the general topic of composition, care should be taken to ensure that backgrounds in photographs are as free from jarring highlights and clutter as possible.

Garden scenes that include people, unless they are the owners or gardeners connected with the garden, are not normally required by publishers unless the pictures depict garden leisure activity, gardening activity, or 'step-by-step' or 'how to' sequences, like planting a tree. Bear in mind when taking these that your model(s) should ideally be wearing clothes that do not date. The fickleness of fashion will render pictures showing distinct styles pretty well unusable once they have gone out of fashion. When a model is included in a picture, it will be necessary to obtain a completed 'model release' form (many examples of which are available on the web).

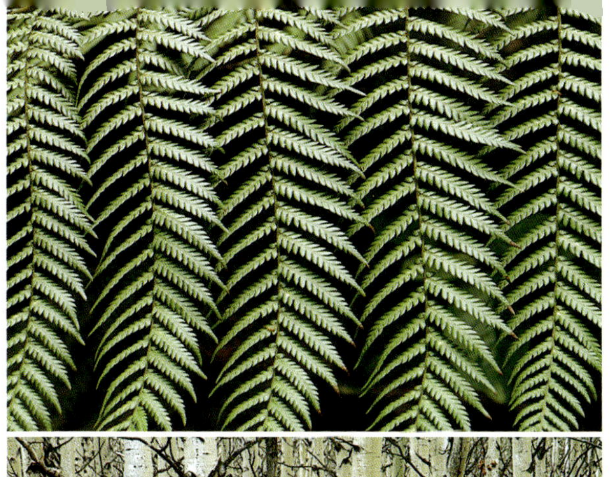

Top: The fronds of this tree fern photographed near Christchurch, New Zealand, form a strong repeat pattern.

**Minolta Dynax 7000i, 35–90mm lens, tripod. f/11 on Agfachrome 50 Professional**

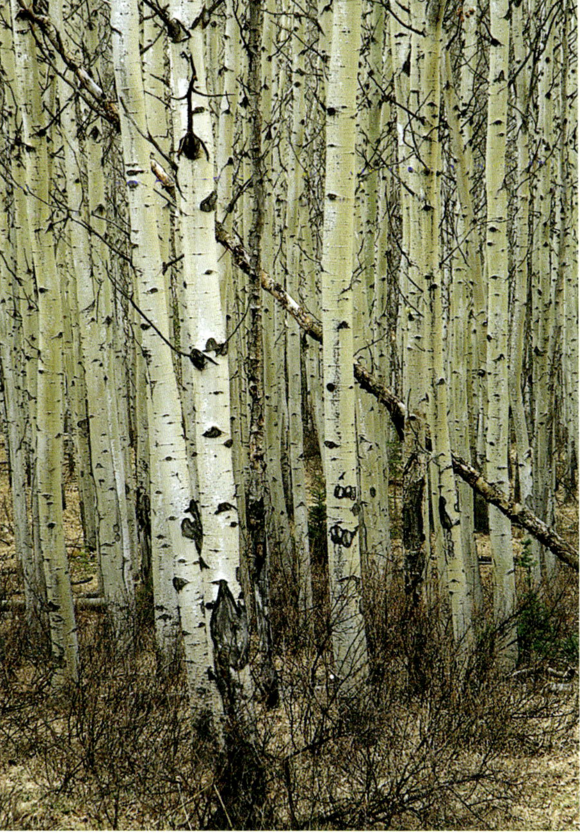

Centre: A stand of American aspens, *Populus tremuloides,* in early spring in Jasper National Park, Canada. The fallen trunk lying diagonally across the frame saves the picture from looking too bland.

**Minolta Dynax 7, 28–135mm lens, 81A filter, tripod. f/16 on Velvia**

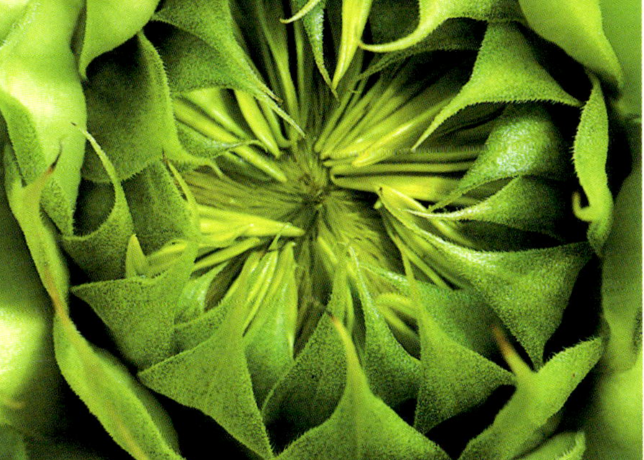

Bottom: Not quite an abstract: a small aperture was required for this initial stage of an opening sunflower bud.

**Minolta Dynax 700si, 90mm macro lens, 81A filter, tripod. f/22 on Velvia**

On location:

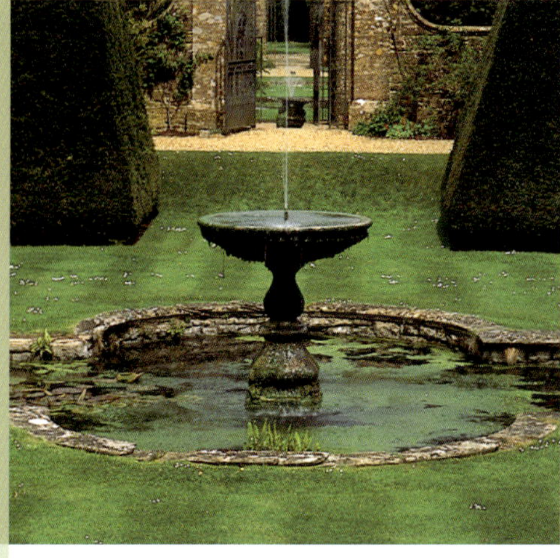

# Formal Gardens

**Various different approaches can be adopted with gardens that might be referred to as formal or 'period'. In terms of composition, general garden scenes can make use of any strong geometric shapes or repeated patterns, while the subject matter should focus on details that would be of interest to students of garden history, such as differing purposes, attitudes and fashions over the centuries.**

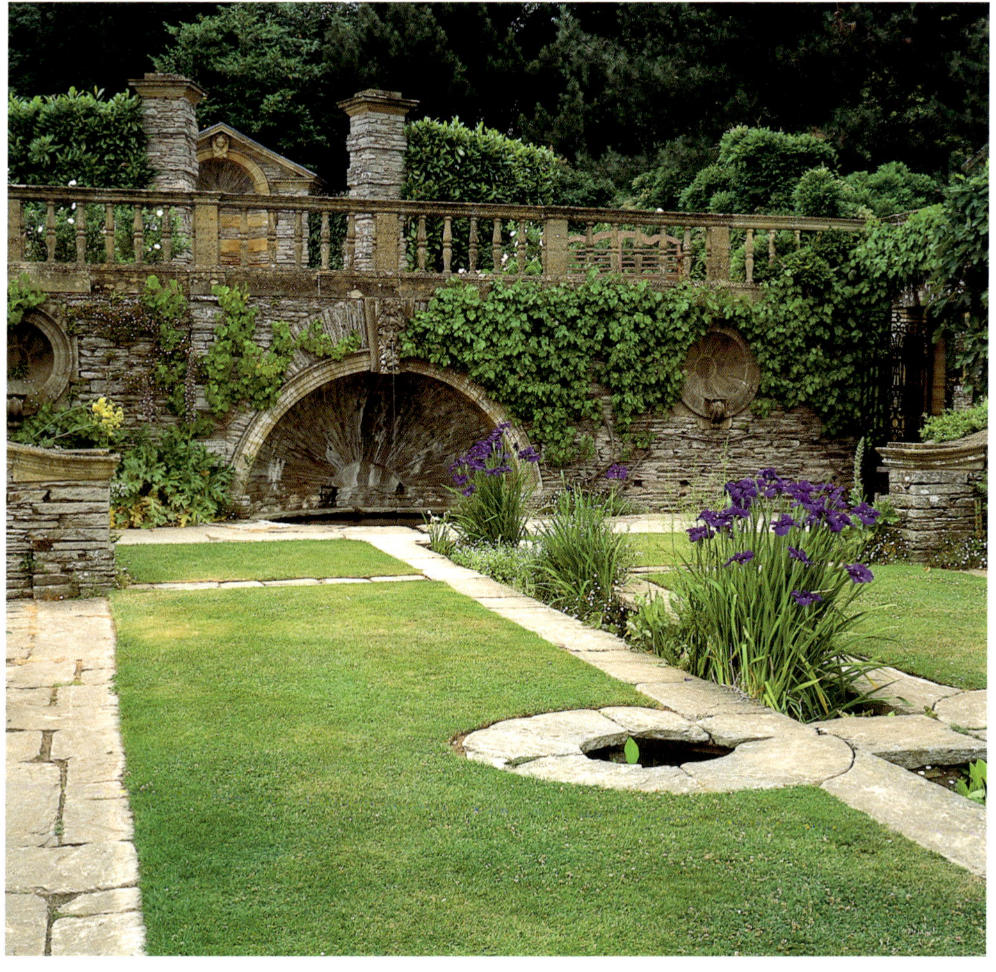

Left: Hestercombe Gardens, in Cheddon Fitzpaine, Somerset, is a superb formal Edwardian garden designed by Sir Edward Lutyens, with Gertrude Jekyll planting schemes. The photograph shows just one small corner of it. This is one of those 'don't miss' gardens.

**Fuji GW670III, 81B filter, tripod. 1/4sec at f/22 on Velvia**

Right: Topiary in all shapes and sizes can be found at Levens Hall, in Kendal, Cumbria. The beds enclosed by the box are filled with colour from spring bedding, which is then replaced for blocks of summer colour with half-hardy bedding plants, as in the picture. The Hall itself dates from the thirteenth century, and some of the topiary from the late seventeenth century.

**Mamiya 645 Super, 80mm lens, tripod. f/22 on Velvia**

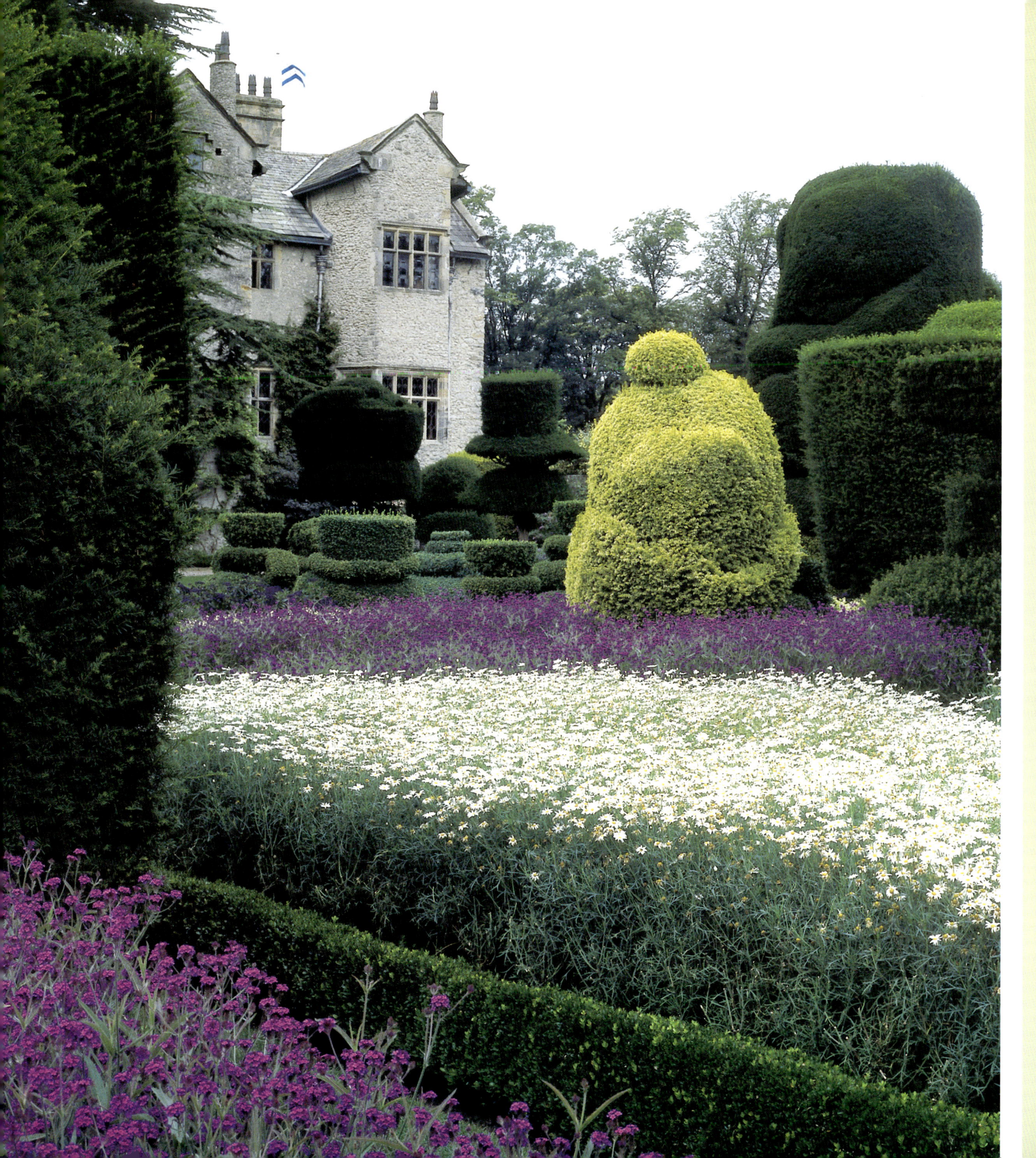

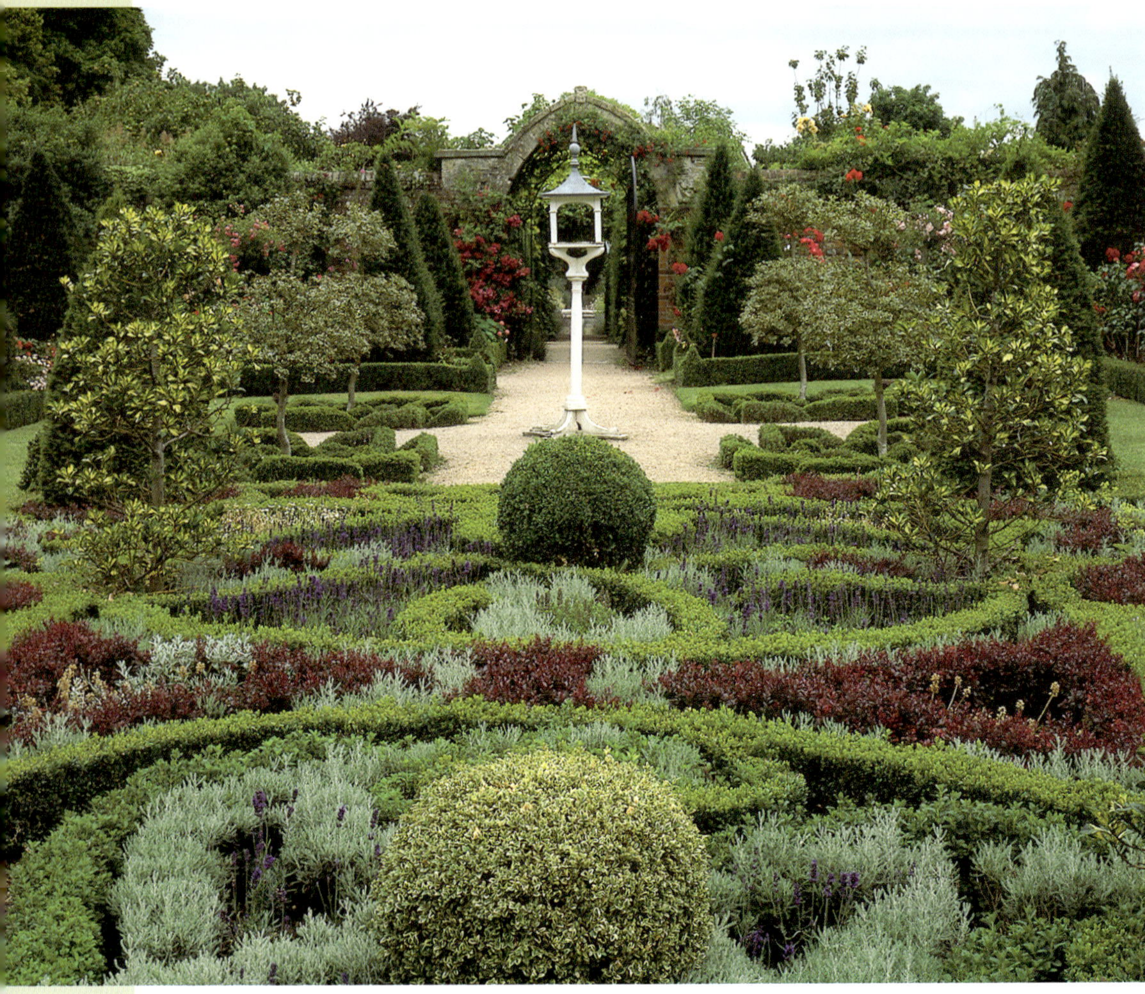

Knot gardens have been part of the garden scene in England since Tudor times, and in essence were originally a manifestation of man's power to tame nature. Instead of the chaos reigning outside in the landscape, an elaborate sense of order was established in the cultivation of low, scrupulously neat hedges, perhaps with small specimen trees pruned into rigid shapes. Formality was the key.

The knot garden featured here is at Abbey House Gardens situated next to Malmesbury Abbey in Wiltshire. A modern twist in this knot garden is the inclusion of a dwarf barberry in the range of plants, imparting a delightful reddish tone to the pattern.

**Mamiya 645 Super, 80mm lens, 81B filter, tripod. 1/4sec at f/22 on Velvia**

Below: This detail from the Celtic Cross Knot Garden shows four plants: *Alchemilla mollis*, *Buxus sempervirens*, *Santolina chamaecyparissus* and *Berberis thunbergii* 'Atropurpurea Nana'. To keep everything sharply defined, I focused manually to a point about one-third of the way into the picture and set a small lens aperture.

**Minolta Dynax 7, 28–135mm lens, 81B filter, tripod. 1/8sec at f/22 on Velvia**

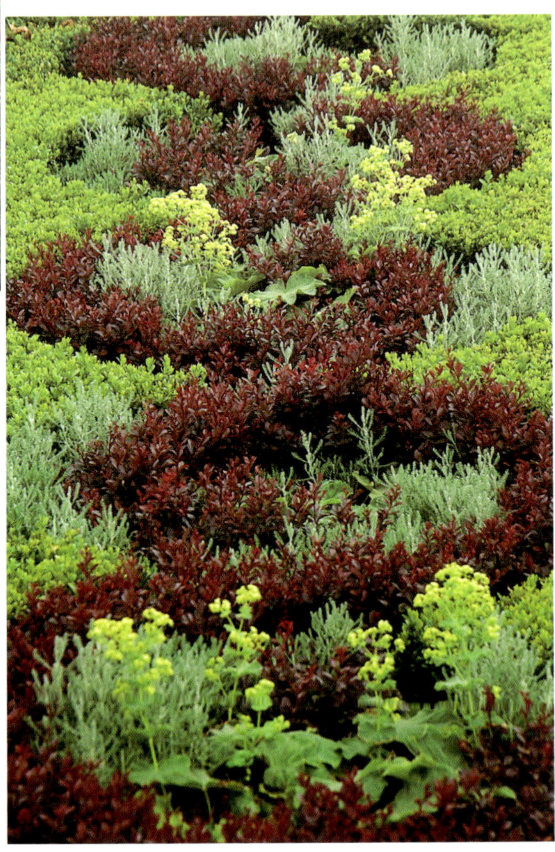

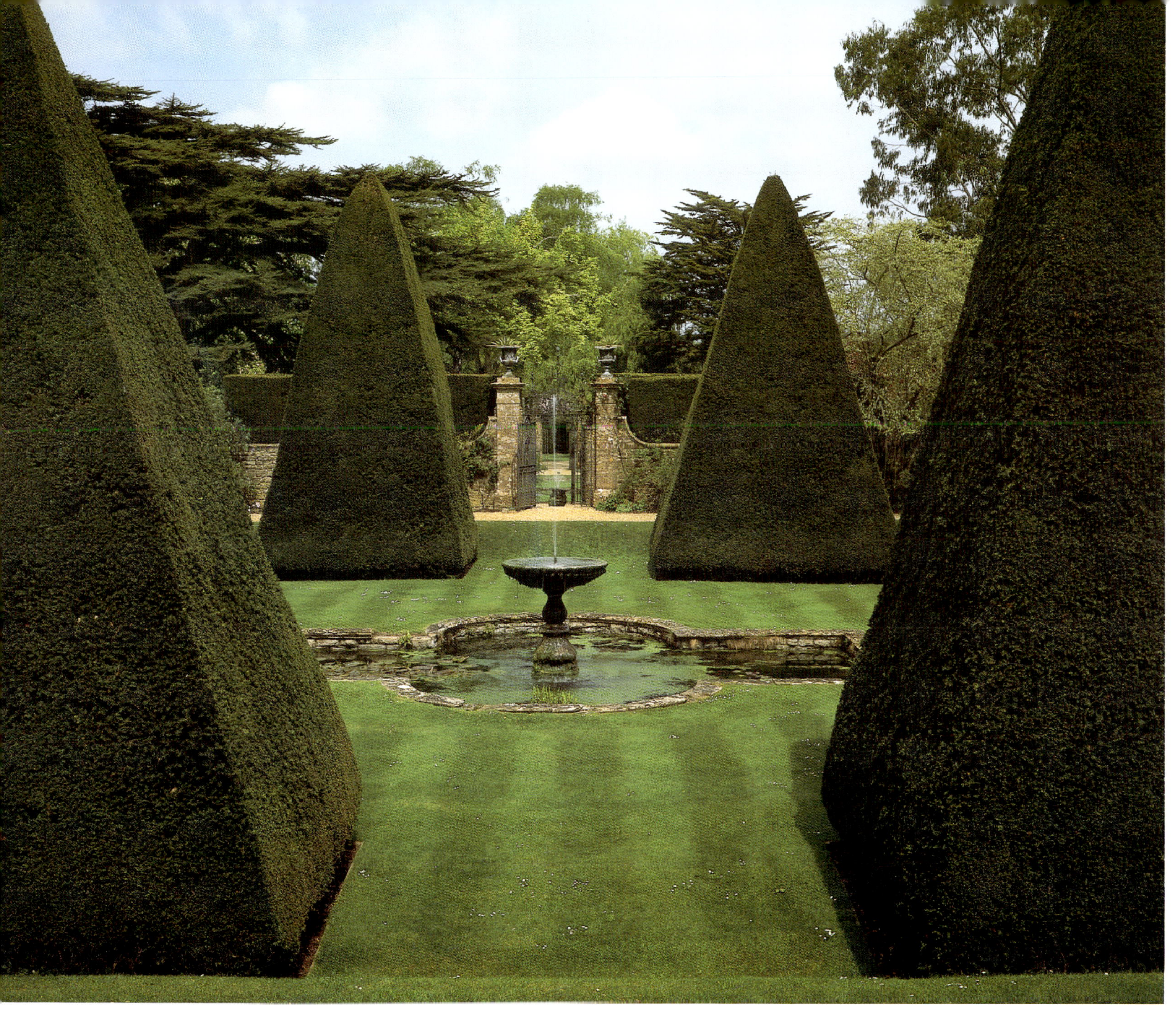

An incident light reading was taken to obtain a satisfactory exposure for this scene at Athelhampton Gardens in Dorset. I didn't want the yew topiary to be too dark, so waited for the sun to brighten it up and treated Velvia as 40 ISO in order to give a little more light to the exposure. The garden was designed in 1891 to be in keeping with the Tudor manor.

**Fuji GW670III, 81B filter, tripod. 1/8sec at f/32 on Velvia**

4

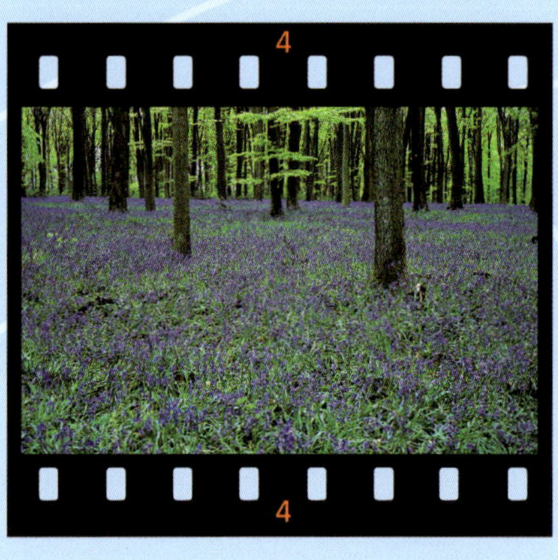


# Exposure and Metering

**To obtain publishable results when working with transparency film, it is essential to combine accurate metering with a sound knowledge of exposure under a variety of conditions.**

In spite of the advances in metering found on present-day cameras, automatic exposure control is not yet foolproof and an understanding of exposure fundamentals is important. This is especially true when working with colour reversal (transparency) film, which requires exposure to be accurate to within about one-third of a stop, or perhaps half a stop on occasions. With print film the situation is considerably easier. This film has far more latitude, of up to three stops over or under, and any mistake in this range can be compensated for in printing.

I have found the matrix, or evaluative, exposure system (in my Minolta cameras this is called 'honeycomb', and 'matrix' in the FinePix S2) to be accurate 95% of the time, and sometimes in difficult lighting situations where I have decided to introduce some exposure compensation, I have found my changes to be unnecessary. Often, though, it is wise to bracket exposures. I tend to let the camera have first say, before trying my own adjustments.

In regard to automatic metering modes where either the aperture or the shutter speed is set, the overwhelming choice in garden photography is to use aperture priority, which enables the photographer to control the depth of field and, subject movement apart, to ignore shutter speeds. I never use shutter priority or program modes, for which there is little call – just aperture priority and manual modes. If subject movement is a problem or shutter speed an issue, the aperture is adjusted to arrive at the best compromise in the circumstances.

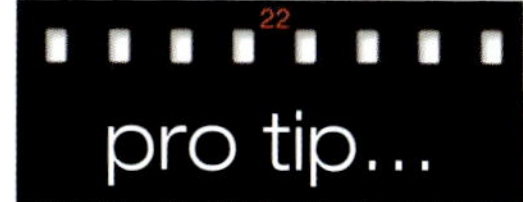


**Transparency film**

Accurate exposure of transparency film is essential because it has narrow exposure latitude. Under- or overexposure of around one-third of a stop is acceptable, but beyond this the mistake is usually too noticeable, especially if the shot is intended for publication.

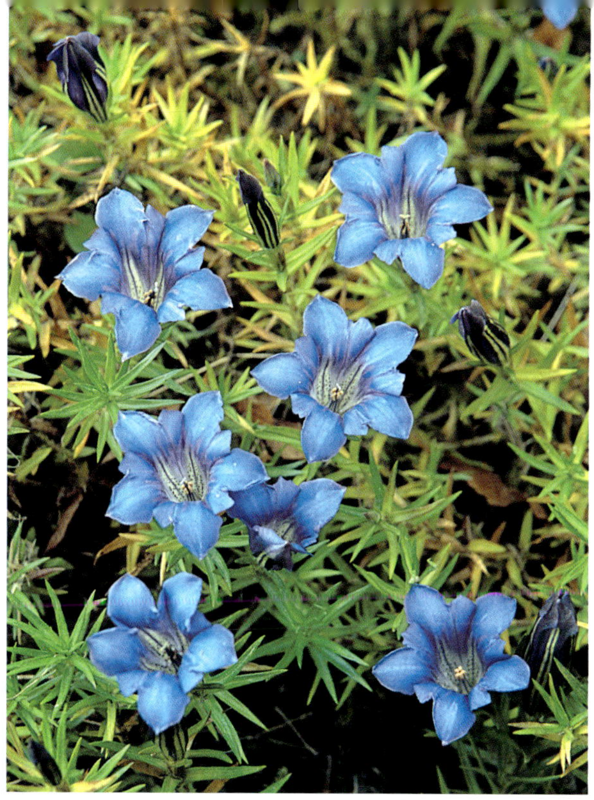

Strong autumnal sunlight coupled with a gusty wind did not bode well for this image of gentians at Sheffield Park Garden, so I asked my wife to shade the flowers and waited for a lull before triggering the shutter.

**Minolta Dynax 700si, 28–135mm lens, tripod. f/16 on Jessops CS 100**

## Equipment: **Hand-held Light Meters**

An alternative to using your camera's built-in metering system is a hand-held light meter, which measures the light falling upon the subject and gives what is known as an incident light reading. The meter is pointed towards the camera from the subject's position or from a position in similar light to that of the subject. There is therefore no question of an extra-bright or extra-dark subject affecting the exposure reading. Hand-held meters can also measure reflected light.

## Equipment: **Types of TTL Metering**

Up to four through-the-lens (TTL) exposure systems are built into SLRs available on the market today, and an understanding of their characteristics is essential for obtaining consistently correct exposure.

**1 Centre-weighted metering** One metering method that has been available for many years is known as 'centre weighted'. With this system the reading is biased towards the central portion of the image, corresponding to the position of the subject in most people's pictures. This normally works satisfactorily, but can be thrown out by unusual lighting conditions, where there is a lot of sky or where the subject is predominantly bright or dark.

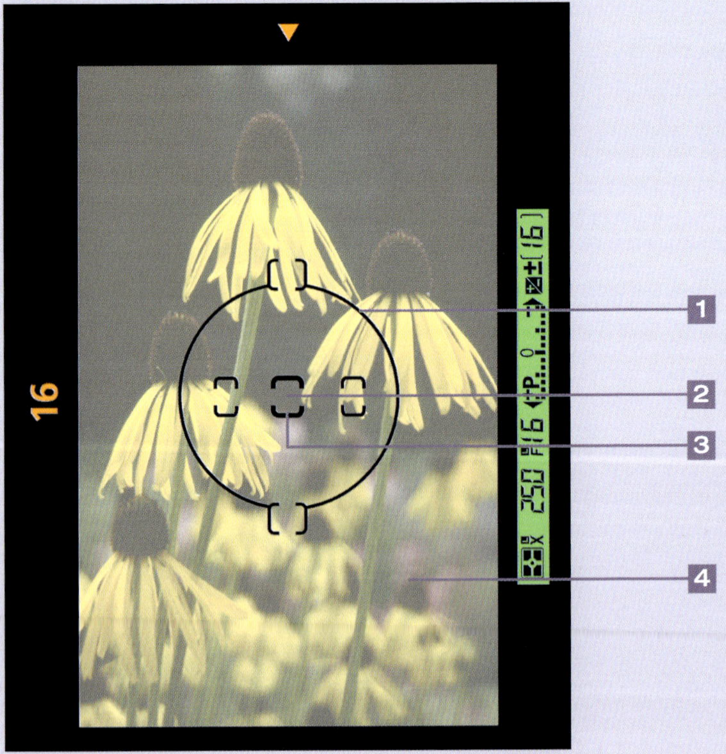


**2 Spot metering** Spot metering measures a very small part of the frame, around 2–3%. A series of readings can be taken and then averaged out by the photographer, or a reading can be taken of a suitable mid-tone (an 18% grey tone) in the picture, such as grass or a rock, and this reading used as the basis for the picture. The important word is 'suitable': the mid-tone must be one that you want to be reproduced as such in the picture.

**3 Partial metering** The third system available on some SLRs is known as 'partial' metering. This is similar to spot metering, but it measures a slightly larger area: the central 9.5% of the frame. This system is useful for scenes where there are big differences in brightness (e.g. between foreground and background) or for subjects that require precise measurement, such as close-up photography.

**4 Average metering** Finally, there is the sophisticated average metering system, which goes under various names according to manufacturer, such as evaluative, matrix or honeycomb pattern. Here, the picture is divided into a series of zones and the system reads each to calculate the exposure by reference to a database held in the meter's computer. Systems vary in their degree of sophistication depending on the camera model.

The Minolta honeycomb-pattern system, for example, is integrated with the autofocus system. It considers the whereabouts, size and brightness of the subject in the frame and gives more emphasis to this area, taking into account whether the image is being taken horizontally or vertically, the degree of backlighting present, and so on. The system works well in all but a few tricky lighting situations, mainly involving very bright or very dark subjects, and these can be recognized with experience and exposures bracketed (see opposite).

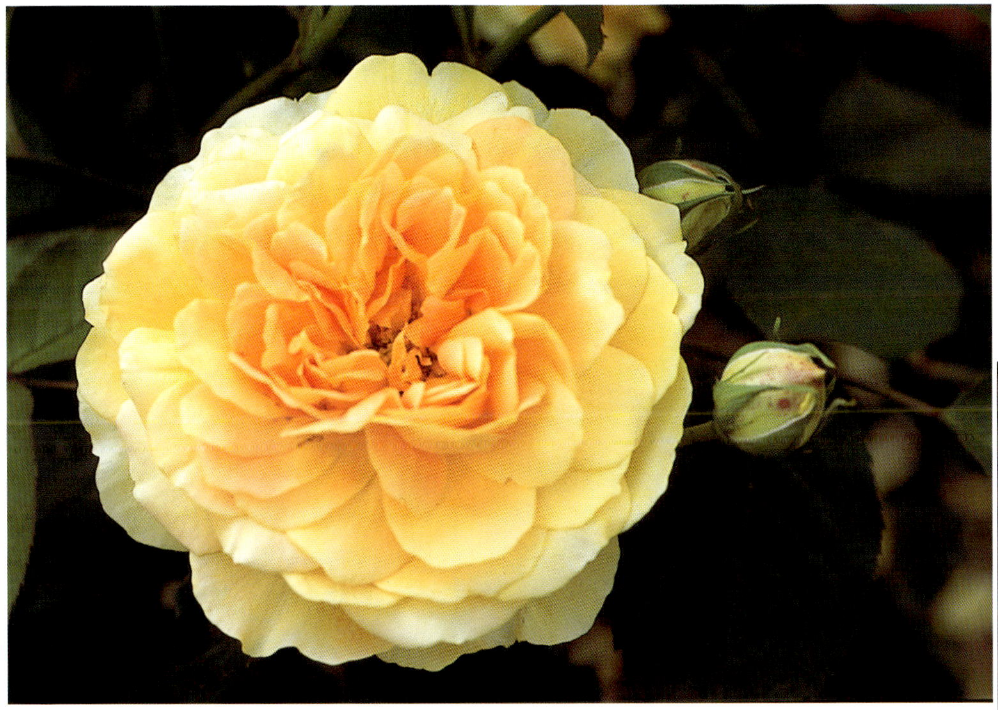

Yellows require correct exposure if they are not to look too dark. Half a stop extra exposure was given for *Rosa* Molineux = 'Ausmol' at RHS Wisley.

**Minolta Dynax 700si, 90mm macro lens, 81A filter, tripod. f/5.6 on Provia 100F**

Below: *Echinacea paradoxa* backlit at Wisley. The dark background of trees was needed to achieve a satisfactory image. A blue sky, if there had been one, would have worked well as a background.

**Minolta Dynax 7, 28–135mm lens, 81B filter, tripod. 1/100sec at f/6.3 on Ektachrome 100G**

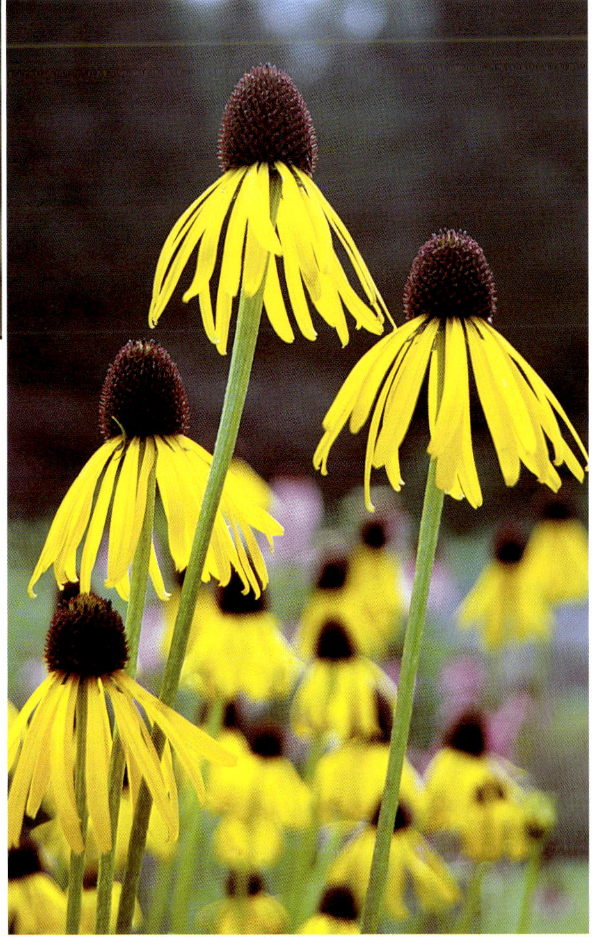

## Bracketing Exposures

When exposing transparency film in tricky lighting situations (or with light and dark subjects), exposure that is correct for the subject and the mood of the picture, as you envisage it, can be difficult to judge. It is in these situations that recourse is made to bracketing. Simply put, this involves taking an extra picture or two at exposure(s) varying by a third or half a stop around the initial accurately metered exposure. By this means at least one of the exposures should be accurate. For example, if your camera's meter indicates an exposure of 1/125sec at f/16 and you feel that a bright subject is influencing the meter to cause underexposure, take a further exposure of 1/125sec at f/13 and another one at f/11.

There are of course many permutations on this, but when you are really unsure take a couple of extra pictures under and a couple more over the exposure indicated by your meter at half-stop intervals. Many cameras have an exposure compensation facility that enables the shutter speed and/or the aperture, dependent on the mode selected, to remain constant.

## Technique: **Photographing Blue Flowers**

Blue can be a difficult colour to capture accurately on film. The problem is known as 'anomalous reflectance' or 'the ageratum effect' after the blue-flowered *Ageratum houstonianum*, a prime culprit. It is caused by the fact that infra-red light, invisible to the naked eye, is picked up by film emulsion, turning the distinctive blue of ageratum or bluebells, another example, a pinkish purple colour.

Some authorities advocate using a mid-blue filter to keep the blues blue, although this will impart a blue cast to surrounding foliage. I have tried a pale blue filter on bluebells on a cloudy day; the blue of the flowers was enhanced but there was a slight effect on the fresh greens of the new foliage of the trees, as can be seen in the image reproduced on the facing page. Although many solutions are touted, my own experience suggests that ageratum shot on Velvia with the sun obscured by cloud looks OK, and bluebells under the conditions already outlined appear close to their true-to-life colour.

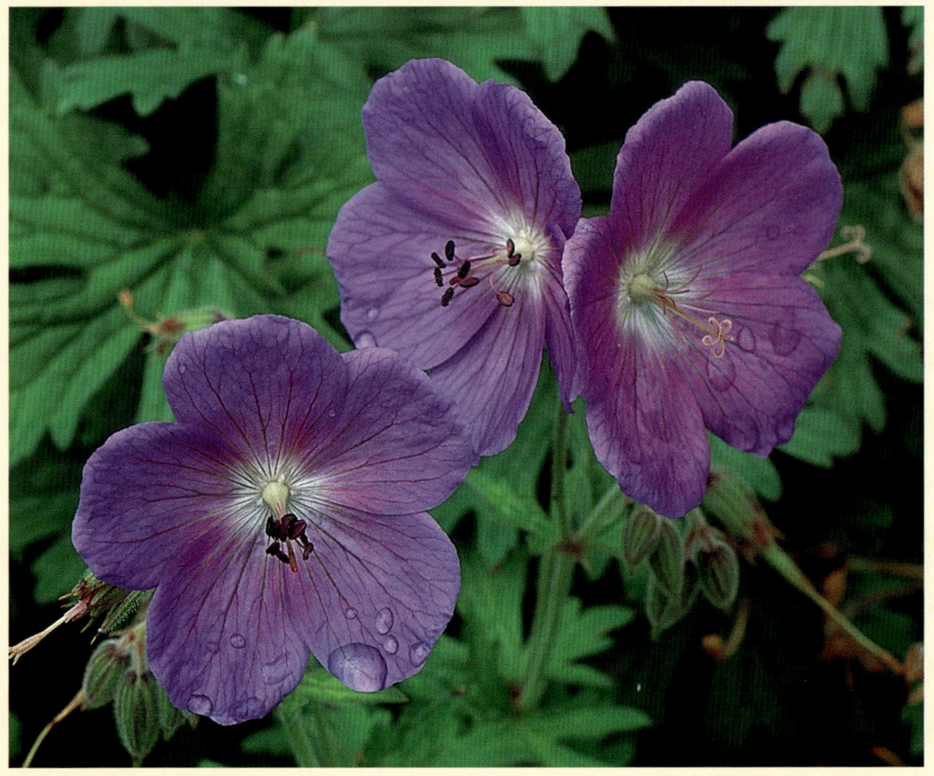

This image of *Geranium himalayense* 'Irish Blue' on Velvia shows the colour faithfully recorded. The exposure was made in overcast light and no filter was used.

**Minolta Dynax 7, 90mm macro lens, tripod. f/5.6 on Velvia**

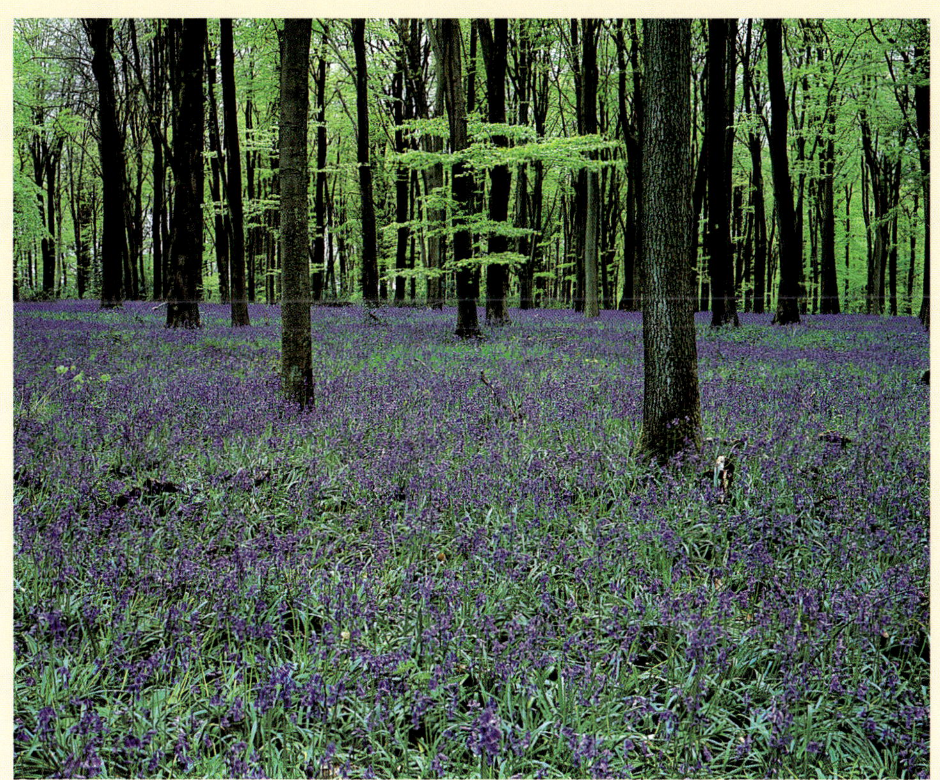

The bluebell is a magnet to photographers, so a little consideration to the problems of capturing the true colour of blue flowers is called for. Some films seem to be more susceptible than others to this problem, but as a general rule bright sunlight on the subject should be avoided, and shooting under a cloudy bright sky will mitigate matters. In a wood full of bluebells, using a short telephoto lens compresses perspective and therefore gives more solid colour. Remember also that a polarizing filter can be used when conditions allow – i.e. when light levels are sufficiently high and no breeze is causing subject movement.

Above: The density of bluebells in this beech woodland was such that the compressing effect of a short telephoto lens was not required to give a solid blue result. The light level in the wood was fairly low, and the wind breezy, so a polarizing filter was not tried as this would have required a further increase in exposure.

**Fuji GW670III, tripod. 1/4sec at f/16 on Velvia**

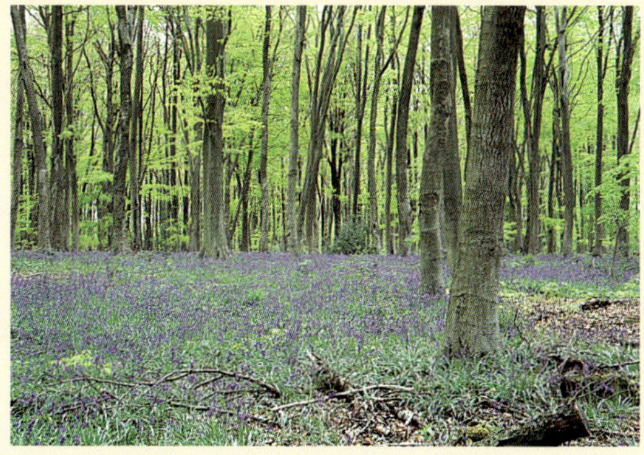

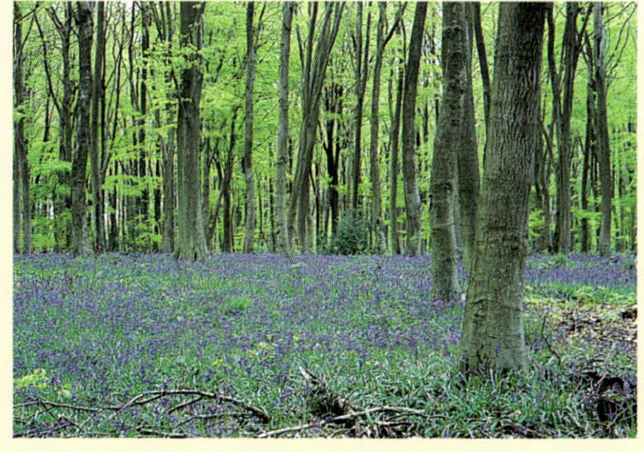

Right: The bluebells here were not flowering in a dense mass and the effect is straggly, particularly in the top picture, for which no filter was used. In the lower picture a pale blue (82A) filter has enhanced the flowers, but at marginal cost to the fresh green of the beech leaves.

**Both shots: Minolta Dynax 7, 28–135mm lens, tripod. 1/2sec and 1sec (respectively) at f/16 on Velvia**

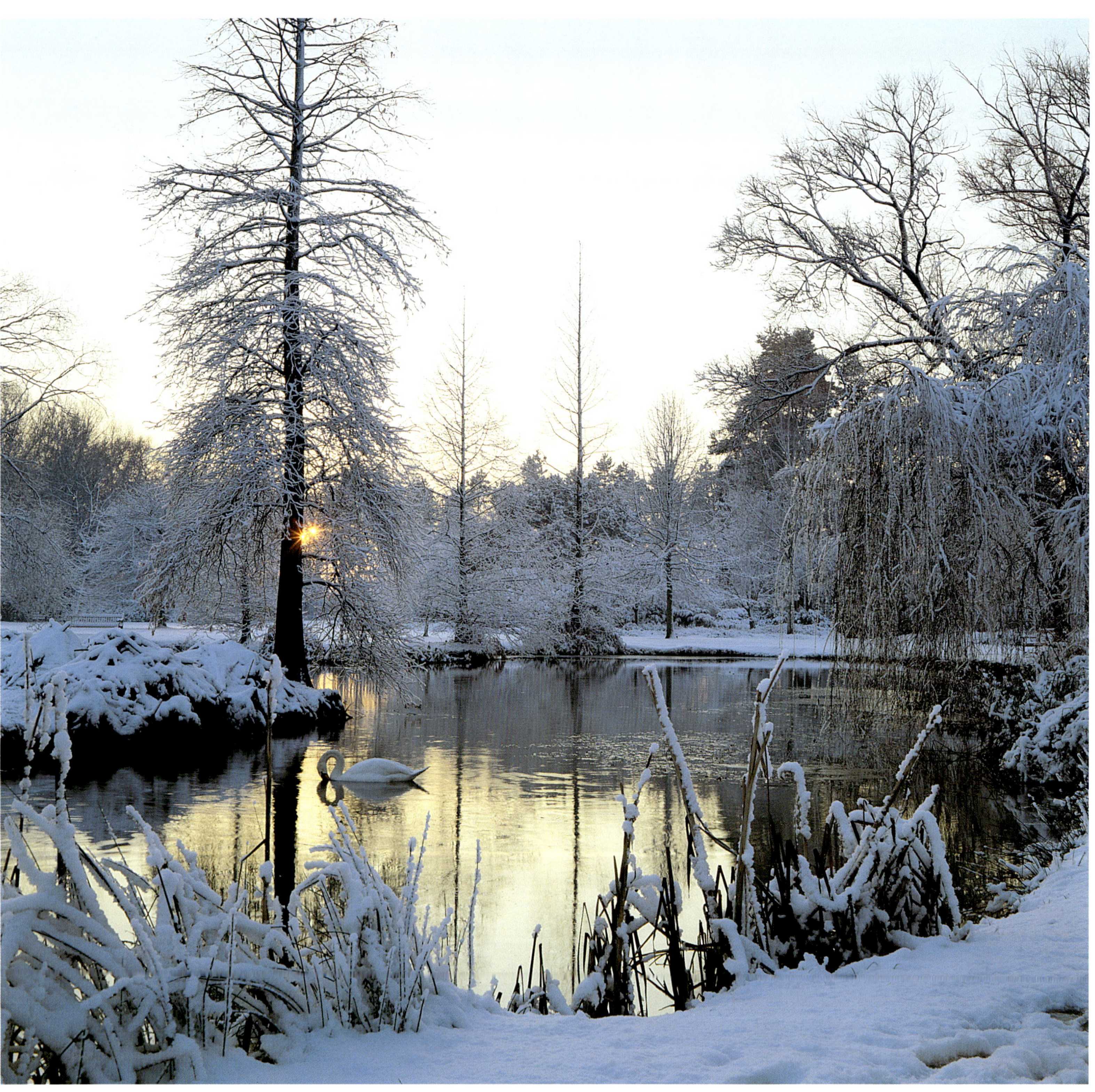

### Difficult Lighting Conditions

Camera exposure meters use reflected light to arrive at their calculated answers, and the reflected light to give a correctly exposed picture is assumed to approximate to that from an 18% grey card placed in the same light as the subject. However, this is not necessarily the case in actual shooting situations. The light reflected off a group of bright yellow flowers will be considerably more intense, and if exposed at 18% grey will be underexposed on transparency film, appearing as a dark yellow. Likewise, a close-up of a dark subject like *Heuchera* 'Chocolate Ruffles' would appear overexposed because the meter had tried to make it lighter, and should be given an adjusted, shorter exposure.

Experience will alert you to potential exposure problems. The degree of adjustment is not easily gauged, however, and to ensure that one exposure looks right it is best to bracket in steps of adjustment. The yellow flowers could have half, one, even one and a half stops added, and the heuchera a further reduced exposure of around one-third of a stop.

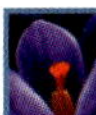

### How to Avoid the Exposure Pitfalls

✓ Before you take any picture, decide which element in it is going to be your focal point and make a meter reading for that.

✓ If in doubt about your exposure, consider bracketing; normally it will only be necessary to bracket either one-third over or under the metered reading.

✓ Where your subject is very dark (dark flowers against dark foliage, for example) or very bright (such as a snowy scene), you will have to adjust your exposure accordingly.

✓ Accurate reproduction of colours can be important if you want to sell your work to gardening books and magazines, so be aware that some colours, especially blues and yellows, may not reproduce as you expected them to on colour film. Adjusting your exposure or using filters can help.

This picture was taken in a hurry as I wanted to catch the swan while it was properly visible and contributing to the picture. Its movement was reasonably slow, which was fortunate because a small aperture was required to ensure a good depth of field. An ambient light meter reading was taken and it must have shown something like 1/4sec at f/22. I was lucky: I only took one shot and if I had had time to think about the snow and *contre-jour* aspects I would probably have got it wrong.

**Mamiya C330f, 80mm lens, tripod. f/22 on Ektachrome 64**

### Technique: **The Sunny f/16 Rule**

The 'sunny f/16 rule' is often mentioned in the literature, and exposure guides on film cartons are based on it. The rule states that when shooting a frontlit scene in bright sunlight in temperate regions, the correct exposure will be one over the ISO number of the film loaded at f/16, or any equivalent aperture and shutter speed. For example, the use of 100 ISO film would give an exposure for average scenes of 1/125sec at f/16, 125 being the nearest shutter speed to 100. In my experience, however, the rule should be treated with caution to avoid a risk of underexposure.

## Case study 2: TATTON PARK, NORTH-WEST ENGLAND

**My wife and I were visiting the north-west of England in a spell of very unsettled weather at the beginning of May 2003. The forecast for the day ahead was poor (mainly cloudy with heavy showers) but Tatton Park, with its superb Japanese Garden, was only ten minutes away from where we were staying and tempting, especially as I had not seen it before. This case study shows just what is achievable during a morning's work, even in conditions not ideal for garden photography.**

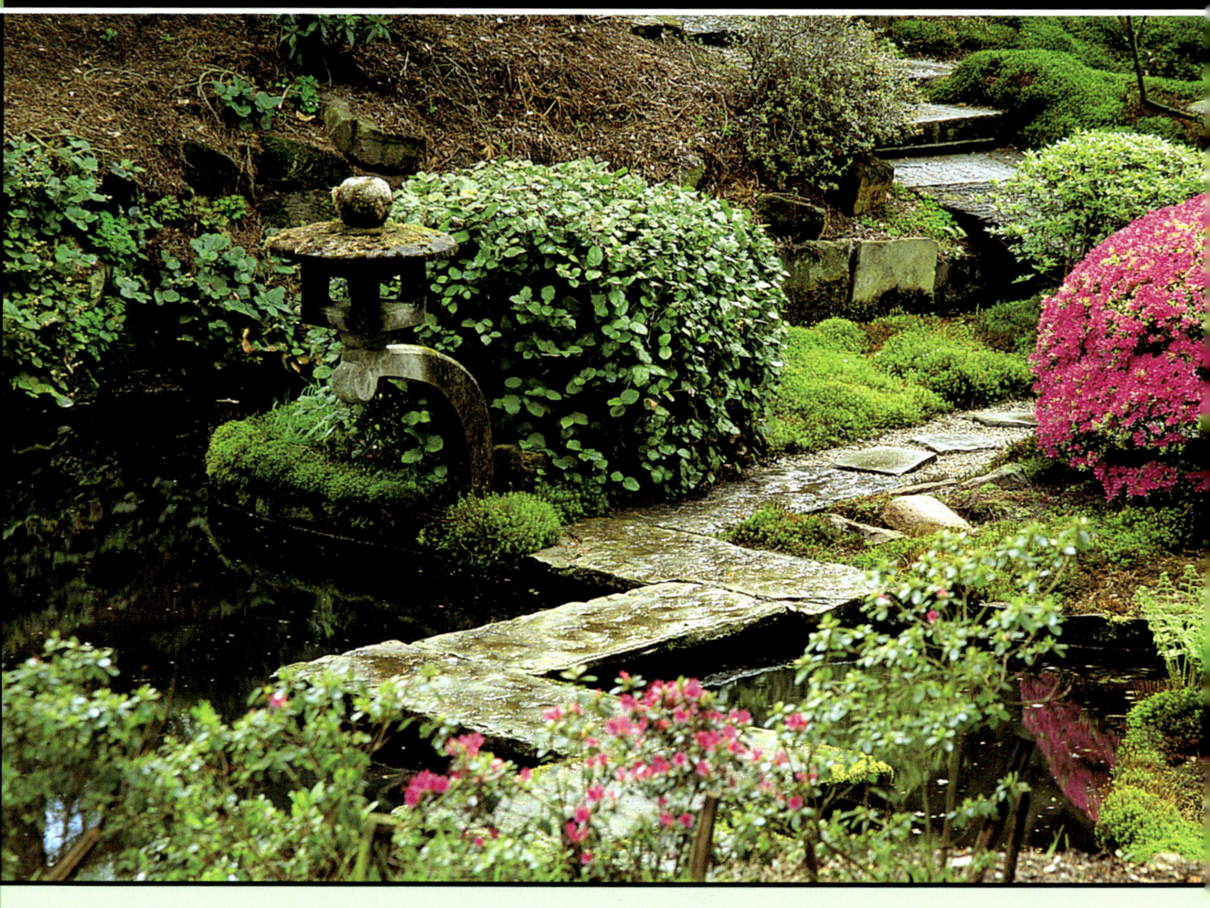

A zoom lens enabled me to isolate the Yatsukashi (Flying Goose Bridge) with its attendant lantern. Even light has enabled detail to be recorded throughout the frame.

**Minolta Dynax 700si, 28–135mm lens, 81B filter, tripod. 7/10sec at f/16 on Velvia**

**Cameras: Minolta Dynax 700si and Fuji GW670III**

**Film: Velvia**

**Lens: 28–135mm zoom**

**Filters: 81A–C warm-ups**

**Notes: Poor weather; overcast with heavy showers**

I normally seek permission for photography before visiting a garden, but this was a spur-of-the-moment decision in view of the weather and the garden's proximity. I hoped that if I achieved anything of note I could retrospectively seek permission to publish the results. In the event, this permission was granted a few weeks later by Cheshire County Council, who administer the Tatton Estate.

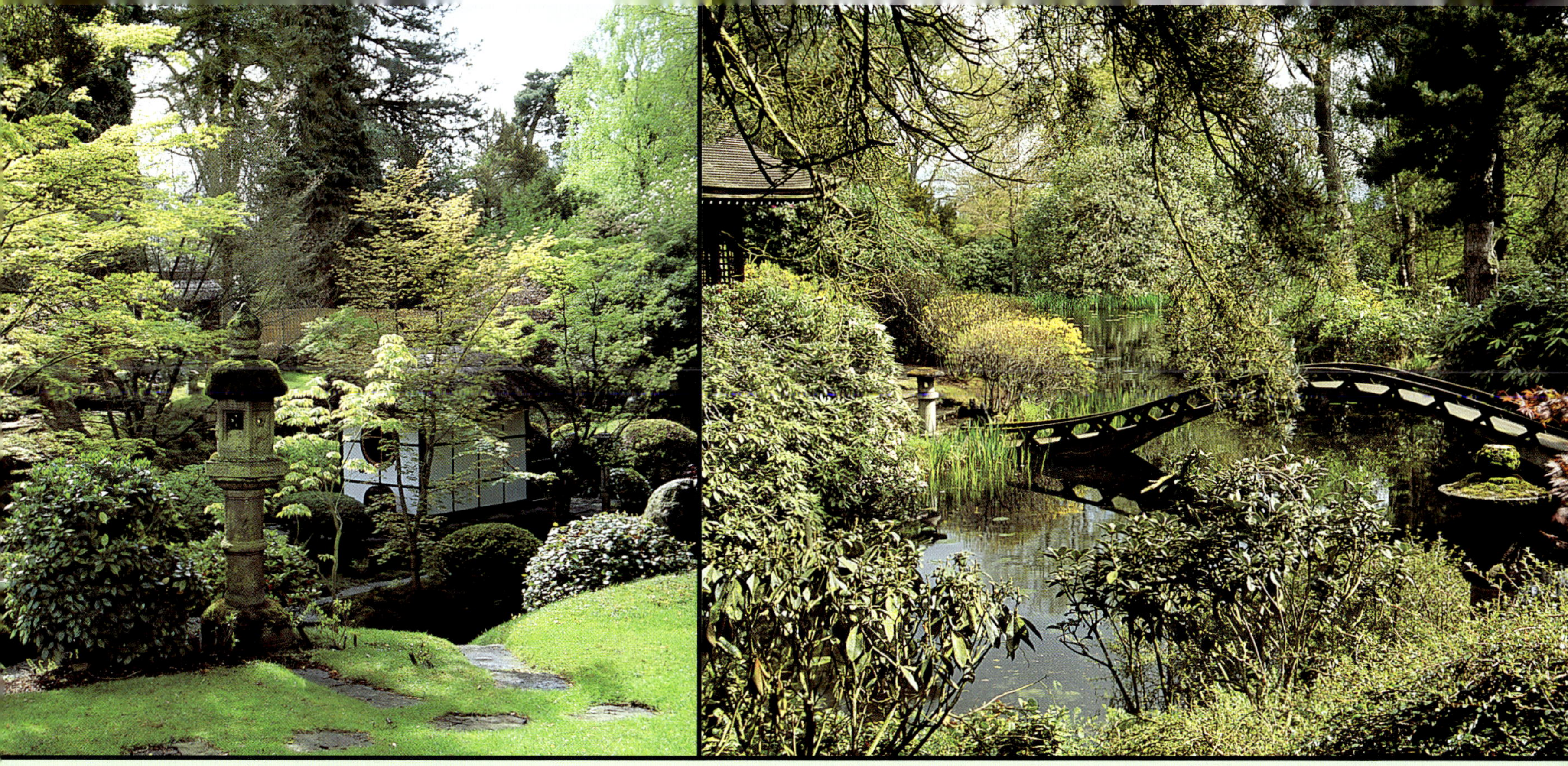

Above left: A fleeting glimpse of sunlight enabled me to take this *contre-jour* picture of the Kasuga lantern and tea house in the setting of the Japanese garden at Tatton.

**Minolta Dynax 700si, 28–135mm lens, tripod. f/11 on Velvia**

**10.00**

On arrival at Tatton, the first hurdle was cleared when no objection was raised at the garden entrance to my using a tripod. I explained my desire to see the Japanese garden and we were directed to a far corner of the grounds. We made our way straight there in order to take advantage of a brief period of good weather, particularly because rain appeared imminent.

Above: The Shinto Shrine and bridge photographed from the garden's perimeter in frontal sunlight.

**Minolta Dynax 700si, 28–135mm lens, 81B filter, tripod. 1/6sec at f/16 on Velvia**

### 10.20

A brief glimpse of sunlight prompted me to take the first photograph: the *contre-jour* image of the latern and tea house shown above (see pages 70–1 for details on *contre-jour* lighting). Light levels were predominantly low, but this was punctuated by occasional glimpses of sunshine, giving a welcome range of lighting conditions. Wind was not a problem, as the location is sheltered by surrounding woodland.

Entry to the garden itself is not allowed and it must be viewed from the perimeter, so the choice of lens was important. Japanese gardens make heavy demands on upkeep and the entry prohibition is wholly understandable.

I took and used both 35mm and medium-format cameras. However, the constant variation in the light levels made medium-format operation difficult – as soon as I had set up the camera and adjusted the aperture and shutter speed, the light would change and the levels had to be re-checked. A 35mm SLR using a zoom lens and aperture priority offered far greater flexiblity, and enabled me to take full advantage of both *contre-jour* and even-light situations.

### 12.30

Following my evident interest in the Japanese garden, I was lent the guide's notes for the garden and given a further set of papers on its background. Such kindness was shown completely out of the blue, but the extra information helped me to ensure that I covered all of the important aspects of the garden.

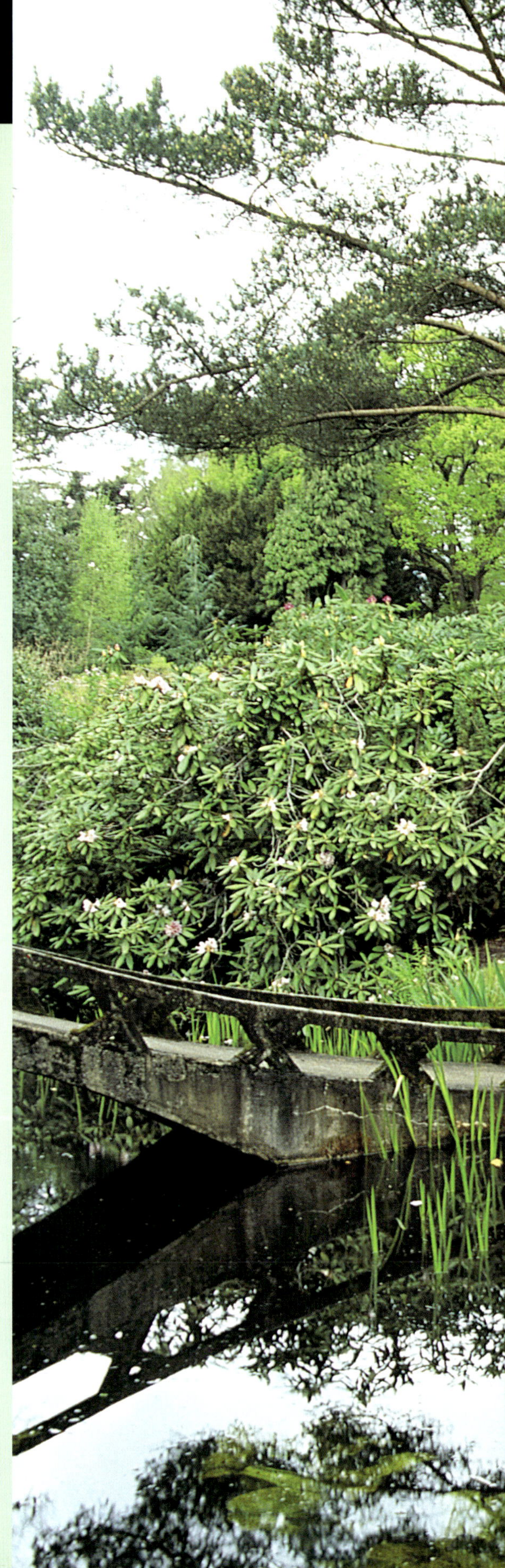

The Shinto Shrine was brought from Japan for the garden's construction in 1910. The steps lead down to the almond-eye bridge, and are designed to produce a perfect reflection in water.

**Minolta Dynax 700si, 28–135mm lens, 81B filter, tripod. 1/3sec at f/13 on Velvia**

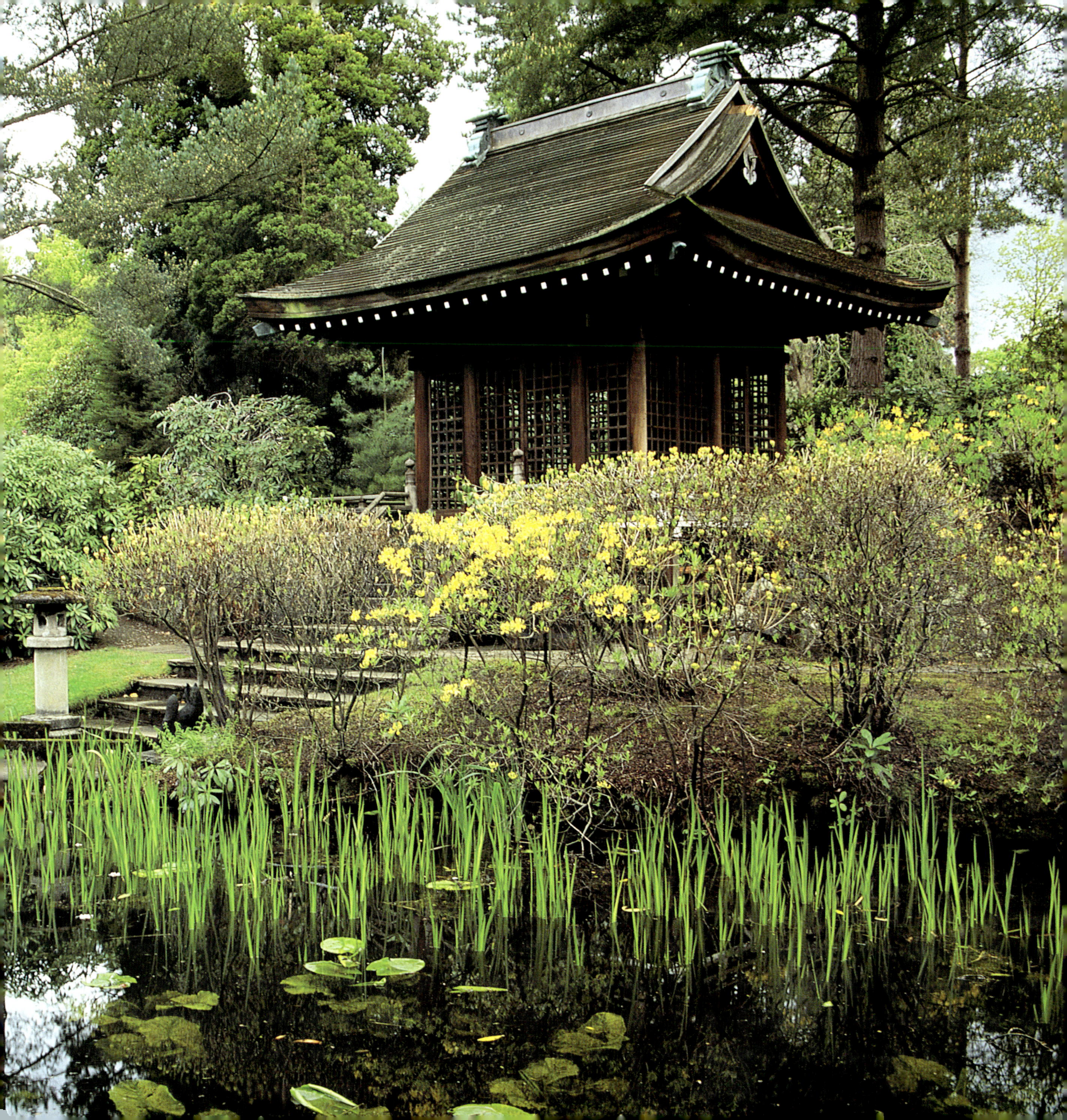

# 5

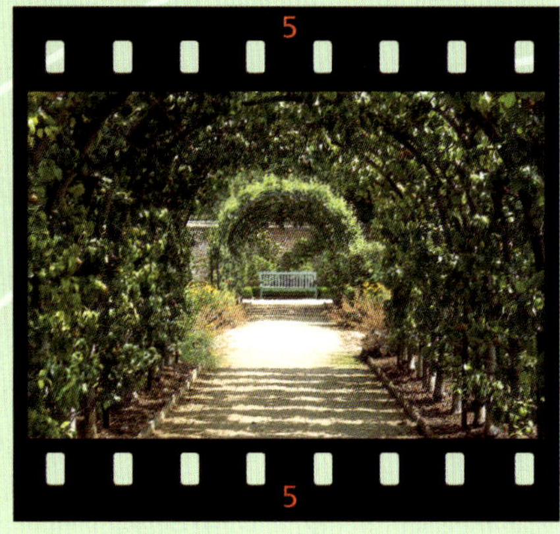

# Light

**Light is everything in photography – after all, the literal meaning of the word is 'drawing with light'. This is achieved through the action of light on film emulsion (or on the pixels of a sensor in digital photography). The quality of light varies widely through the year and throughout a single day, and therein lies much of the appeal of photography.**

An ideal light for garden photography is that soft, diffused light we sometimes get on days that are overcast but bright, with the mere hint of a shadow. If these conditions are accompanied by little or no wind we have a garden photographer's heaven. Colours will be saturated, ugly shadows absent and the choice of aperture unfettered by subject movement.

Of course, conditions do not normally match this ideal, but the fleeting conditions of nature give the photographer some of the best chances for producing outstanding pictures. Mist or fog with the outlines of trees and plants receding into the distance present an opportunity to produce a tranquil, ethereal mood. Misty conditions yielding to the slanting rays of an autumnal sun give another chance for taking out of the ordinary pictures, although these opportunities are generally short-lived. Fleeting too can be the sparkle on frost-encrusted leaves on a winter's morning – the sun can melt the crystals before one's very lens. Rain also provides opportunities; gentle rain can give a lovely soft light and sun shining on drenched foliage light of another quality. The use of reflectors, diffusers and flash can make improvements to the quality of light where necessary, and another option is simply to be patient and wait for a cloud to dampen down the contrasty shadows of a strong sun or for a lull in the breeze.

## Direction of Light

The direction of light is important. It can have a dramatic affect on the appearance of a finished image, and so needs to be considered carefully before each shot is taken. There are three main possibilities:

**Frontal** Frontal lighting is often considered as rather boring, but for many situations in garden photography it can be used to good effect, perhaps best by positioning the camera at a slight sideways angle to it

Below: The leaves of the conifer *Taxodium distichum* change colour before they are shed in autumn. Side lighting was used here with an 81B filter to give extra punch to the tree's russet tones. Sheffield Park Garden, East Sussex.

**Minolta Dynax 700si, 28–135mm lens, 81B filter, tripod. f/8 on Jessops CS 100**

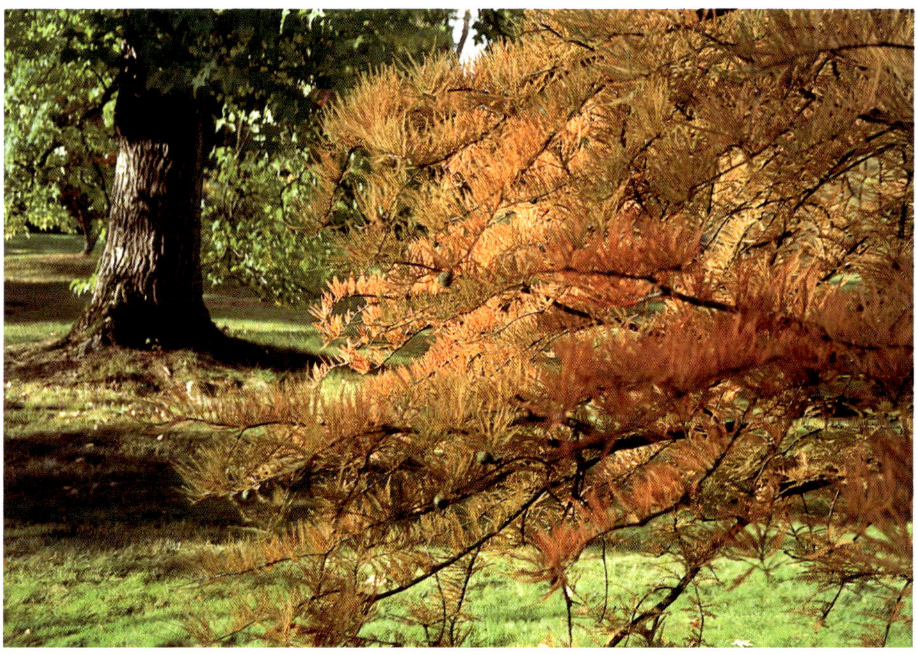

in order to impart a hint of modelling to the subject. Close subjects and views like garden scenes can be spoilt by dark shadows on a sunny day. By opting for frontal lighting these are reduced to a minimum and any pitfalls with exposure calculation avoided, assuming the subject's brightness is average.

pro tip...

**Side lighting**

Positioning the camera side-on to the direction of the light enables full use to be made of a polarizing filter, always a help in giving a picture an extra dimension and lifting it out of the ordinary.

Side With side lighting, subjects are provided with texture and solidity, and depth is imparted to the scene. For example, the shadows of a distinctively shaped plant, such as a cordyline, cast on paving can be employed as an integral part of a picture's composition. Depending on the range of contrast present in a scene, an important decision may have to be made on whether to expose for the highlights or the shadows. The latter course will result in overexposed highlights, and as a rule of thumb this is not the better course to take. Normally it is preferable to expose for the highlights and lose shadow detail.

## Equipment: **Lens Hoods**

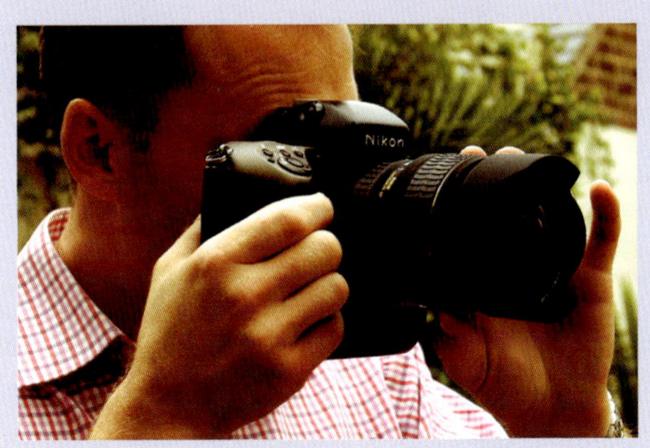

When photographing against the light flare can be a problem, and the lens needs to be shielded by fitting an adequate lens hood. Even one's hand held so as to create a shadow over the front lens element or filter will do the job perfectly adequately.

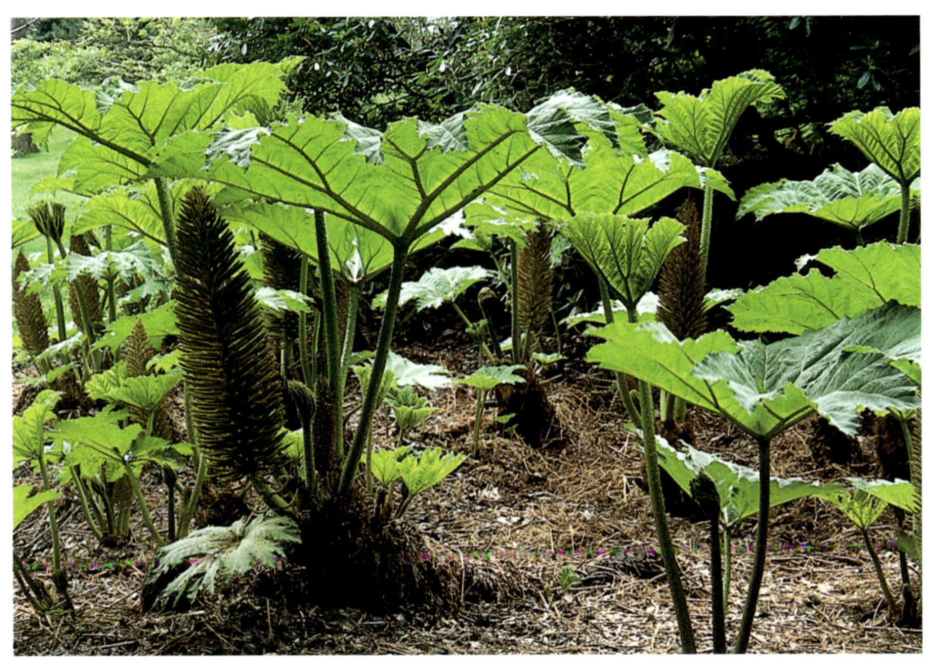

Contre Jour Photographing a single bloom or even a whole scene against the light (the photographic term is *contre jour*) adds drama and reveals texture and outline. A run of the mill subject shot with flat frontal lighting can be made dramatic and arresting when pictured with the light coming from behind. Exposure will need to be considered because the brightness of the light can fool the camera's meter into under-

Left: Backlit leaves of *Gunnera manicata* at Clyne Gardens, Swansea, South Wales.

**Minolta Dynax 700si, 28–135mm lens, 81B filter, tripod. f/11 on Provia 100F**

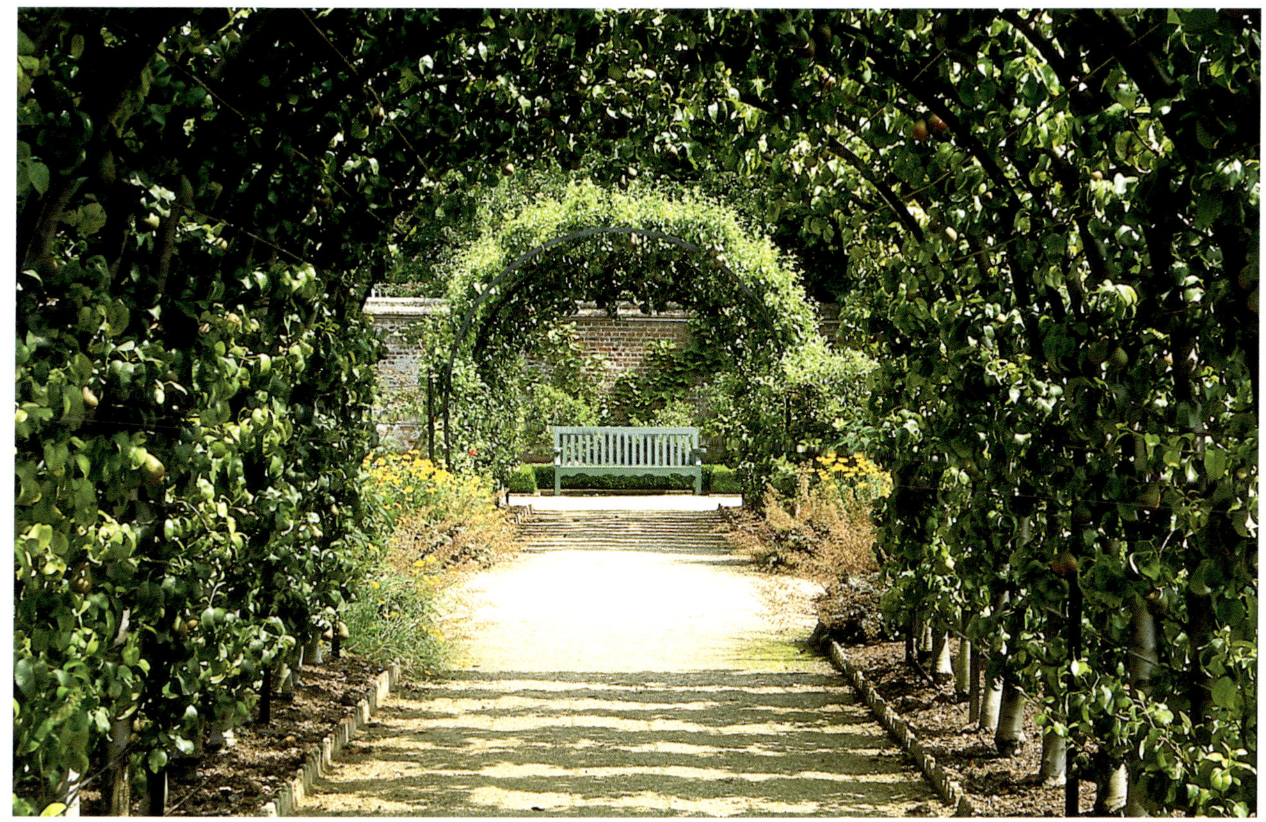

Left: Shadows cast by trained fruit trees on the path beneath are an essential element of this scene in the walled kitchen garden at West Dean in West Sussex.

**Minolta Dynax 7, 28–135mm lens, 81B filter, tripod. f/22 on Velvia**

exposure. In these situations I normally bracket with exposure increasing by half a stop or so. Remember: to avoid any possibility of eye injury, on no account look through the viewfinder directly at the sun.

## Close-up Photography

Lighting plays a vital part in successful close-up photography. Using natural light is straightforward and the available light can be enhanced either by using a reflector or a touch of fill-in flash. The effect of using a reflector is immediately apparent and can be gauged by adjusting the distance it is placed from the subject and the angle at which it is held. High-contrast sunlight can be modified by using a reflector or, better still, a diffuser.

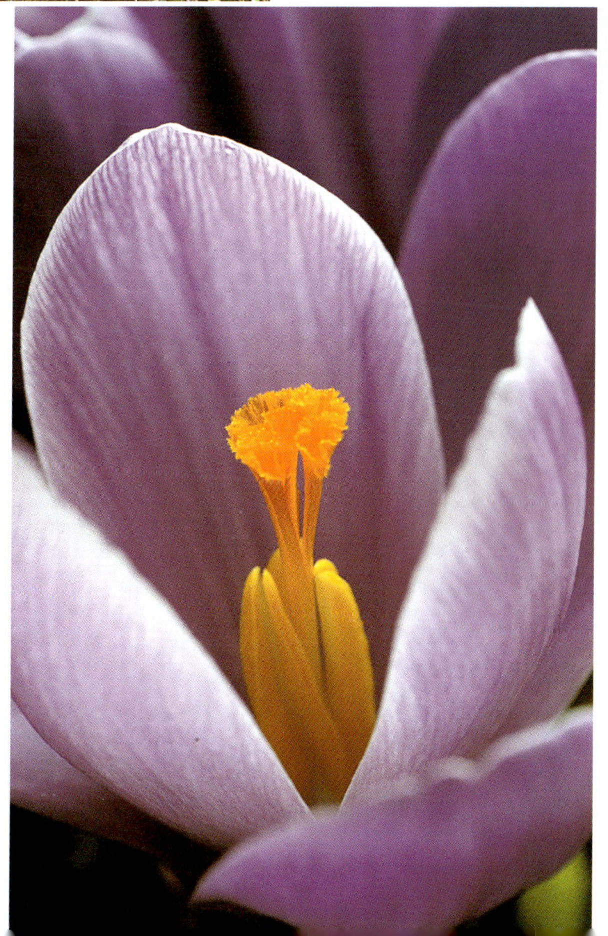

Right: A close-up of *Crocus vernus* 'Remembrance', taken indoors under natural light. The film plane was positioned parallel to the stamen to ensure that it remained in focus.

**Minolta Dynax 700si, 90mm macro lens + 1.4x teleconverter, 81A filter, tripod. 1sec at f/8 on Provia 100F exposed at 200 ISO**

## Technique: **Colour Temperature**

Daylight film is manufactured to deliver colours accurately in midday sunlight (or with flash), when the light's colour temperature (measured on what is known as the Kelvin scale) is 5500°K. Midday sunlight assumes a mixture of blue sky and white cumulus cloud, but sunlight's temperature varies depending on weather conditions and the time of day. At dawn and dusk it is around 3000–4000°K and more reddish light is emitted, caused as the sun's rays travel further through the atmosphere. A warm cast can, of course, be beneficial to the result of dawn and dusk pictures. However, if 'correct' colours are required it is necessary to fit a blue 80 or 82 series light-balancing filter. On the other hand, under a deep blue sky colour temperature can be 10,000°K or more. This temperature will give a bluish cast to colour film, which can be corrected with a suitable warm-up filter. Greens, in particular, benefit from the use of warm-up filters.

In the field it is difficult to know what the colour temperature is without a colour-temperature meter. In any event, I limit myself to a restricted range of filters, an important reason being that filters can affect flower colours. For this reason I rarely use a warm-up filter when photographing blue or bluish flowers.

The chart below shows which filters to use to help correct colours on daylight-balanced film in some frequently experienced summer lighting situations, assuming that a degree of correction is required. The list, I stress, is a purely personal one.

A summer's afternoon at Nymans, West Sussex, with fair-weather cumulus dotting the sky, but what was the colour temperature? Certainly over 5500°K because the result with an 81B filter seems fine.

**Fuji GW670III, 81B filter, tripod. f/32 on Velvia**

| | **Colour temperature** | **Filter** |
|---|---|---|
| Clear blue sky | >10,000°K | 81EF (rarely) or 81C |
| Hazy sunlight | c.9000°K | 81C or 81B |
| Overcast light | c.7000°K | 81B |
| Lightly overcast sky | c.6500°K | 81B or 81A |
| Mean noon sunlight | 5500°K | 81A or None |
| Early morning sunlight | 4000°K | 82A |
| Late afternoon sunlight | 4000°K | 82A |

This series was taken over the course of a few minutes during the early afternoon of a summer's day at Great Comp Garden in Kent. The sky was clear blue, and the colour temperature undoubtedly high. The effects of each change of filter are slight, but most noticeable on foliage colour. If there had been any areas of paving or rock in the picture the effect on those materials would have been evident too (see page 110 for details on photographing stone).

**All shots: Mamiya 645 Super, 80mm lens, tripod. 1/15sec at f/16 on Velvia**

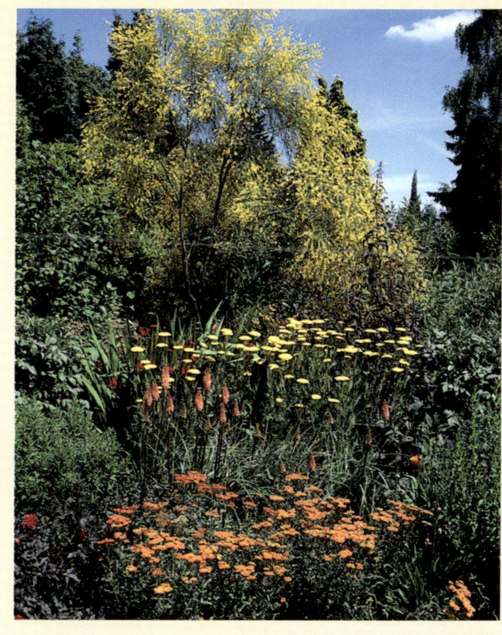

No filter

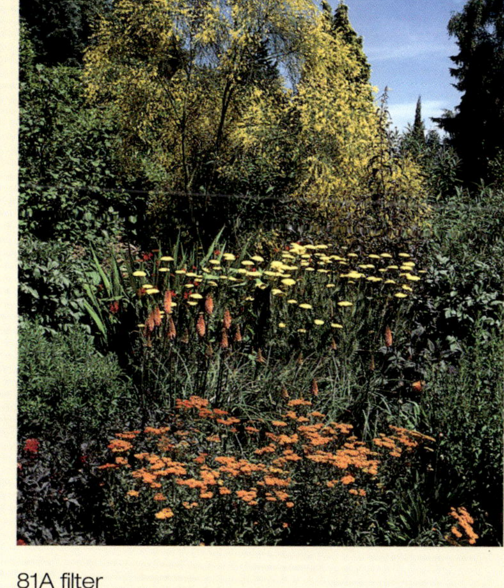

81A filter

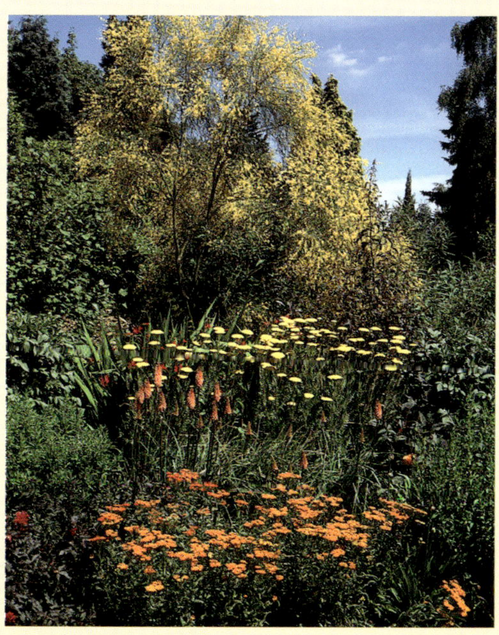

81B filter

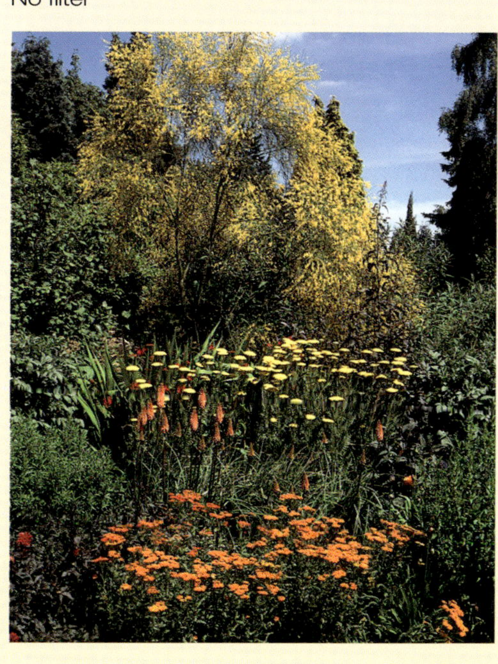

81C filter

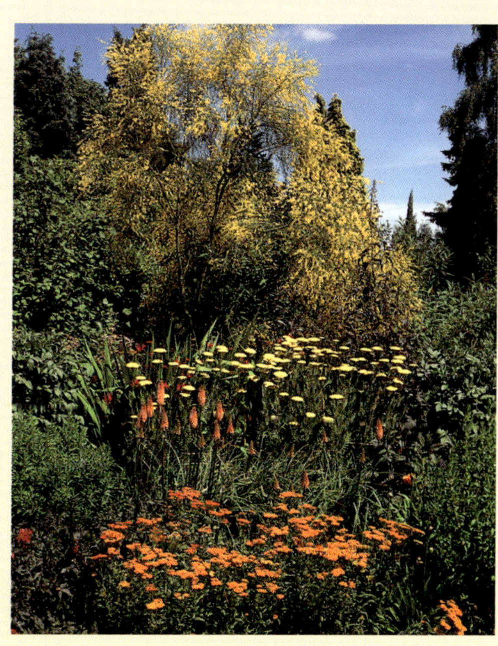

81EF filter

## Equipment: **Teleconverters**

Recourse to a teleconverter will increase image size, but there will be a drawback in loss of light. Teleconverters, also referred to as converters or extenders, are generally available in two strengths, 1.4x and 2x. They are lenses that are placed between the camera and the main lens, and multiply the image size by their respective strengths. Teleconverters were considered to degrade the image to some extent, but now quality has been improved to the point where they can confidently be expected to produce excellent results. The light loss with a 1.4x teleconverter is just under a stop; two stops of light are lost with a 2x teleconverter. Teleconverters are used extensively for wildlife photography where their light weight is a real plus point.

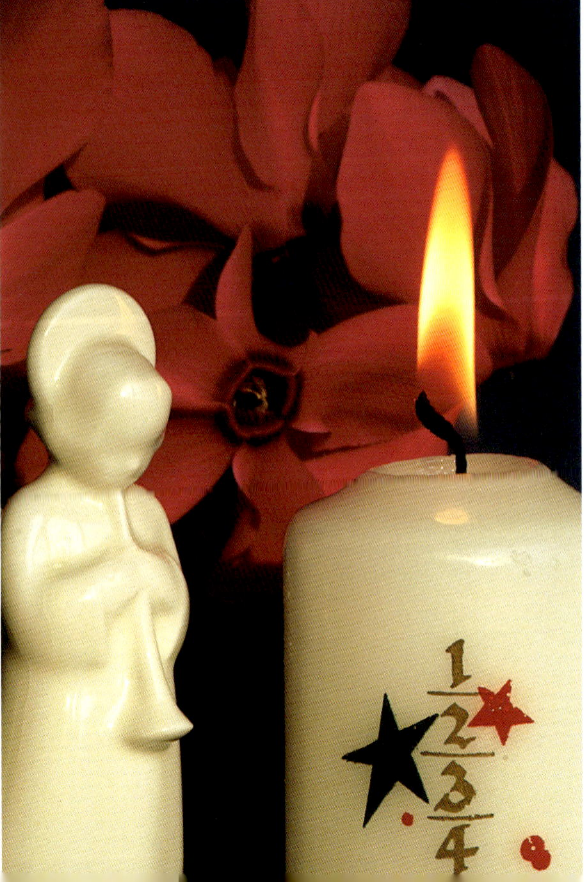

A red cyclamen has provided the background to this 'home studio' Christmas scene photographed by available light from a window.

**Minolta XG-M, 90mm macro lens, tripod. f/32 on Fujichrome 100 Professional**

### Flash

As far as electronic flash is concerned, photographers can be divided into two groups: those who employ it frequently and those who do not. I must confess to being numbered in the second group. The main drawback of using flash is that it can be difficult to visualize exactly what its effect will be on the image. Its use can create unpleasant contrast with dark shadows, and this puts many off using it, but in horticultural photography flash certainly does have its applications. The secret is to achieve a result where the viewer is unaware that flash has been used.

**Ring flash** I haven't tried any of the specialized macro flash units on the market, but I do use ring flash occasionally and have found that it can produce good results. However, the power of the units is limited. Subjects therefore need to be fairly close to the lens, especially if a small aperture is to be used. With a 90mm macro lens an aperture of f/8–f/11 is just about possible with 100 ISO film for a subject about 6in (15cm) away. To give a little more room for manoeuvre – i.e. up to f/13 – I use Provia 100F and up-rate it to 200 ISO. I occasionally use ring flash as fill-in flash to provide both even illumination of orchids and an effective method of throwing light into the throats of cymbidiums.

**Off-camera flash** A separate flash used off camera allows much greater flexibility than one built into the camera. The intensity of the light can be diffused with a light piece of material over the flash gun's lens or the light can be bounced using a white reflector, a wall or a ceiling for subjects such as a vase of flowers.

## Technique: **Fill-in flash**

Flash can be employed instead of a reflector as fill-in light to reduce contrast in bright sunlight or to throw light onto a subject in lower light situations. When using flash in these ways (also referred to as 'slow-shutter sync') the shutter speed is set automatically to increase the background exposure and flash output is decreased to maintain correct subject exposure. In the past this was a complicated mental exercise, but with the advent of dedicated TTL flash it is now a simple operation. Indeed, some cameras have a flash exposure-compensation button that makes it possible to fine-tune an exposure and achieve a natural-looking result.

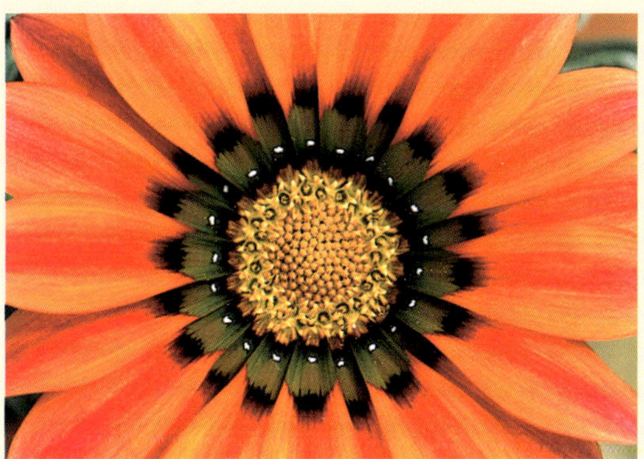

A touch of flash (slow-shutter sync) has been given to this image of a gazania in order to soften the shadows caused by ambient light.

**Minolta Dynax 700si, 90mm macro lens, 81A filter, tripod. 1/3sec at f/16 on Velvia**

Right and below right: Two images of *Passiflora vitifolia* in the orchid house at RHS Wisley. The first was obtained solely using natural light, while a ring flash was used to take the second. This gives a slightly more saturated red, but inevitably the background is black.

**Both pictures: Minolta Dynax 7, 90mm macro lens, 81A filter, tripod. f/5.6 on Velvia**

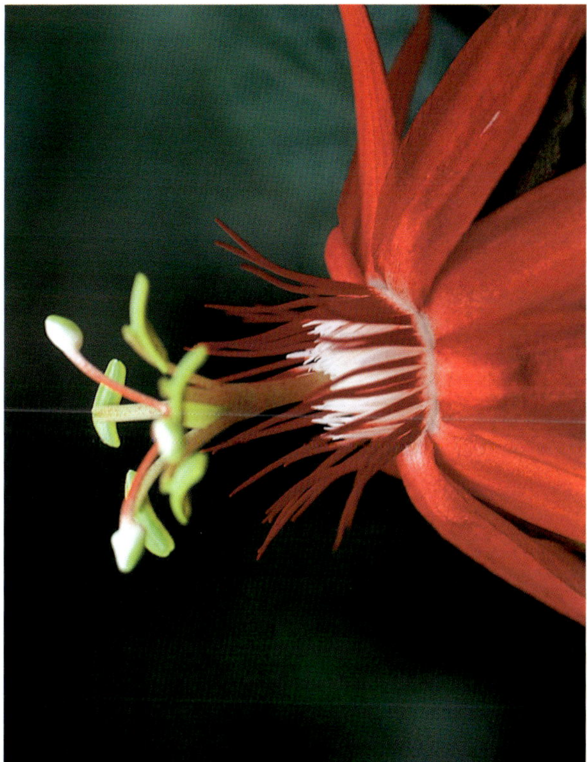

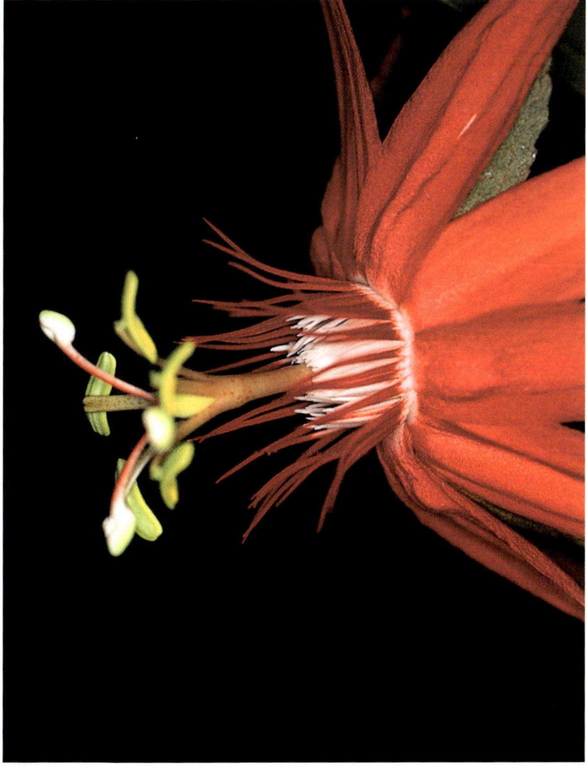

On location:

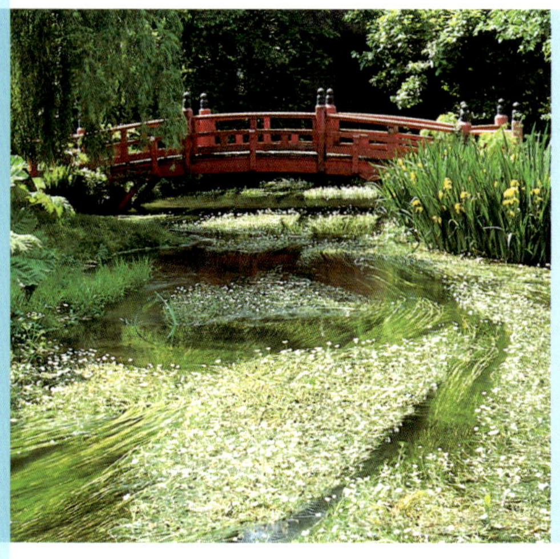

# Water in the Garden

**Water in a scene always fires my imagination and has me looking around for ways to incorporate it into a picture. Its reflective qualities offer special opportunities for securing memorable images whether the light is bright or soft. Frontal light, especially low sunlight, will guarantee superb reflections and backlighting off water can be employed for silhouetted effects, but be wary of flare.**

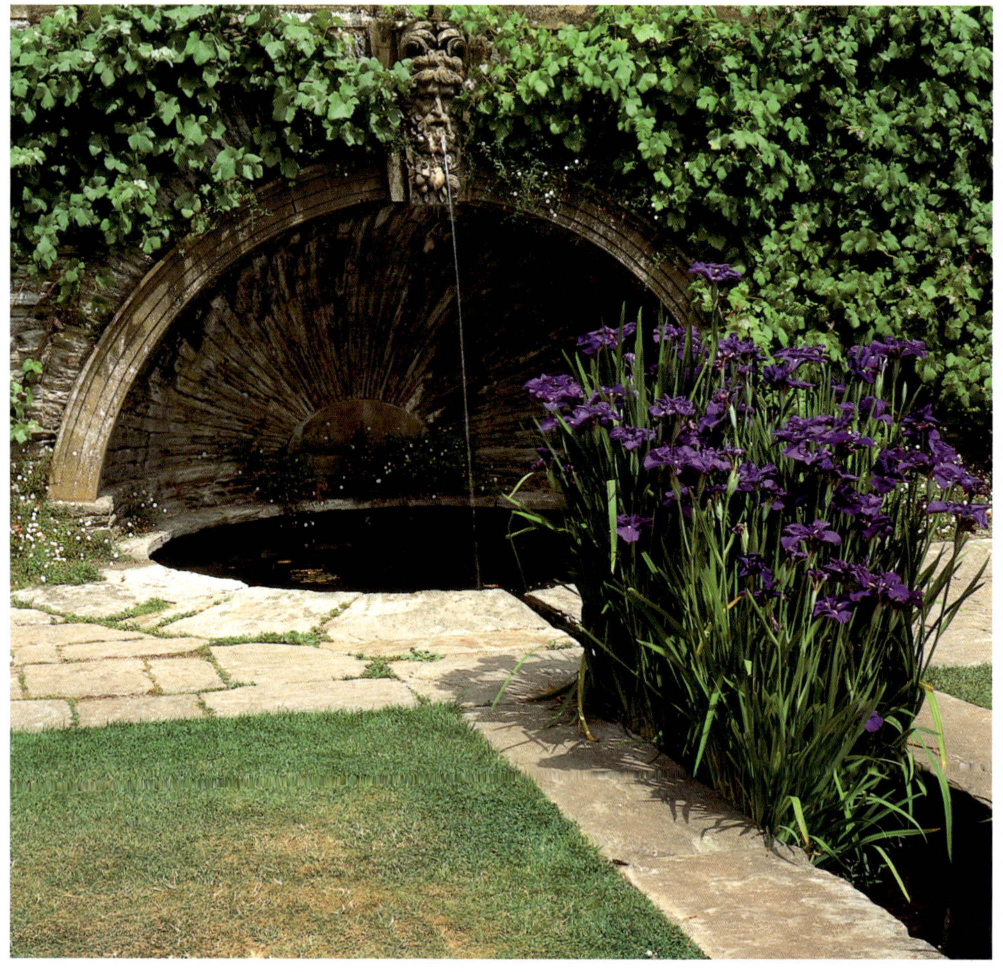

In the Lutyens-designed formal garden at Hestercombe, narrow canals or rills run along two sides of the sunken parterre known as the Great Plat. These rills emanate from deep hemispherical pools recessed into the stone walls. The picture illustrates the importance of light: stronger shadows would have rendered the hemisphere dark and forbidding, but the weak sunlight has highlighted the water spouting from the mask.

**Fuji GW670III, 81B filter, tripod. 1/8sec at f/27 on Velvia**

Right: Scotney Castle, Kent. The ruin of this romantic castle, dating from the fourteenth century, is the centrepiece of the garden that straddles a hillside leading down into the valley where the castle is located.

**Mamiya C330f, 180mm lens, tripod. f/32 on Velvia**

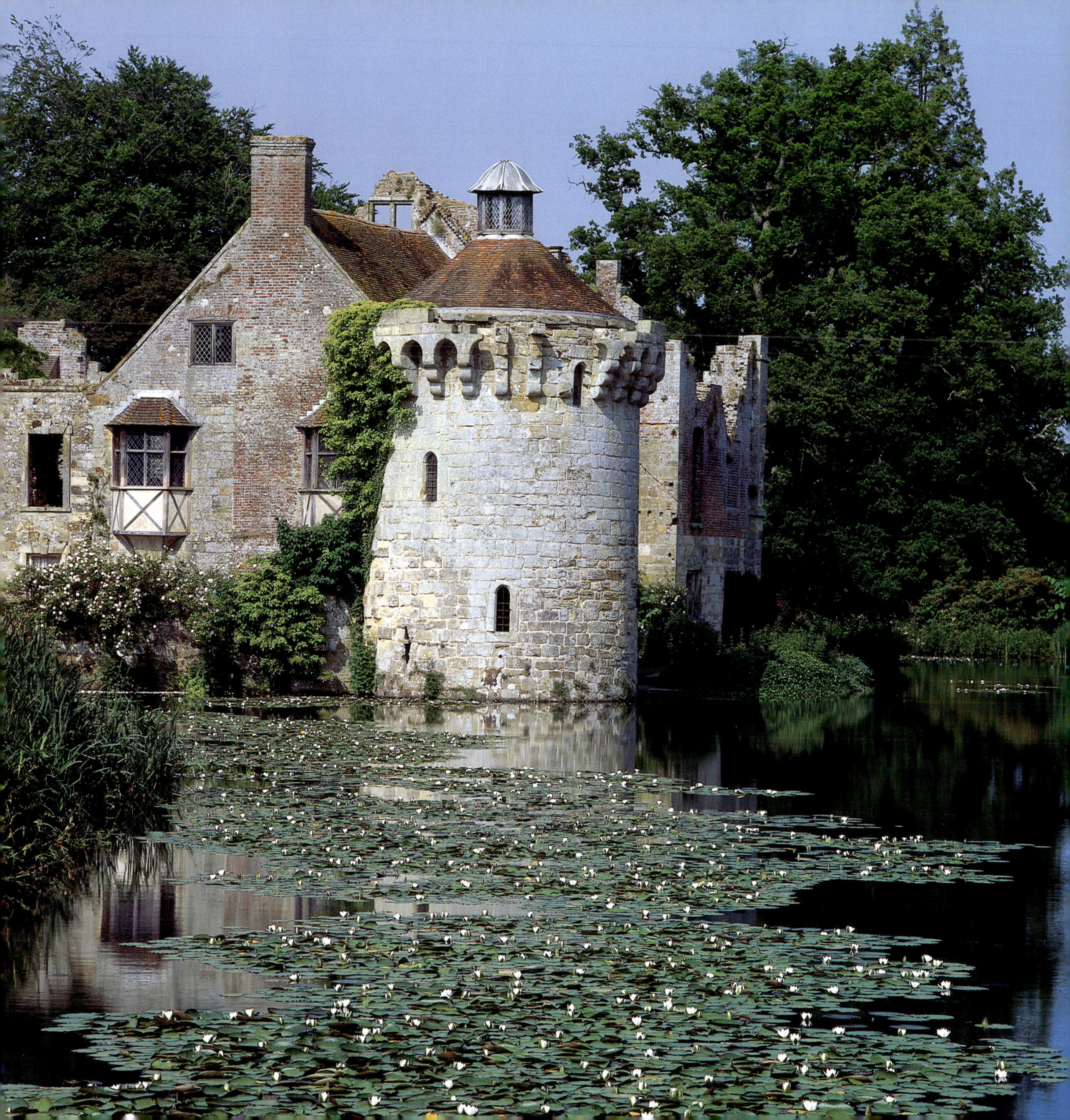

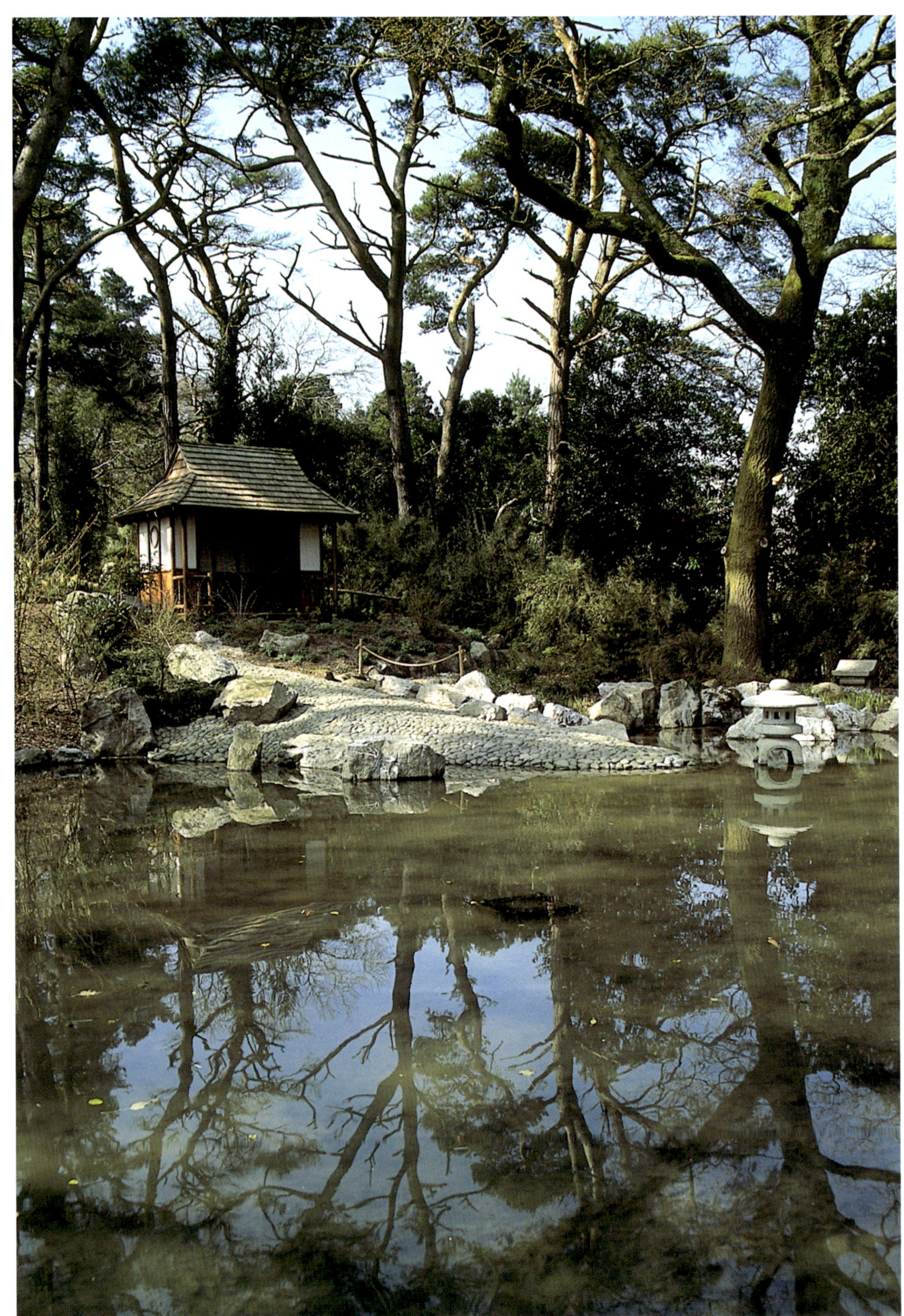

A half-and-half composition, which succeeds because of the reflections in the lake and the placement in the picture of the Japanese Summer House in the Okakkei ('borrowed scenery') Garden at Pine Lodge in Cornwall.

---

**Minolta Dynax 7, 28–135mm lens, 81A filter, tripod. 1/10sec at f/11 on Velvia**

Right: A diffuser held over this tropical waterlily, Nymphaea 'Director George T. Moore', in the glasshouse at RHS Wisley in Surrey, eliminated shadows cast by framework supporting the glazing.

**Minolta Dynax 7, 90mm macro lens, diffuser, tripod. f/22 on Velvia**

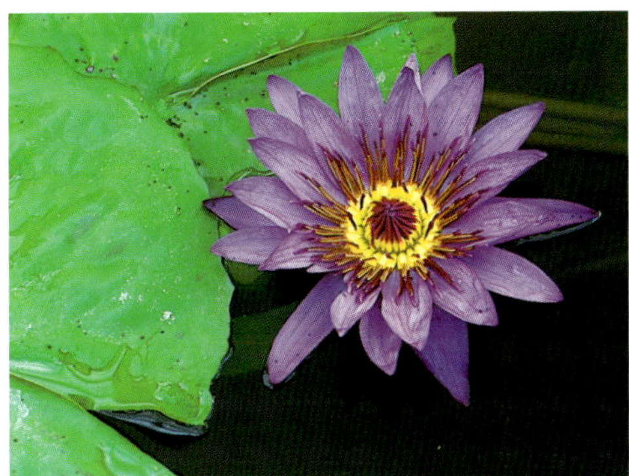

Below: A carrier stream of the Wiltshire Avon at Heale House Garden, with flowering River Water-crowfoot on its surface, sweeps past a clump of *Gunnera manicata* towards the Nikko Bridge, positioned to give the picture balance.

**Minolta Dynax 7, 28–135mm lens, 81B filter, tripod. 1/4sec at f/20 on Velvia**

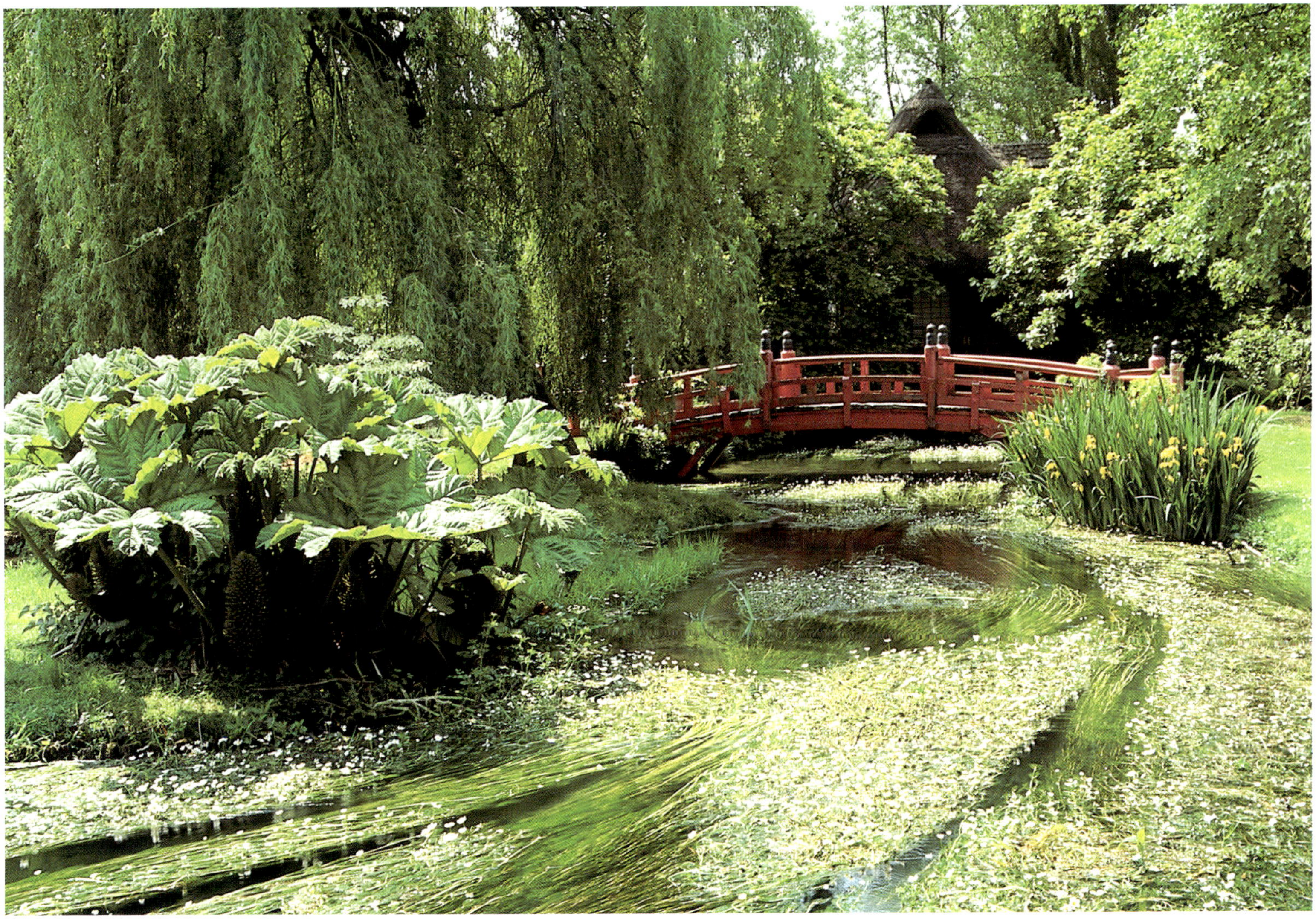

# Part two:
# **In the Garden**

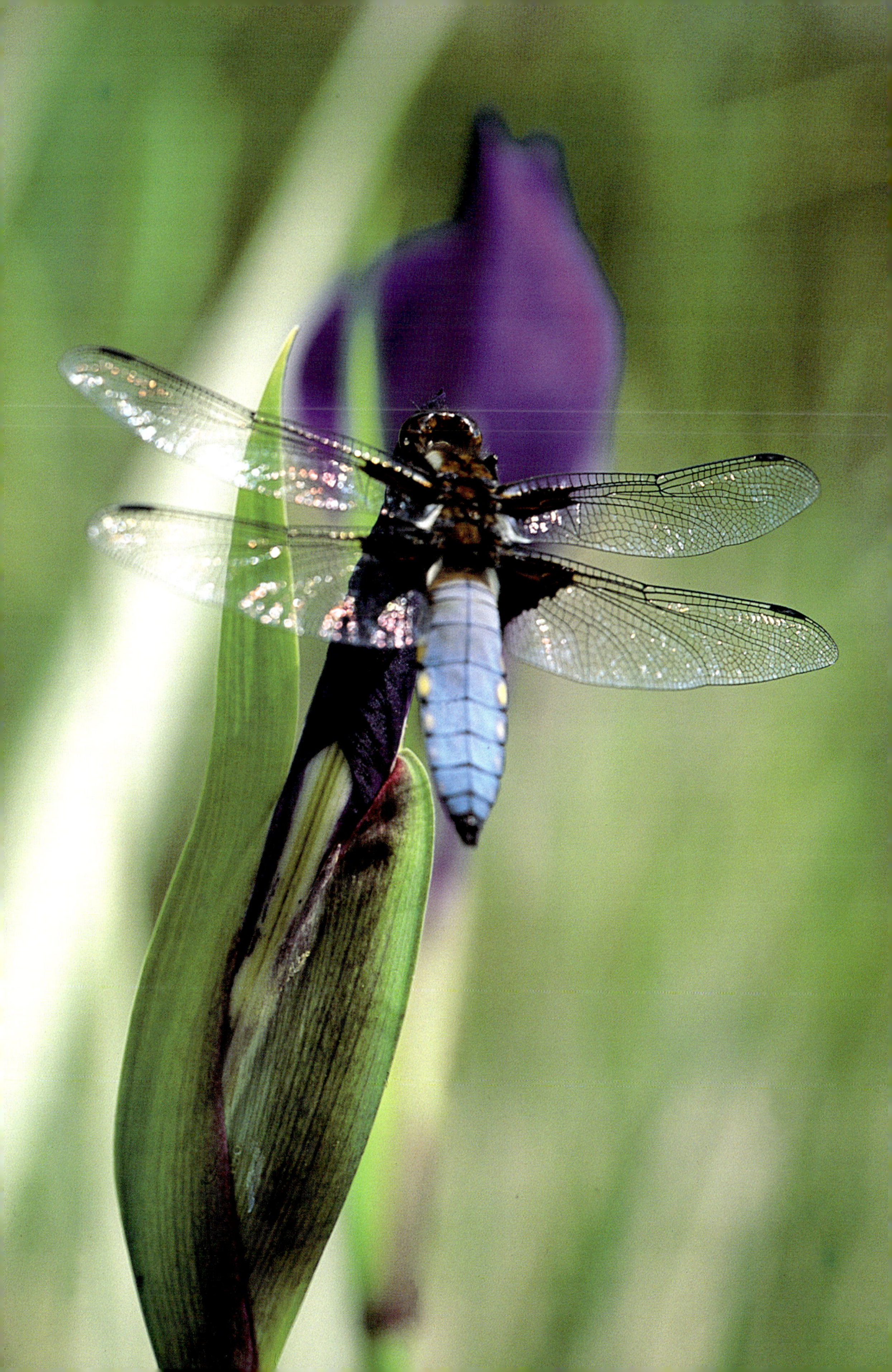

6

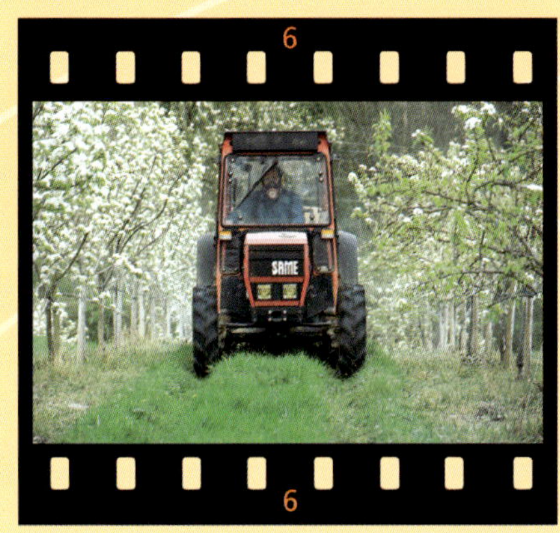

# The **Seasons**

**The cycle of the seasons, with the gradual change in a garden's appearance as one week succeeds another, is fascinating to the gardener and a feast of visual action for the photographer.**

It pays to know at least something about what you are photographing. Let's take late summer in a fruit orchard as a simple example. Some 'Discovery' apples will look pretty colourful at this time of year, but will they still be there and looking even better in a few weeks? Is it a waste of time to photograph them now or will they be harvested soon? Clearly, it would be useful to know that 'Discovery' is in fact an early dessert variety harvested in late summer. Again, a clump of *Stachys byzantina* 'Big Ears' would be enhanced as a saleable picture if the texture of the grey 'lambs' ears' leaves, an adaptation against drought conditions, could be shown by selecting a viewing angle that emphasizes their felted texture.

## Capturing the Seasons

The pictures on this page show four views of the statue of Pan at the Royal Horticultural Society's garden at Wisley taken in each of the four seasons. They illustrate the opportunities photographers in temperate regions have for obtaining varied images throughout the year. Because of its form with the body of the Arcadian god on a tapering pedestal shaft, this statue is more properly referred to as a 'term', and it was manufactured by Haddonstone, who specialize in high-quality decorative stonework.

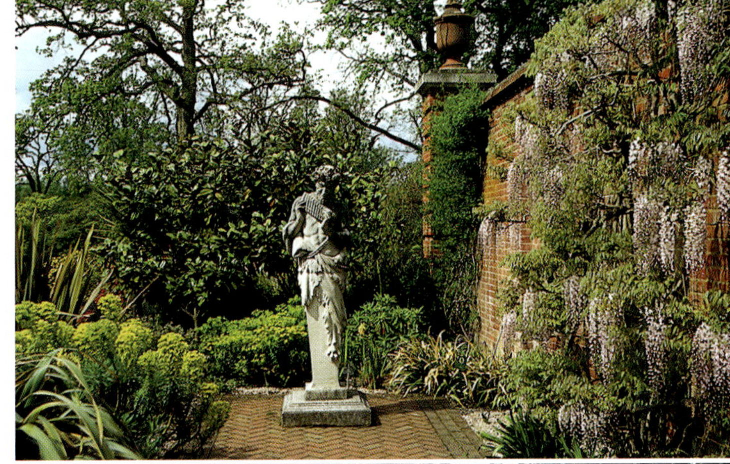

Top: A spring day at RHS Wisley with wisteria and euphorbia.

**Minolta Dynax 7, 28–135mm lens, 81B and polarizing filters, tripod. 1/15sec at f/8 on Velvia**

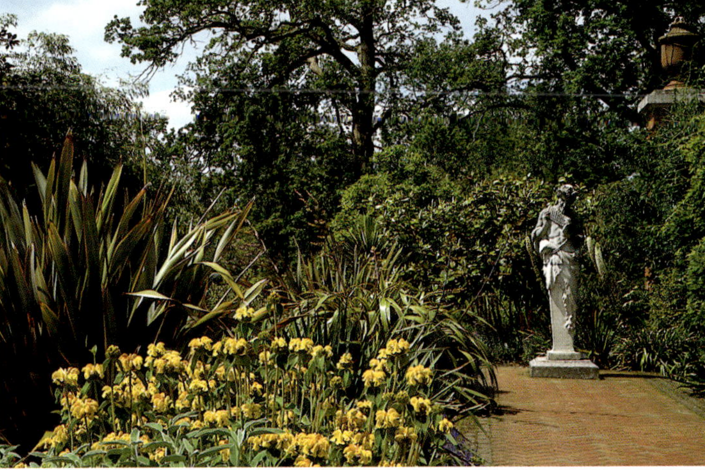

Second top: Summer. In the foreground is *Phlomis lycia*.

**Fuji GW670III, 81B filter, tripod. f/32 on Velvia**

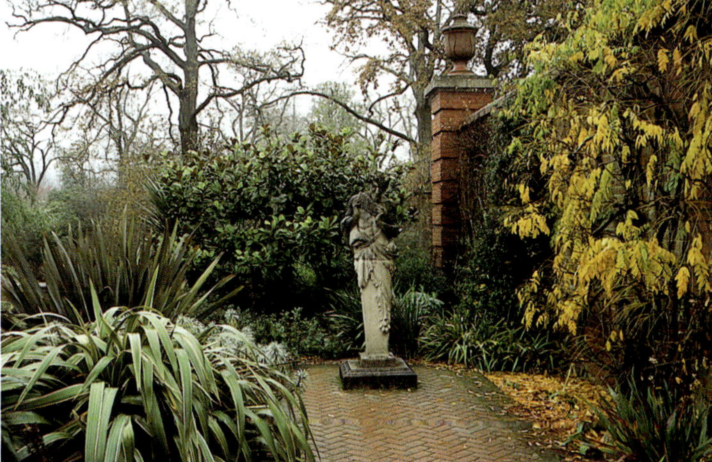

Right: Autumn colour.

**Minolta Dynax 700si, 28–135mm lens, 81B filter, tripod. 1/3sec at f/11 on Provia 100F**

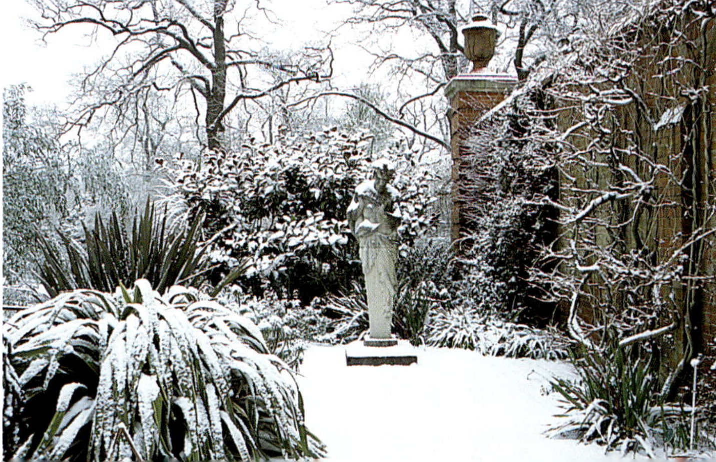

Bottom: Snow was still falling as I took this shot.

**Minolta Dynax 7, 28–135mm lens, tripod. f/16 on Provia 100F**

A spring image in a Sussex pear orchard. I used a zoom lens to fill the frame with tractor and blossom.

**Minolta Dynax 700si, 70–300mm lens, tripod. f/11 on Provia 100**

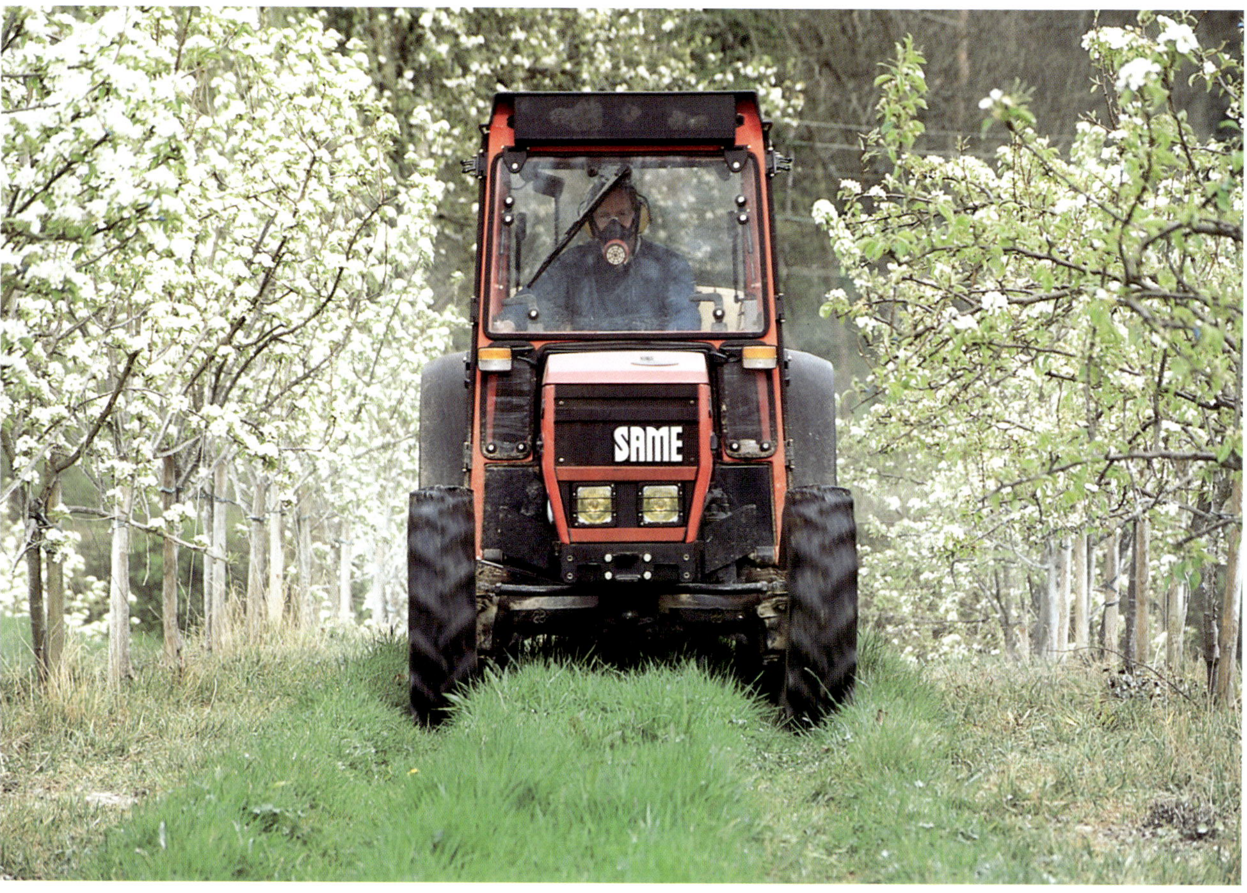


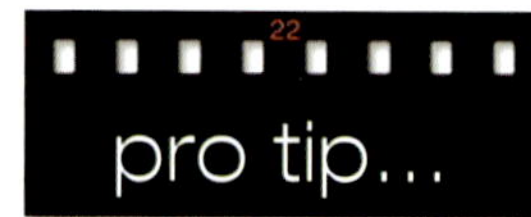


**Forecasts**

Both gardeners and garden photographers closely follow weather forecasts, which are normally a good guide to photographic possibilities, even though days don't always turn out quite as expected.

## Spring

Spring is, of course, the season when the garden wakes up from its winter's rest. Fresh, verdant greens are everywhere and multitudes of bulbs, herbaceous plants, shrubs and trees waste no time in producing flowers and blossom in a kaleidoscope of colour. If you are undecided as to which transparency film to go for, now is the time to experiment!

It is advisable to capture the season on film as soon as each scene is approaching its best because spring weather is notoriously changeable and heavy rain, wind or a late frost can devastate a perfect picture-in-waiting overnight. Subjects that are particularly appealing in spring include colourful bedding displays with tulips, wallflowers and so on, and woodland gardens with a dazzling show provided by rhododendrons, azaleas, magnolias and the like. There is so much of interest and delight, it is just a matter of being out and about and alert to the picture-taking opportunities that spring offers.

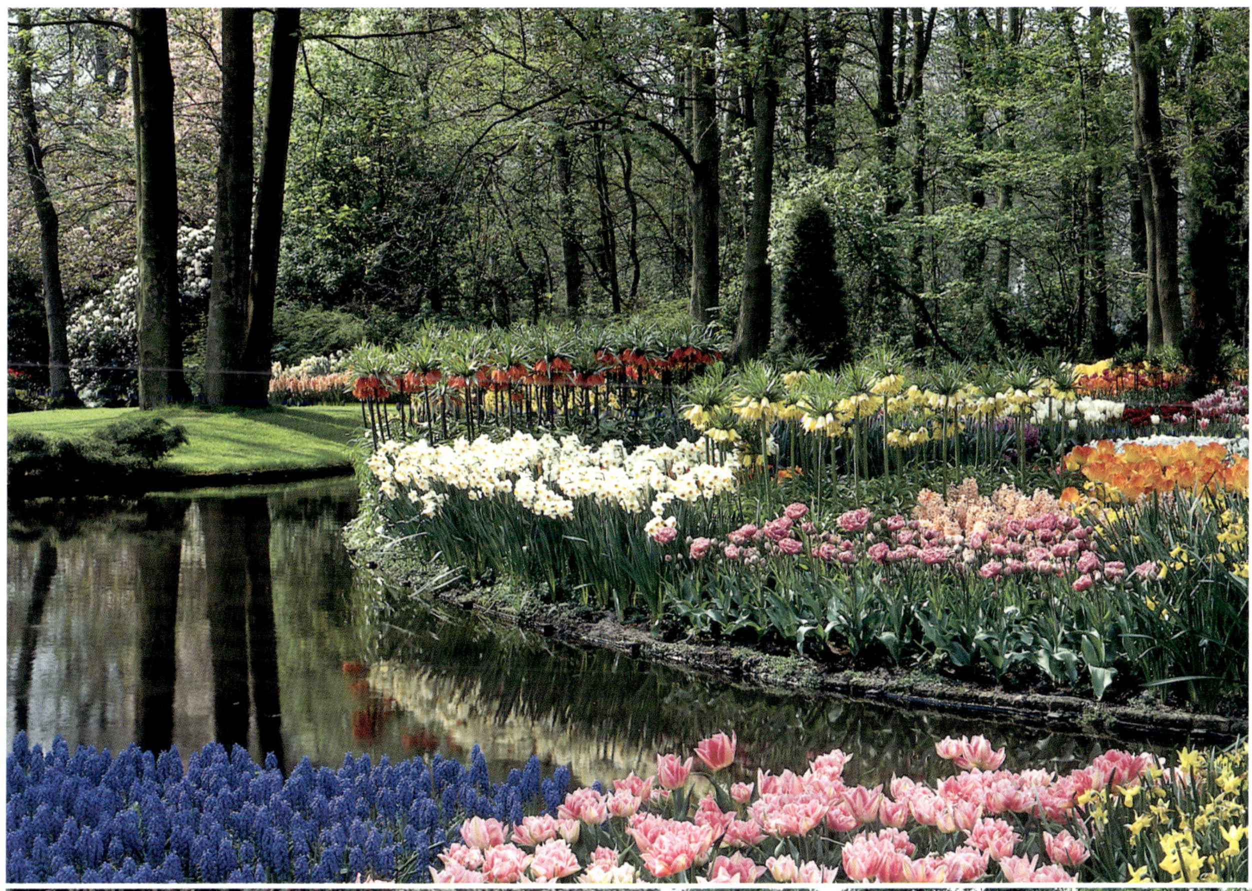

Left: Spring bulbs at Keukenhof, Lisse, in the Netherlands; concentrated spring colour that has to be seen to be believed.

**Mamiya 645 Super, 80mm lens, tripod. f/22 on Fujichrome 100 Professional**

Below: Subdued late-spring light has resulted in an absence of contrast and even lighting over this whole scene in RHS Wisley.

**Fuji GW670III, 81B filter, tripod. f/32 on Velvia**

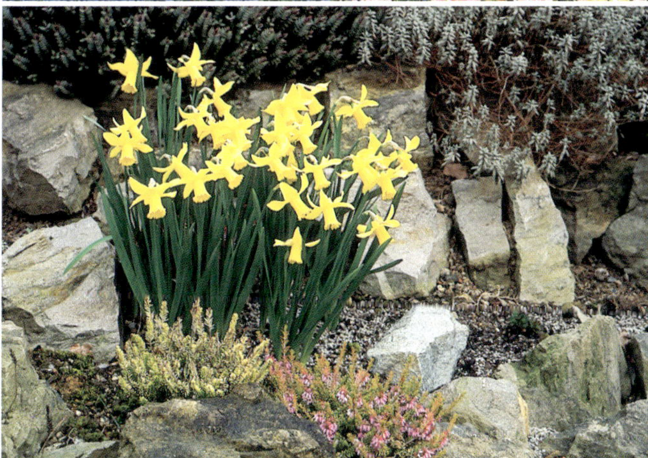

An early spring image of a dwarf narcissus heralds a busy season to come for the garden photographer.

**Fuji GW670III, 81B filter, tripod. f/11 on Velvia**

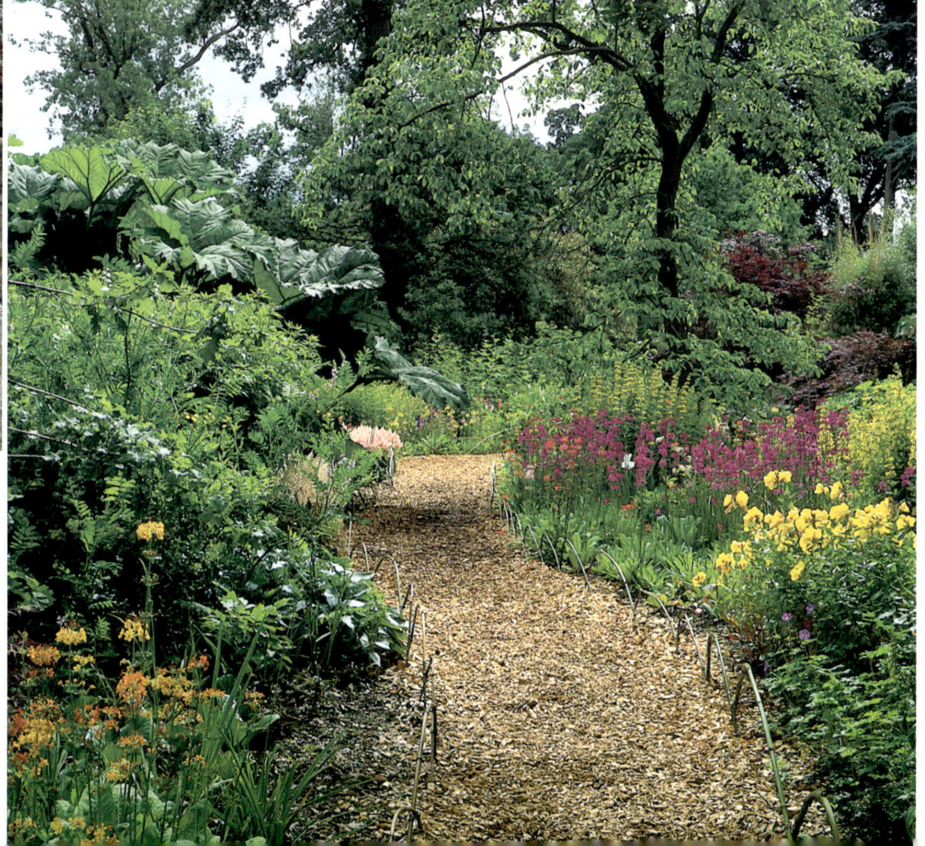

Right: This group of *Meconopsis* x *sheldonii* was flowering near the primulas at Harlow Carr in early summer and conditions were perfect for plant photography (even light and almost no breeze to sway the petals), allowing a slow shutter speed.

**Minolta Dynax 700si, 28–135mm lens, tripod. 1/6sec at f/16 on Velvia**

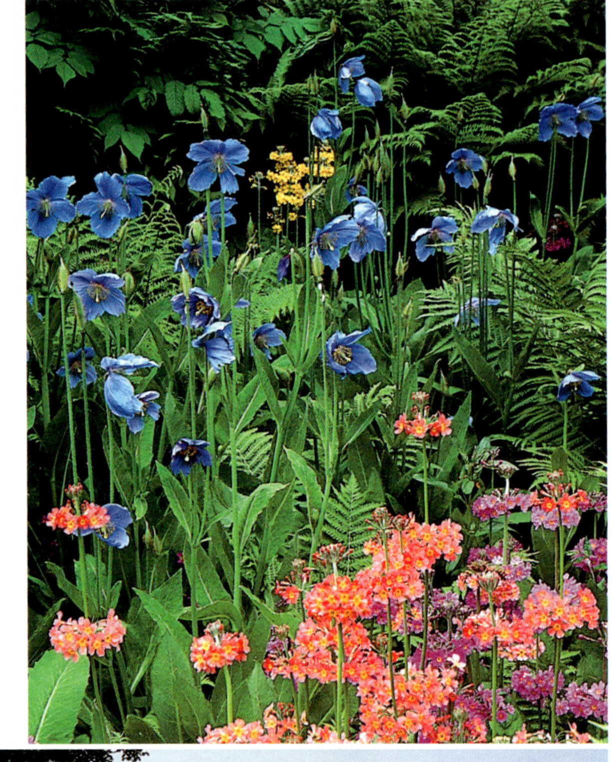

## Summer

Like spring, summer provides more subjects than a photographer can comfortably cope with, and one can only try to scratch the surface of possibilities. Water gardens can be at their very best in late spring and early summer, as can herbaceous borders once the season has progressed a bit. From high summer the kitchen garden provides many subjects, some of them decorative, and plantings carried out in the 'naturalistic' style can be stunning from now until the end of autumn.

Summer light can be harsh, creating high levels of contrast, and often it is advisable to stop shooting for a few hours around noon when the sun is high in the sky, modelling light is poor and shadows dense. The light is softer and altogether better earlier in the morning and later in the afternoon. I must admit, though, that I often disregard the middle of the day 'ban' and seek out subjects that are comparatively unaffected. In any event, a day of continuous sunshine with no alleviating cloud can be unusual, and white cumulus cloud can act as a wonderful giant reflector for garden scenes.

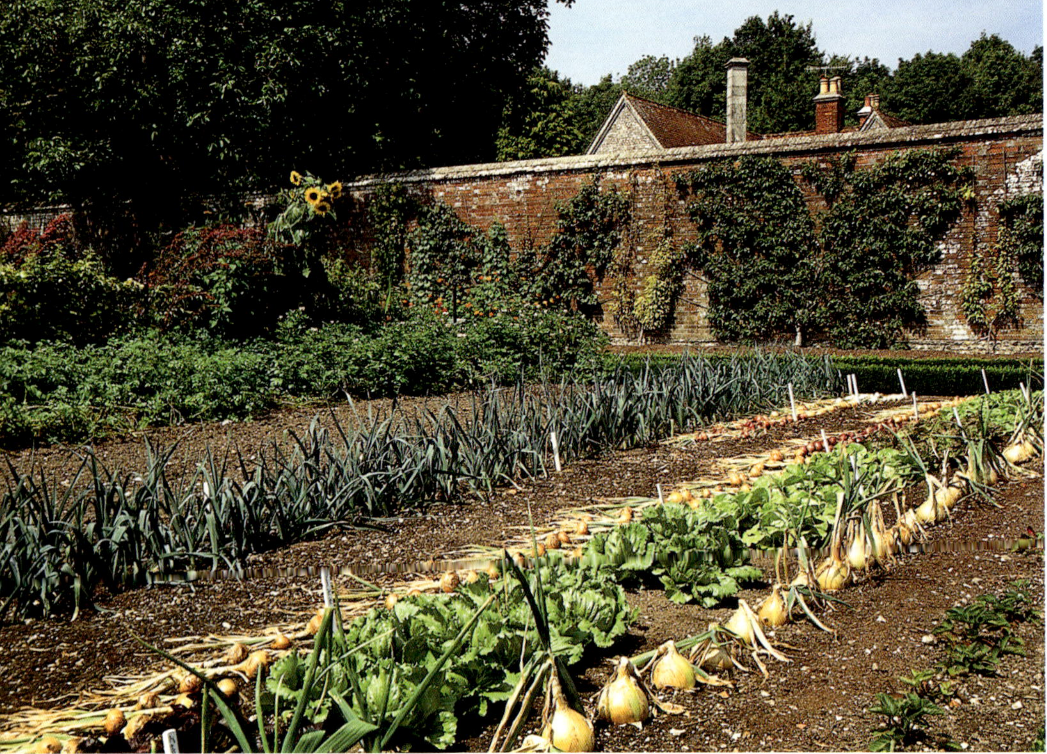

Left: Shot in late summer, this traditional kitchen garden, at West Dean in West Sussex, has a mix of vegetables, fruit and flowers.

**Minolta Dynax 7, 28–135mm lens, 81B filter, tripod. f/16 on Velvia**

Right: High summer colour in one of the walled gardens at RHS Wisley.

**Fuji GW670III, 81B filter, tripod. f/32 on Velvia**

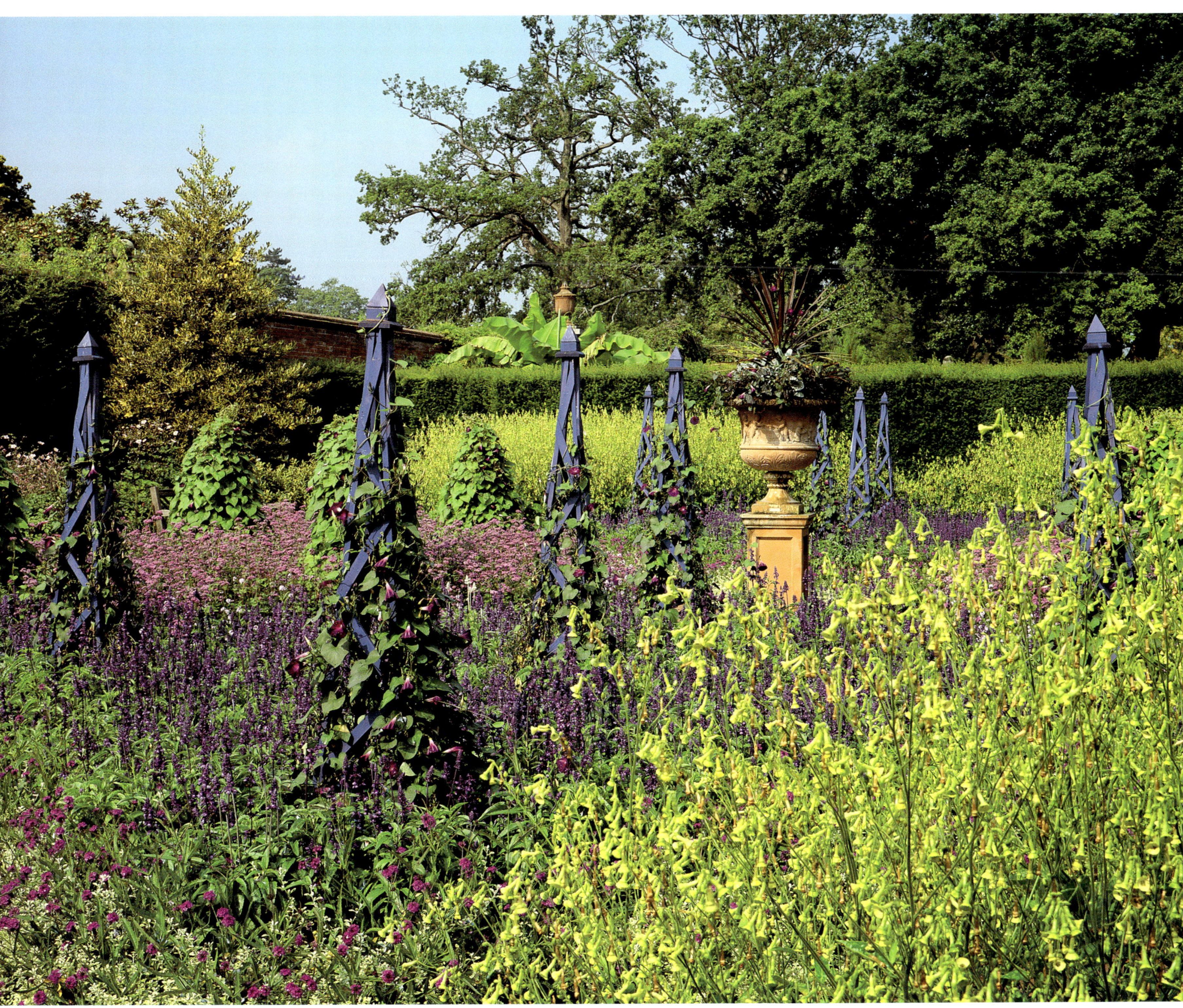

## Autumn

Autumn is a magical season for gardens and garden photographers, though the effects are often short lived. Mists are fleeting (although these can be faked, see below) and autumn foliage can be gone overnight following wind and rain. The maxim is to be out and about, making the most of the photographic opportunities while they are there.

The fiery colours of autumn demand attention. What a frustrating business it must have been for photographers before the advent of colour film! Some grasses are at their best at this time of the year with, for example, the seed heads of the many cultivars of *Miscanthus sinensis* illuminated by slanting sunlight. Fruit is also an obvious autumnal subject, as are the seed heads of plants such as *Clematis tangutica*.

### Technique: **Faking Mist**

Something approaching misty or foggy conditions can be contrived on a dull day by breathing onto the lens and waiting to trip the shutter at an opportune moment as the condensation clears.

Below: The view of *Parrotia persica* as it really was.

**Minolta Dynax 700si, 28–135mm lens, 81B filter, tripod. 1/4sec at f/8 on Provia 100F**

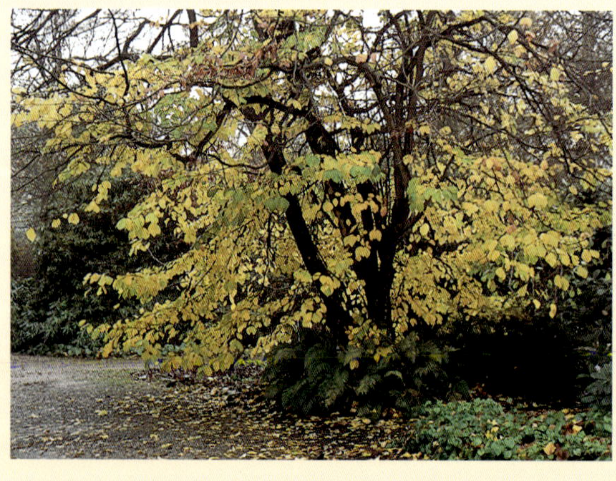

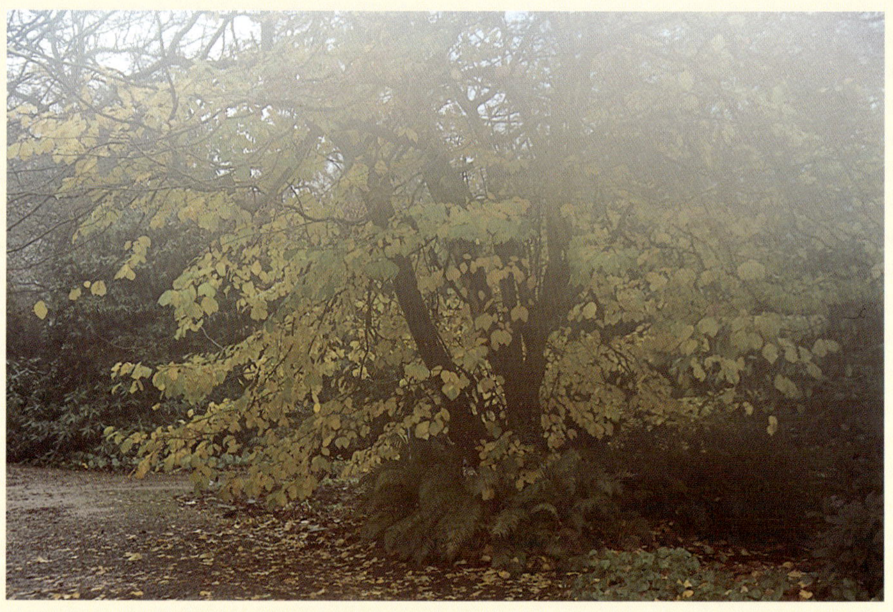

Above: An autumnal, overcast day at Wisley. It was not misty; this effect was simply achieved by breathing on the 81B filter.

**Minolta Dynax 700si 28–135mm lens, 81B filter, tripod. 1/4sec at f/8 on Provia 100F**

Below: A small aperture ensured that most of this carpet of leaves from *Betula uber* at Wisley is in sharp focus.

**Minolta Dynax 7, 28–135mm lens, 81B filter, tripod. f/22 on Velvia**

Right: On an overcast afternoon, the flames of this bonfire provided most of the light.

**Minolta Dynax 700si, 70–210mm lens, polarizing filter, tripod. f/5.6 on Fujichrome 100 Professional**

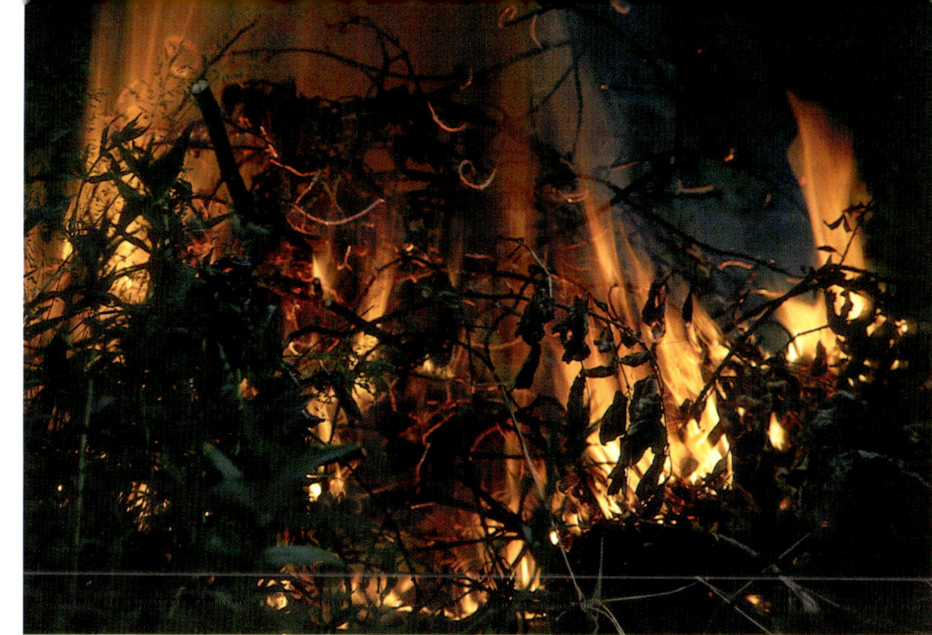

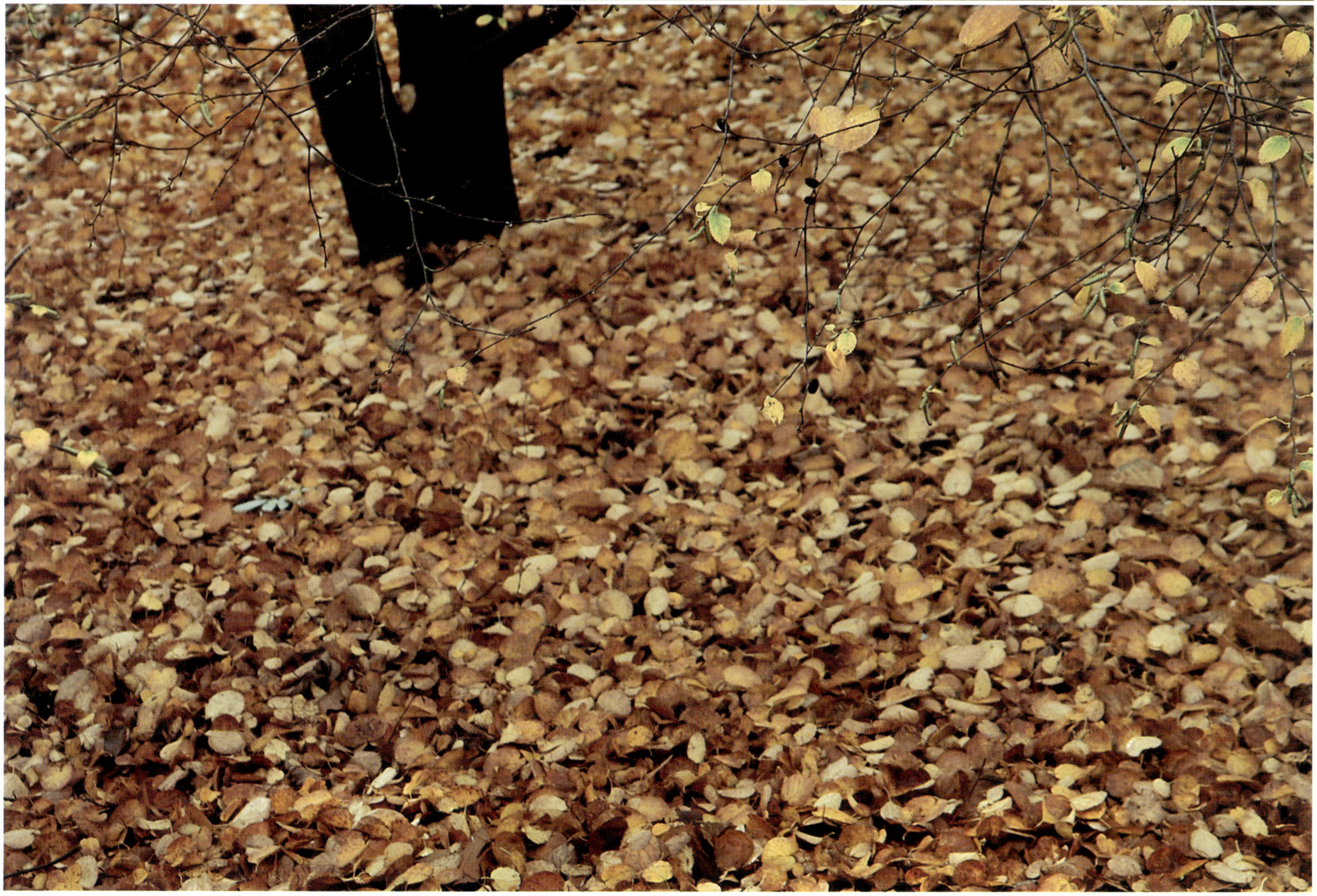

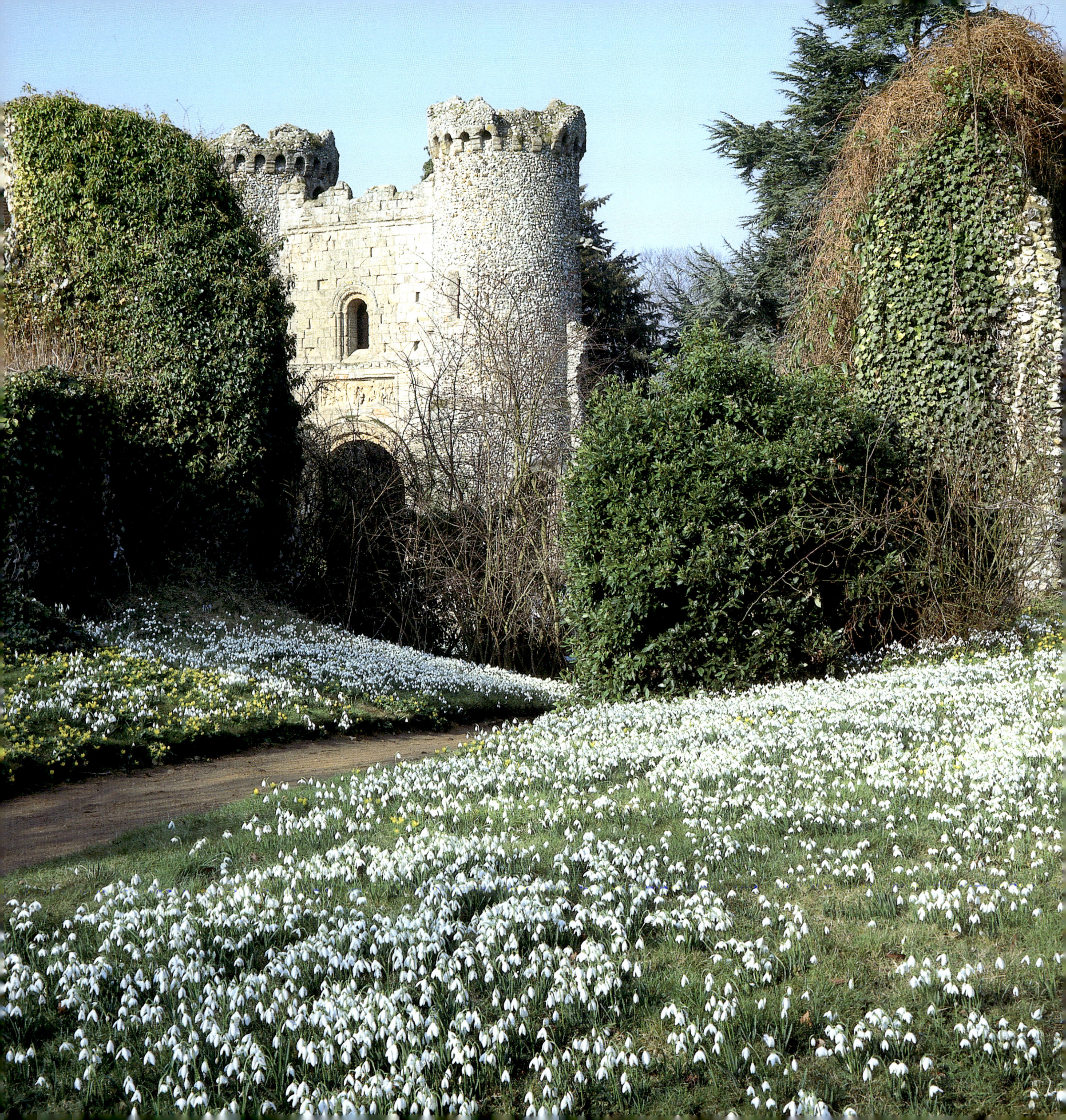

### Winter

Admittedly, subjects are fewer on the ground in winter, but frost and snow open up a wonderful new range of photographic opportunities. Beware of underexposing snow scenes (see overleaf).

Personally, I enjoy wintertime photography, even in the absence of frost or snow, provided the light is reasonable. The hustle and bustle of spring and summer are absent, as are the crowds in the case of public gardens. Granted, subjects have to be searched for, but at the same time it is fairly obvious where any photographic interest lies: make for the hellebores or perhaps the yellow- and orange-flowered branches of witch hazels, under-planted perhaps with snowdrops. The reds and yellows of dogwood stems are superb in winter sunlight, as are those of some of the willows.

Left: Spring doesn't seem so far off once sheets of snowdrops brave cold winter days. In this view at Benington Lordship, Hertfordshire, the snowdrops clothing the castle moat (now dry) and lining the old church wall combine with the bright yellow flowers of winter aconites to set off the gatehouse of the Norman castle ruins.

**Mamiya C330f, 80mm lens, tripod. f/32 on Velvia**

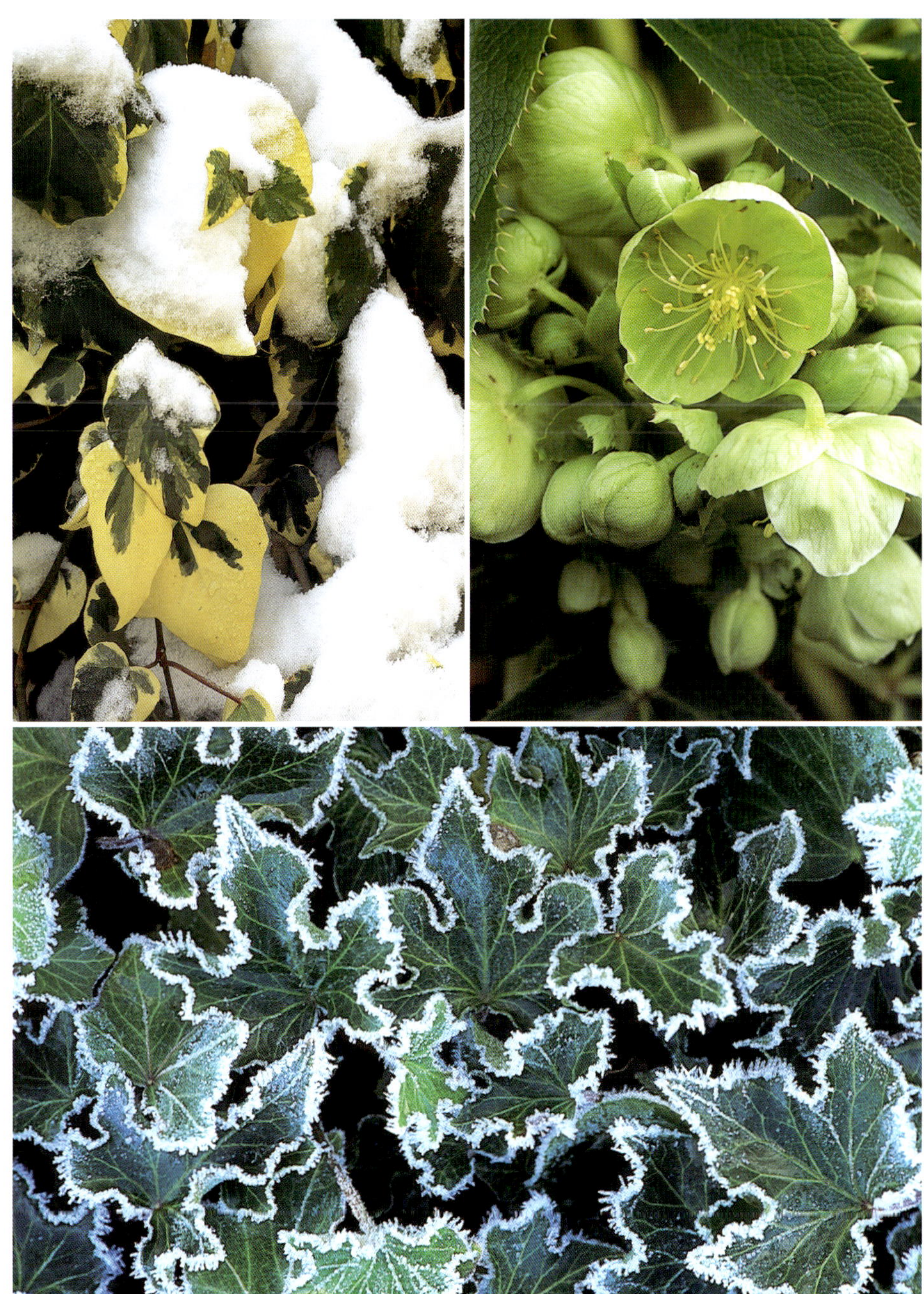

Top left: A gold reflector threw some light onto this *Hedera colchica* 'Dentata Variegata'.

**Minolta XG-M, 90mm macro lens, gold reflector, tripod. f/32 on Velvia**

Top right: A 'Rule of Thirds' (see page 47) image of *Helleborus argutifolius*. RHS Wisley.

**Minolta Dynax 7, 90mm macro lens, 81A filter, tripod. f/16 on Velvia**

Above: Frost crystals on *Hedera helix* 'Ivalace' at RHS Wisley. A picture taken before the winter sun got to work.

**Minolta Dynax 700si, 180mm macro lens, tripod. f/22 on Velvia**

## Technique: **Photographing Snow**

Snow poses a particular problem when metering a scene, but fortunately it is an easy one to understand. The key is to keep in mind the 18% grey situation (see page 63). A reflected-light exposure meter, as found in cameras with autoexposure, will treat snow as being 18% grey instead of white, and it will underexpose the shot as a result. Therefore extra exposure must be given, particularly when using transparency film, as this has less exposure latitude.

The amount of extra exposure required will vary between half a stop and two stops, and this must be judged according to ambient light levels and the proportion of snow in the scene being photographed; the more snow there is, the more compensation required. In any event, it is best to bracket exposures – as shown in the example on the facing page – unless an incident light reading can be taken. Remember that too much compensation will result in overexposure and a loss of detail in the final image.

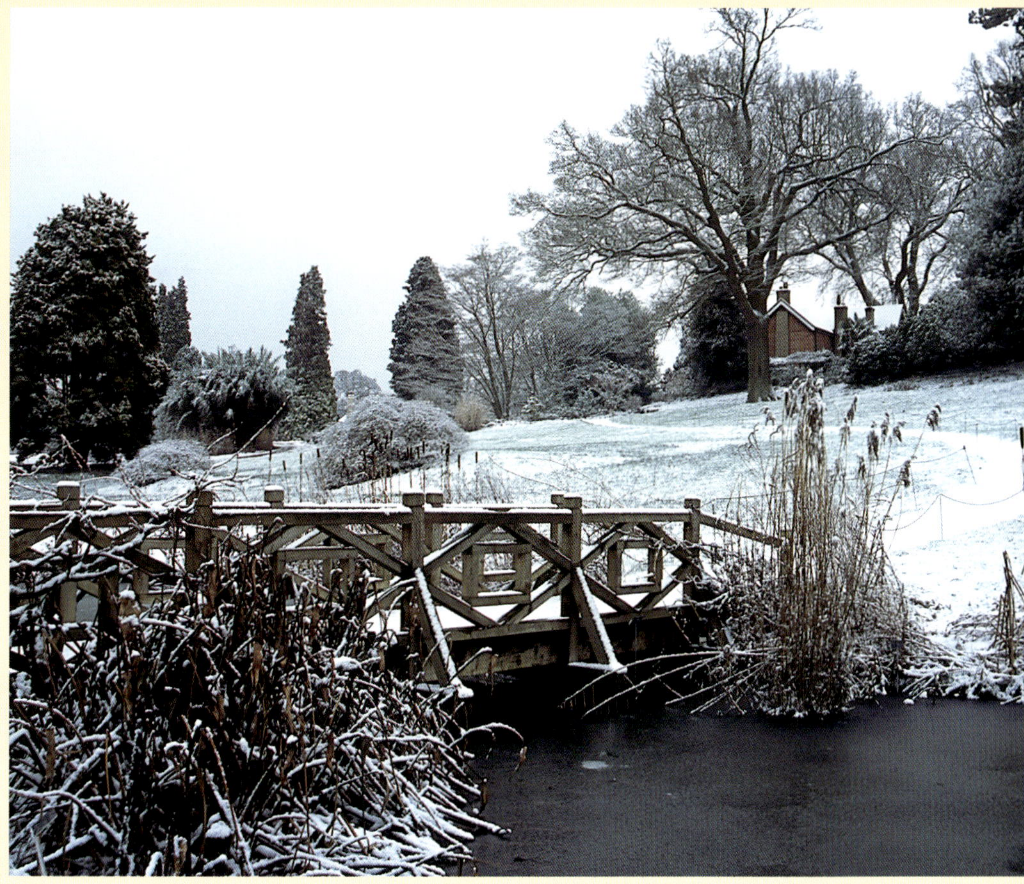

In this almost monochrome scene, the exposure was increased by one stop to keep the snow suitably white. RHS Wisley.

---

**Minolta Dynax 700si, 28–135mm lens, tripod. f/11 on Provia 100F**

Snowflakes were drifting down from a leaden sky at Wisley, and the main exposure in this sequence was based on an incident reading from a hand-held meter. I then increased exposure in half-stop stages. The second image (bottom left) is certainly acceptable for publication, but marginally inferior to the first. The third and fourth (below centre and right) are overexposed. Notice how areas of detail have been lost, especially in the fourth image.

**All shots:**
**Minolta Dynax 7, 28–135mm lens, tripod. f/16 on Provia 100F**

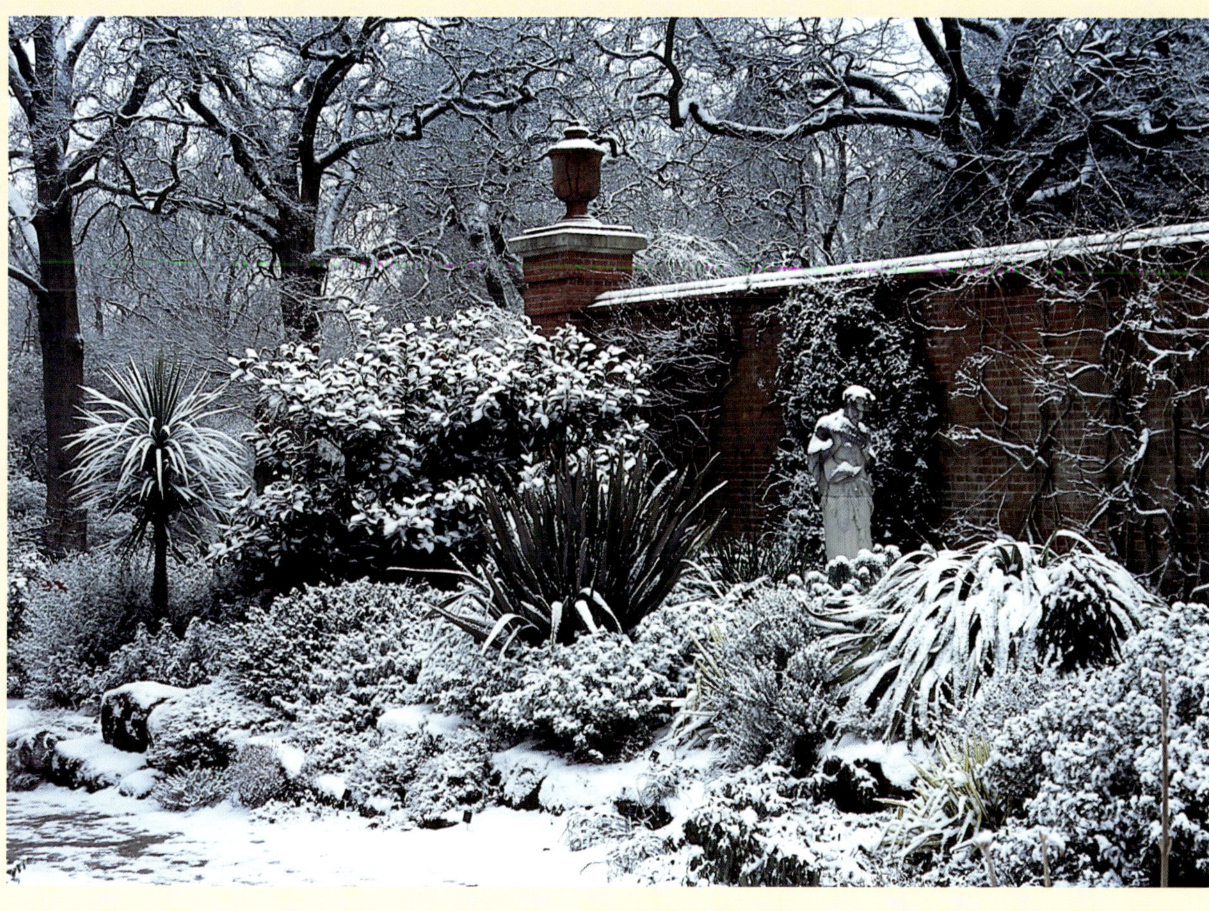

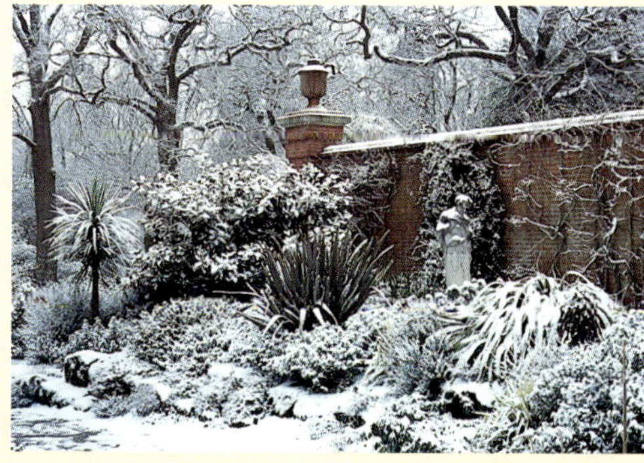

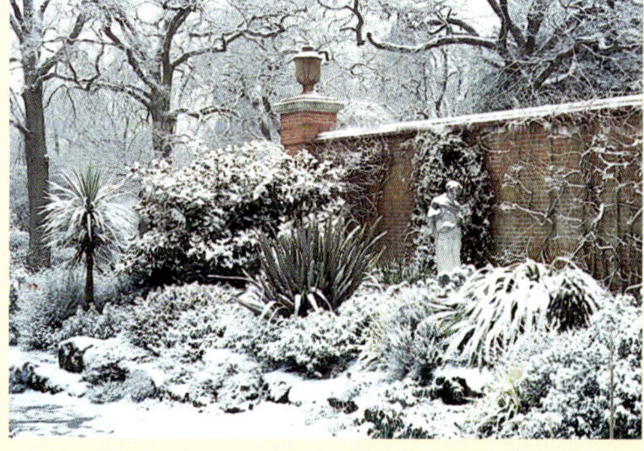

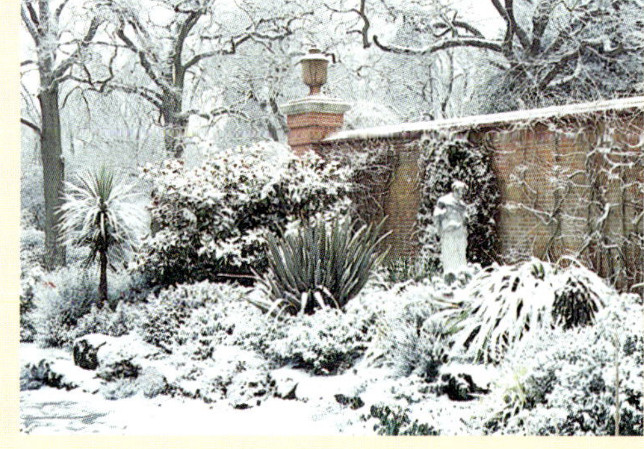

7

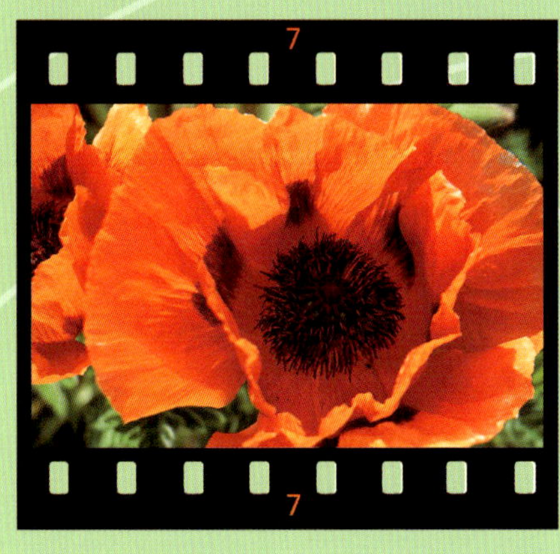

# Plant **Portraits** and Plant **Associations**

**When the phrase 'garden photography' is mentioned, the impression normally conveyed is that of the photography of individual plants in flower, and this coincides with the majority of requests picture libraries receive from clients.**

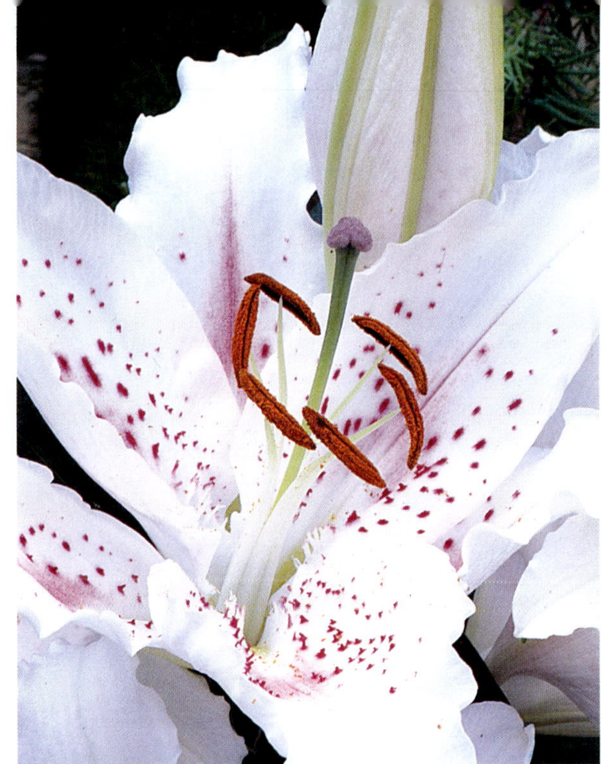

Lilies were the top plant in a recent British favourite-flower poll. This is *Lilium* 'Muscadet'.

**Minolta Dynax 700si, 90mm macro lens, tripod. Provia 100**

In 2002, a British television programme polled viewers on which were their favourite flowers. The lily took first place with the following (in alphabetical order) taking the next nine places: clematis, daffodil, delphinium, fuchsia, iris (bearded), poppy, primula, rose and sweet pea. With this in mind, I consulted two picture libraries specializing in horticultural images to find out which flower subjects are currently most frequently requested by their clients. The flowers listed above figured in the answers I received, but with the two provisos: specified cultivars are usually requested and very often these are required in a garden setting in association with other plants. The particular cultivars asked for can either be established favourites or the newer varieties.

Bear in mind also that plants are subject to the dictates of fashion. For example, plants like gladioli and tagetes are currently out of vogue, while *Verbena bonariensis* and *Cerinthe major* 'Purpurascens' have been 'in' for some time. Some South African gems and late daisy-flowered plants that fit in well with the 'naturalistic' style are increasing in popularity, and it is now said that gladioli and dahlias are due for a comeback as well.

### Plant Associations

The category of plant photography summed up by the phrase 'plant associations' is another one frequently requested by publishers. We photographers are very much in debt to gardeners and garden designers

### Taking the Perfect Plant Portrait

✓ Picture libraries require pin-sharp plant portraits photographed in good, even light with unfussy backgrounds.

✗ Even if there is a slight blemish on a leaf or flower it will be only too apparent on film. Don't waste time on a lost cause – it may be that a perfect example is waiting just around the corner.

✓ An extra something can be added to pictures of individual blooms by spraying them with water drops from a spray bottle. This should not become standard practice, but can work well.

✓ Be aware of current trends in garden photography and the requirements of publishers and picture libraries. As well as watching relevant TV programmes and reading the press, trends in image-library styles and subject matter can be researched online. For more on researching markets, see Chapter 10 (page 130).

Below: Lavenders, eschscholzias and others provided this colourful mixture at RHS Hyde Hall. A small aperture gave sufficient depth of field, but I decided against using any filters, relying on Velvia to do justice to the plants' colours.

**Minolta Dynax 7, 28–135mm lens, tripod. f/22 on Velvia**

when it comes to plant associations. Their imagination and skill conjures this web of colour, form and texture to grow and flower in harmony and provide ephemeral impressions to delight the eye. As photographers we therefore need planned and successful associations, and we need the good fortune to be present to photograph them in good conditions.

Our reactions to them, from the point of view of colour, are often subjective. I am very catholic in the range of colour associations which please me but I have to admit to liking blue or purple with yellow, even something as straightforward as a yellow sunflower contrasted against a blue sky. Try this with a polarizing filter together with a warm-up filter.

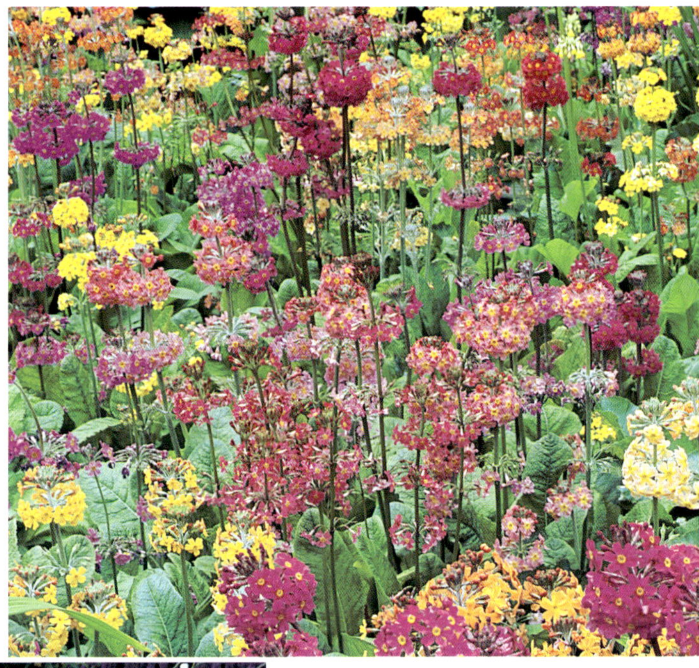

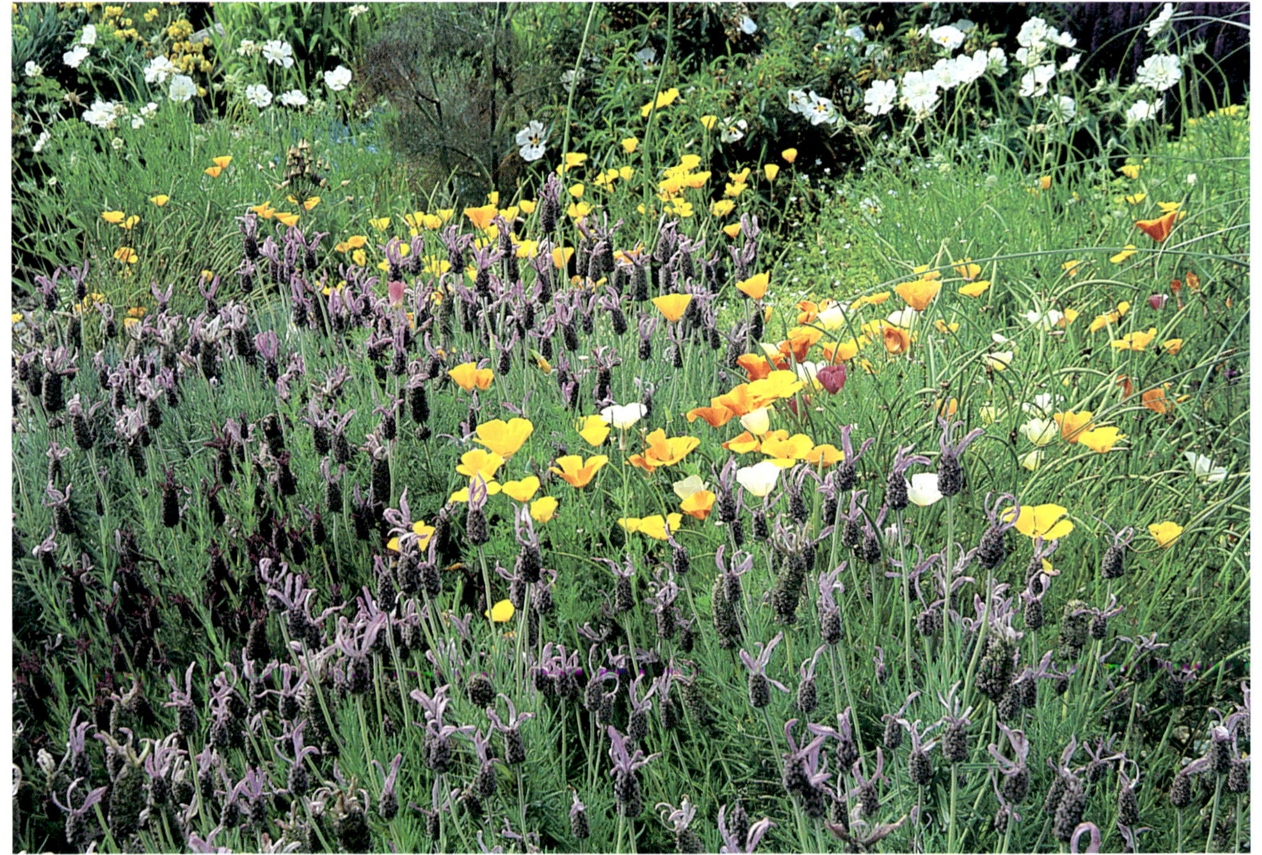

Above: An amazing variety of shades of primula hybrids at RHS Halow Carr. The hybrids come about through the self-hybridization of five species: *pulverulenta*, *bulleyana*, *beesiana*, *burmanica* and *chungensis*.

**Minolta Dynax 7, 90mm macro lens, 81A filter, tripod. 1/6sec at f/22 on Ektachrome 100G**

Left: A gold reflector threw warm light onto this bunch of grapes.

**Minolta Dynax 700si, 90mm macro lens, 81A filter, tripod. f/8 on Velvia**

Centre: Natural light only was used for this orchid.

**Minolta XG-M, 90mm macro lens, tripod. f/22 on Velvia**

Right: This *Delphinium elatum* 'Blue Dawn' was taken with no breeze and the sun obscured by a large cumulus cloud.

**Minolta Dynax 7, 28–135mm lens, tripod. 1/20sec at f/20 on Ektachrome 100G**

Right: I had to wait for a lull in the breeze to get this shot of *Papaver orientale* 'Pizzicato'.

**Minolta Dynax 700si, 90mm macro lens, 81A filter, tripod. f/5.6 on Velvia**

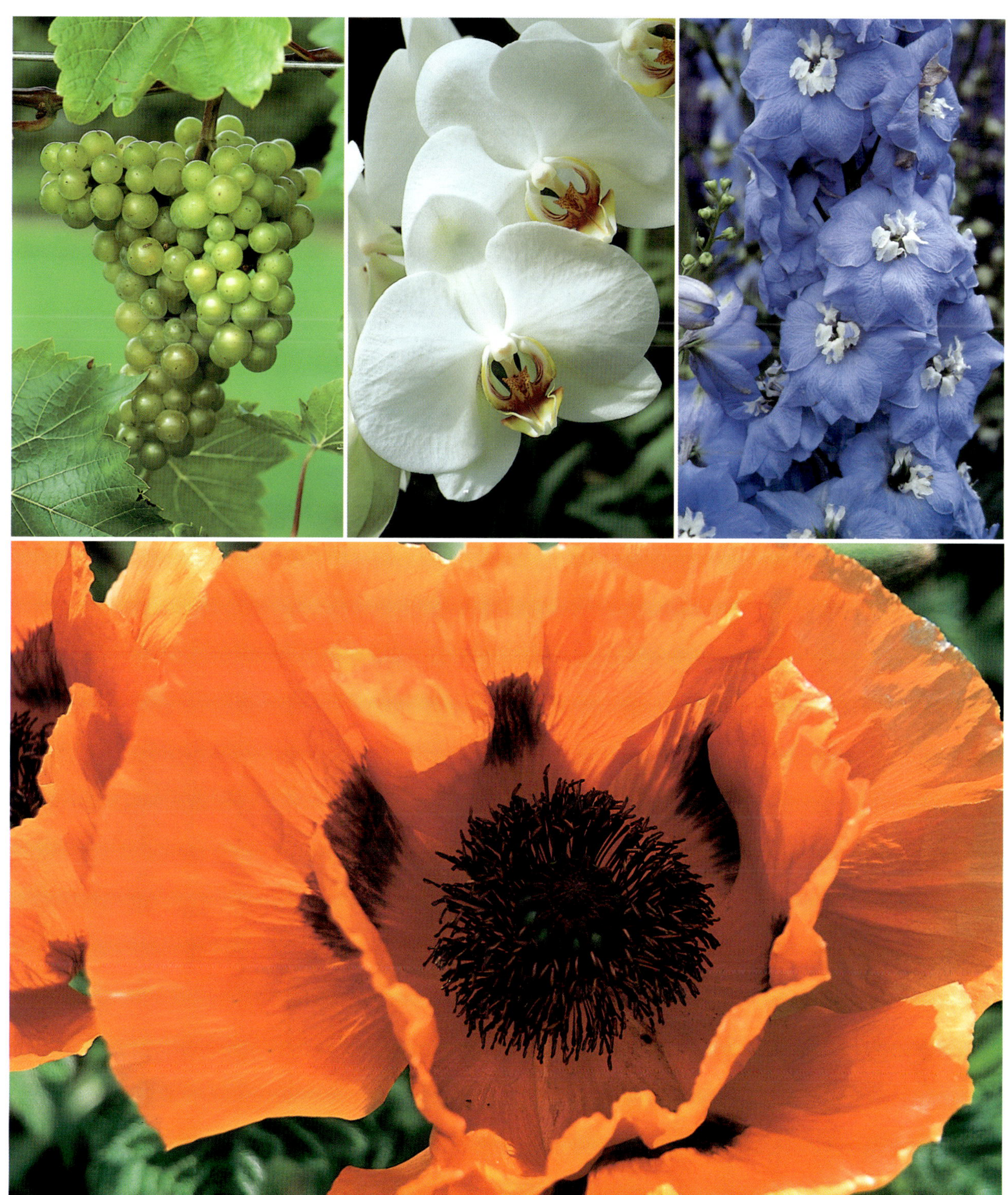

## Technique: **Understanding Colour**

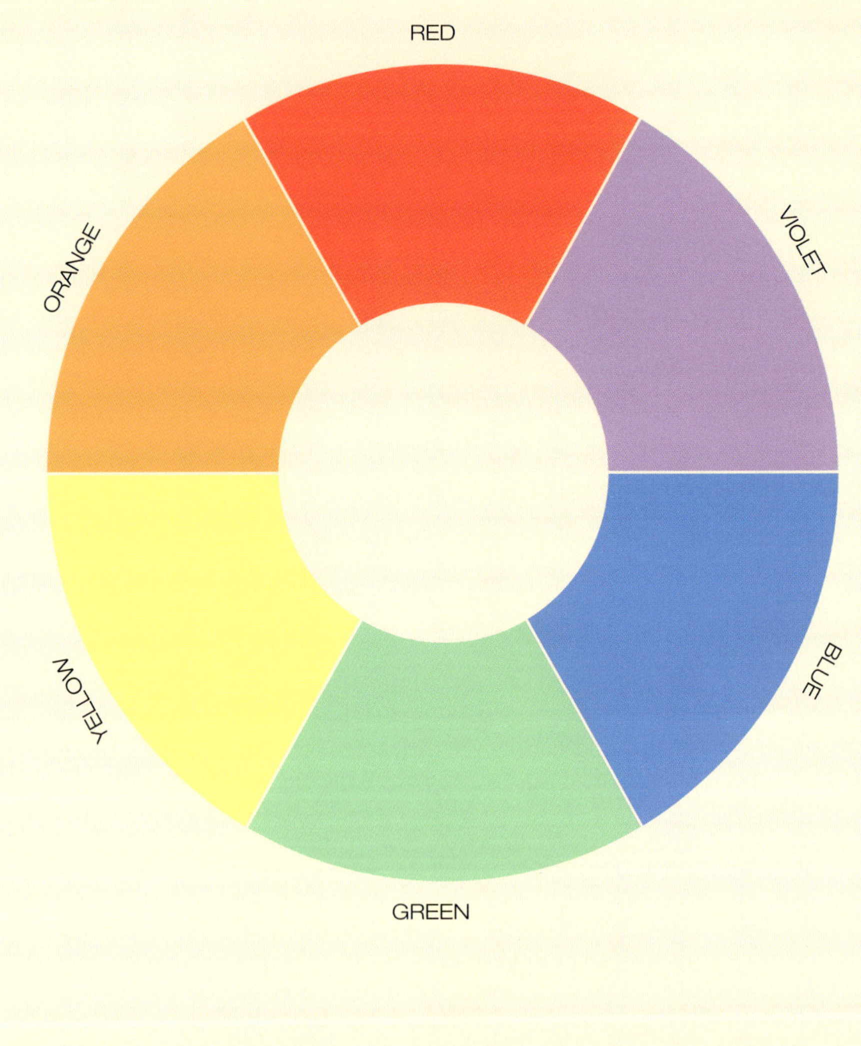


Colour pictures are often best improved by reducing the number of colours present to a minimum. On the colour circle (see left) yellow and violet are opposite each other and are known as complementary or contrasting colours, whereas colours next to each other on the circle, such as yellow and orange which 'go' with each other are known as harmonious colours.

Red, orange and yellow are warm colours, whereas green, blue and violet are known as cool colours. Each colour has a range of tints or tones produced by the addition of white or black.

Use the colour circle to assist you in giving mood to a picture. For maximum impact use complementary colours together (yellow with violet, for example) and if a more restful effect is sought use colours or their tints next to each other on the circle.

The colour wheel has much relevance in the natural world. Taking a rowan tree as an example, it is interesting to note that when the berries are ripe they are orange/red, contrasting with the green of the leaves and making them noticeable to birds. What blackbird or thrush would be interested in a harmoniously coloured non-orange rowan berry?

Right: These bluebells and violet blossoms are harmonious colours and produce a relaxing image.

**Fuji GW670III, tripod. f/32 on Velvia**

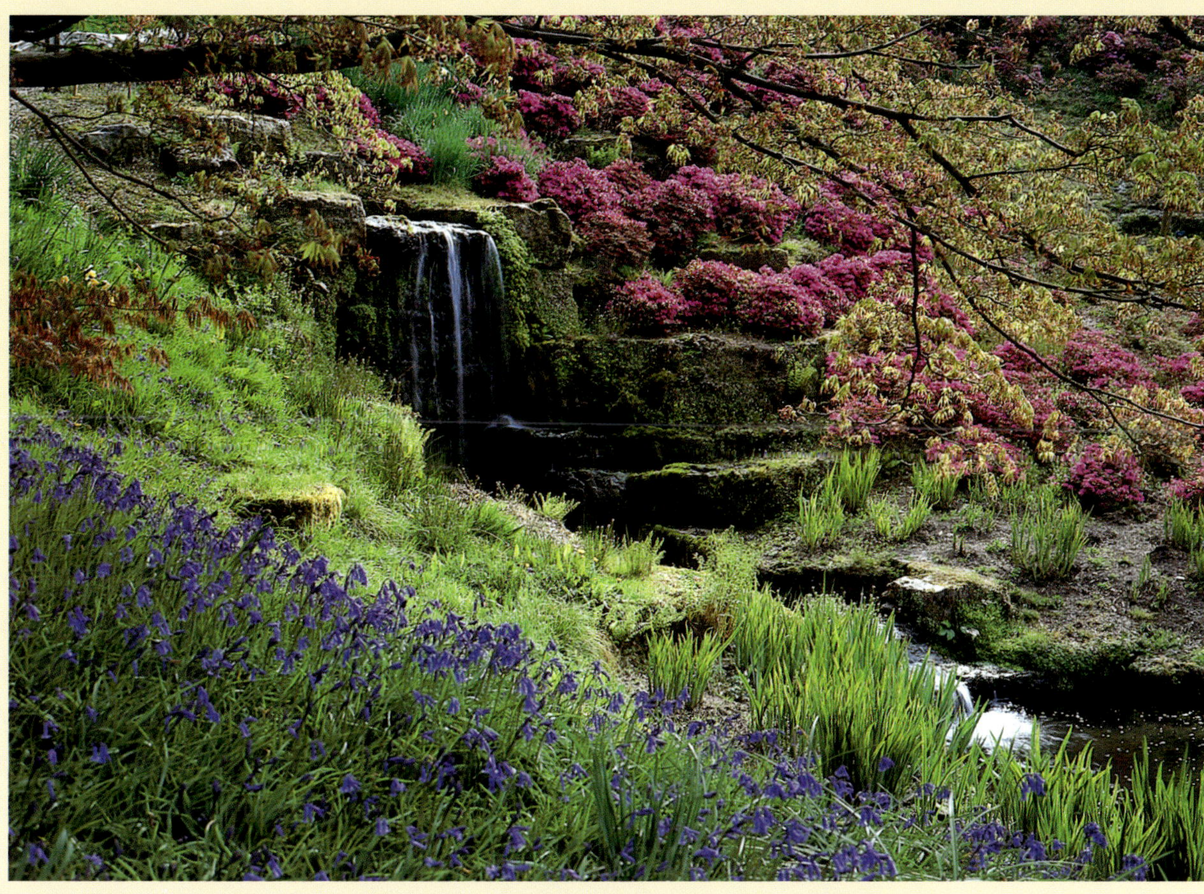

Below: This crocus photo achieves its impact from the contrasting colours of violet and orange.

**Minolta Dynax 700si, 90mm macro lens with 1.4x teleconverter, 81A filter, tripod. 1/6sec at f/3.5 on Provia 100F exposed at 200 ISO**

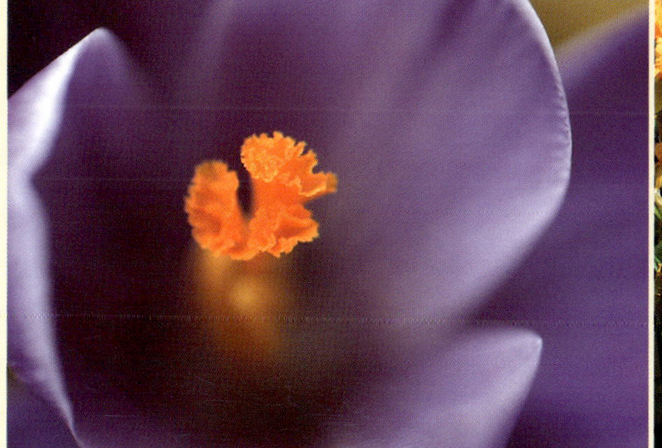

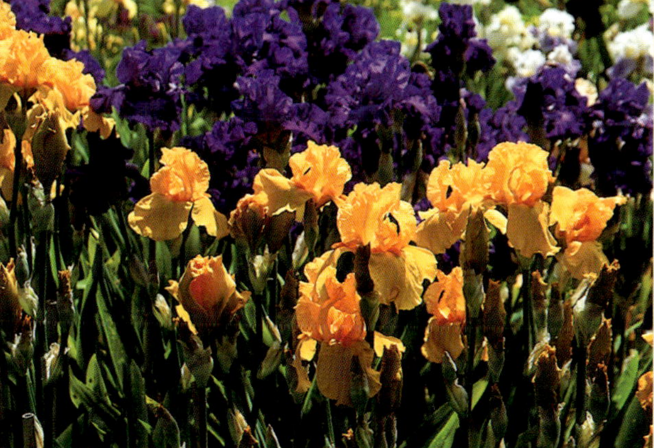

Left: *Iris* 'Feu du Ciel' in association with *Iris* 'Mer du Sud' creates a stunning combination of colour.

**Minolta Dynax 7, 28–135mm lens, 81B and polarizing filters, tripod. 1/10sec at f/10 on Velvia**

## Equipment: **Using Filters to Improve Colours**

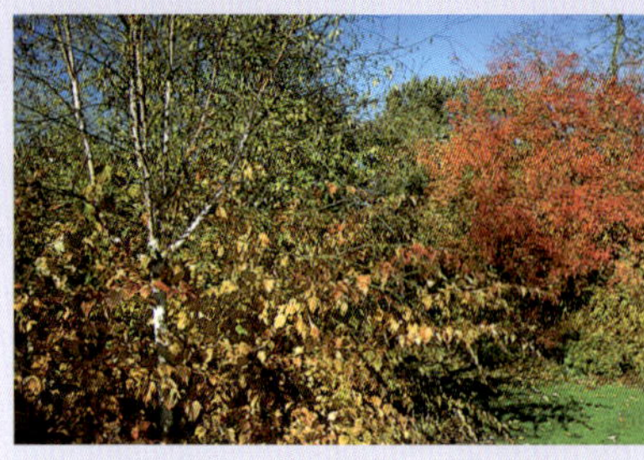

Autumn colours were enhanced by the use of warm-up and polarizing filters in this scene at Wisley.

**Minolta Dynax 700si, 28–135mm lens, 81B and polarizing filters, tripod. f/16 on Velvia**

A polarizing filter will increase the colour saturation on flower portraits and plant associations, and can improve a picture, perhaps in conjunction with a warm-up filter. Warm-up filters can improve the appearance of greens in a picture. On the other hand, if you wish to give a dreamy feeling still fit the warm-up filter but try breathing on it for a mist-like, ethereal effect.

I used a macro lens to get up close to this *Fuchsia* 'Beacon' lit by the afternoon sun. A stone-coloured sheet of cardboard provided a plain background.

**Minolta XG-M, 90mm macro lens, tripod. f/8 on Kodachrome 64 Professional**

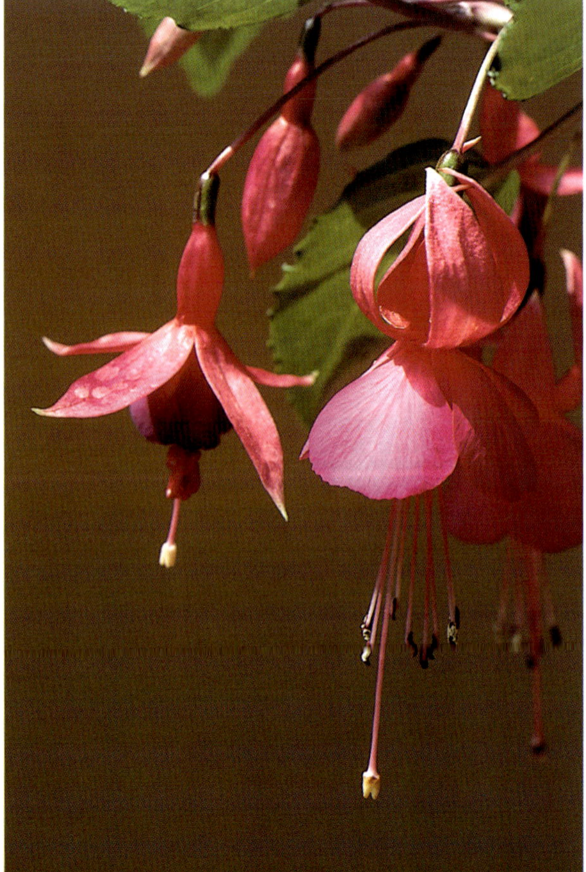

### Going Close Up

Close-up photography is a fascinating part of garden photography, and finding suitable subjects is an absorbing task in itself. Good technique is essential when taking close-ups. Any movement of the subject or lapse in focusing will be magnified and ruin the picture. Use of a tripod is therefore mandatory, as is the ability to focus the lens manually. The use of a cable release or remote electronic shutter release will further help in guaranteeing a pin-sharp image.

For this branch of garden photography, an SLR is ideal as parallax (see Glossary, page 146) problems are absent. Additionally, light that is not entirely ideal can be improved for plant portraits by the use of fill-in flash or by using a reflector or diffuser.

The starting point for close-ups is generally considered to be one-tenth life size, a ratio of 1:10, upwards. Life-size (1:1) means that the image of the subject is the same size on the film as it is in reality. Strictly speaking, macro photography starts at a minimum ratio of 1:1, although it is generally accepted to start at a ratio of 1:4.

Depth of Field In general garden scenes, about one-third of the depth of field at any given aperture extends from the point of focus back towards the camera, and about two-thirds extends away from the point of focus. In close-ups, however, this ratio changes to about one-half in front of the point of focus to one-half behind it. This is one of the main reasons for choosing a camera with the facility to preview the depth of field. Even then, at small apertures the viewfinder image can be very dim. If your camera does not have a depth-of-field button, it is a matter of careful focusing and second-guessing the aperture (or bracketing the aperture).

## Technique: **Keeping Your Close-ups in Focus**

In order to have any chance of depicting a three-dimensional subject as sharp in a close-up picture it is necessary to stop the lens down and position the film plane in the camera as parallel as possible to the subject. When taking the photograph of the moth orchid (right), for example, the film plane was placed parallel to the flower's petals, the lens stopped down and a focus point one-half of the distance between the front of the lip and the petals was chosen. Use of the depth-of-field button confirmed the bloom was sharply defined front to back.

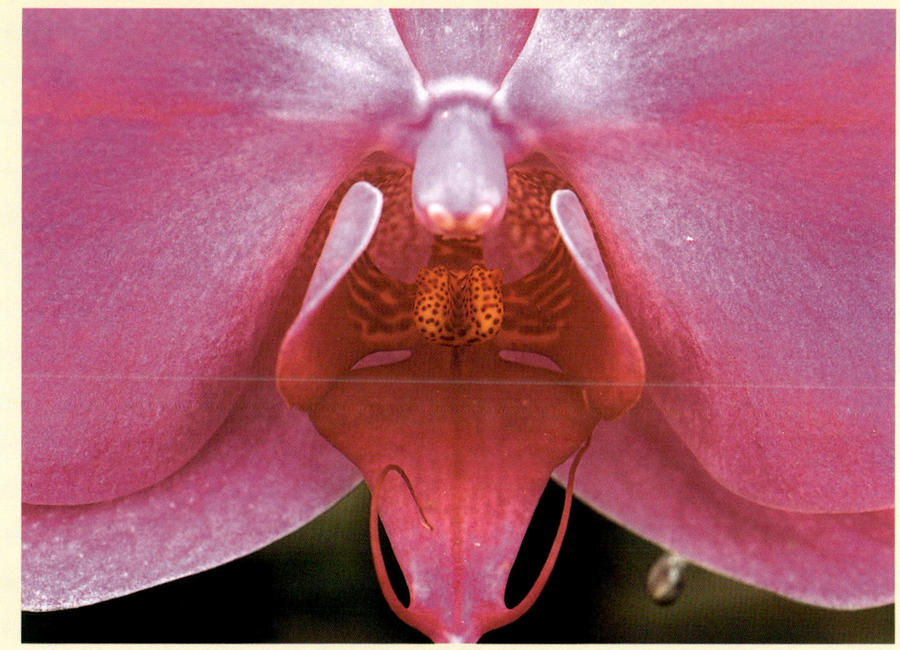

Above: Critical focusing with the lens stopped right down to f/32 ensured that all parts of this moth orchid were sharply recorded.

**Minolta Dynax 7, 90mm macro lens, 81A filter, tripod. f/32 on Velvia**

Below left: With the camera at this angle to the subject, not all of the flower head will be in focus. Below right: Adjusting the camera position so that the film plane is parallel to the flower means that more of the subject will be sharp.

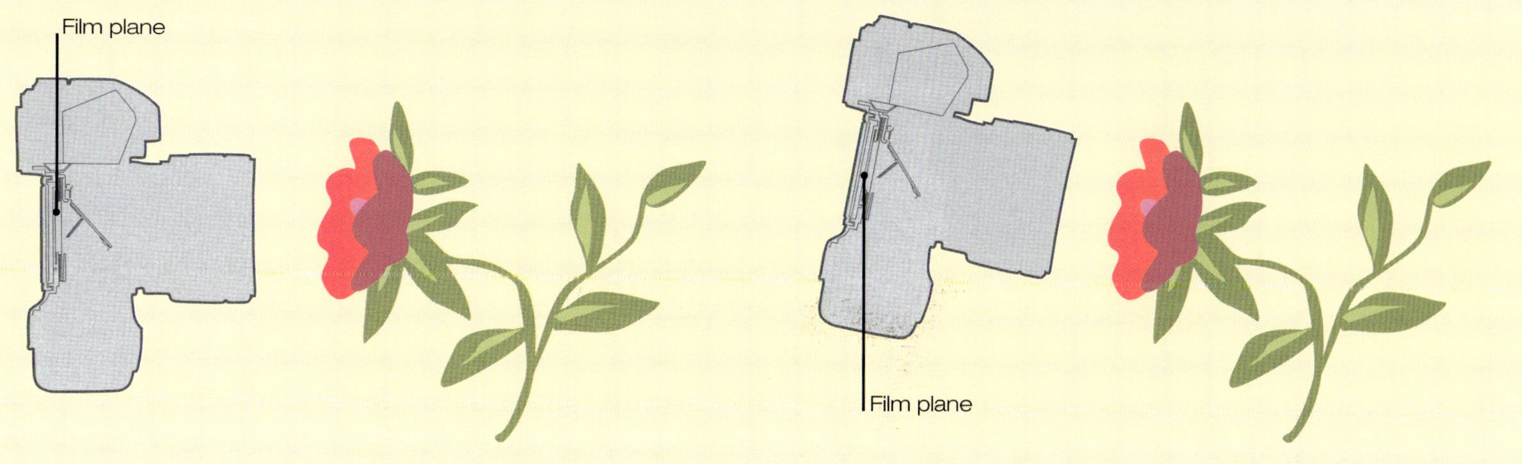

## Equipment: **Close-up Accessories**

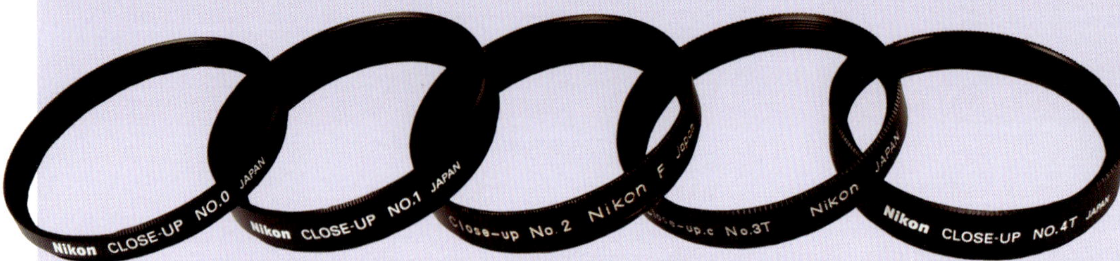


### Close-up Lenses

Close-up lenses are attached to the front of the lens in the same way as a screw-in filter, and are available in strengths of +1, +2 and +3 dioptres (in ascending order of magnification).

### Extension Tubes

Extension tubes usually come in sets of three different lengths and, unlike close-up lenses, one set will fit all of a camera system's lenses. The more extension given to the lens, the greater the magnification, but there is a corresponding loss of light and this entails a longer exposure. In itself this is operationally acceptable if the camera is mounted on a tripod and the subject stationary. The close-up potential of extension tubes is greater when used with the shorter focal length lenses of 50–100mm. Taking 35mm SLRs as an example, a 50mm lens with 50mm extension will focus to give an aspect ratio 1:1; a 100mm lens would need 100mm of extension to give the same ratio. Remember, though, that some of this extension will already be built into the lens barrel for focusing purposes.

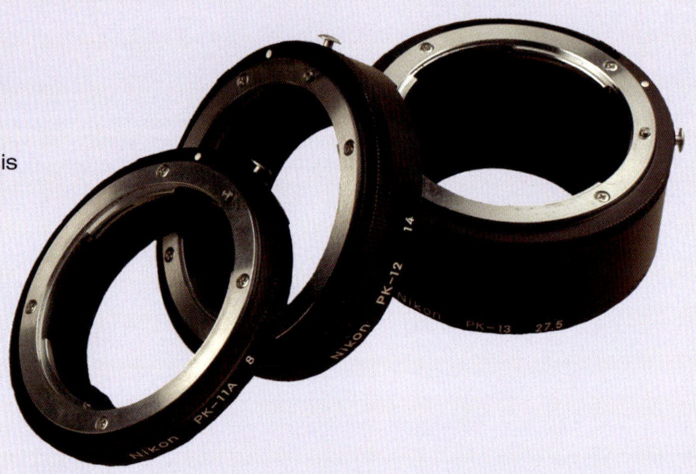


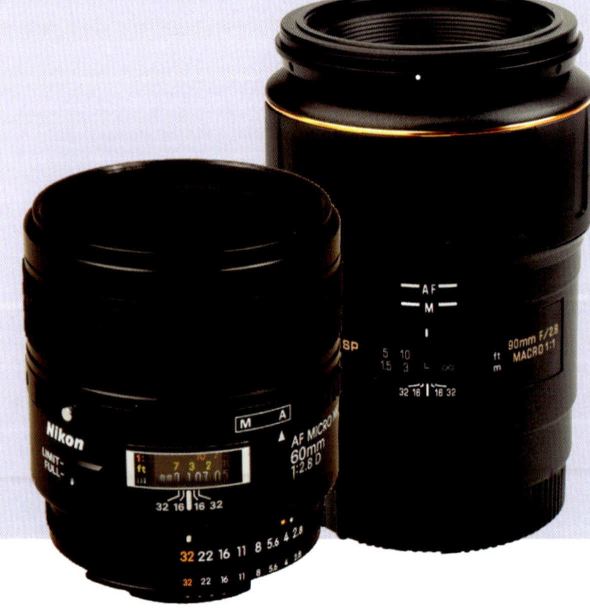


### Macro Lenses

By far the most satisfactory and convenient solution is to use a proper macro lens. A Tamron 90mm macro lens is a favourite lens of mine for 35mm work. It's very sharp, of course, and the image in the viewfinder is bright, making manual focusing (utilized for most macro work) easy to carry out. Another advantage of using this 90mm short telephoto, with its more restricted field of view, is the ability to isolate the subject and, if necessary, utilize its f/2.8 aperture to control the background.

Below: The regularity of the spines of *Echinopsis scheliana* provides a strong pattern in this detail.

**Minolta Dynax 7, 90mm macro lens, tripod. f/16 on Velvia**

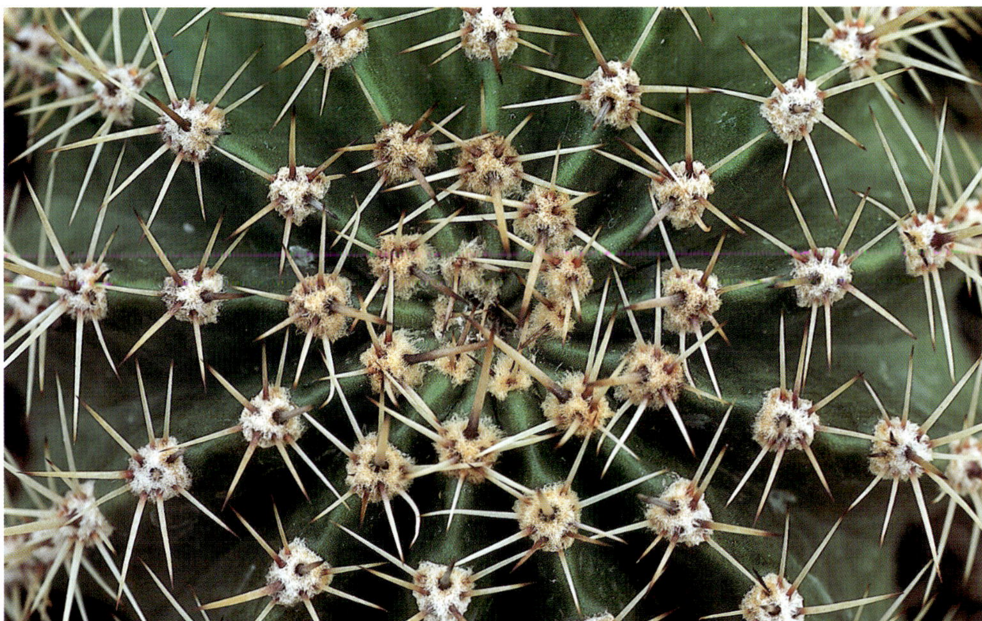

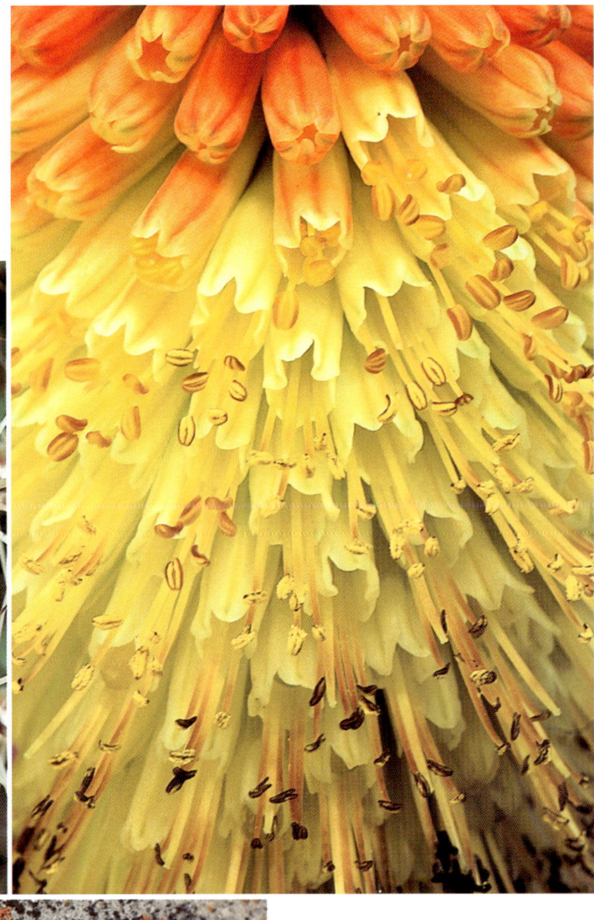

Right: Lichens on rock in the cool clear air in Banff National Park, Canada, make a colourful abstract when photographed close up.

**Minolta Dynax 700si, 180mm macro lens, tripod. f/16 on Provia 100**

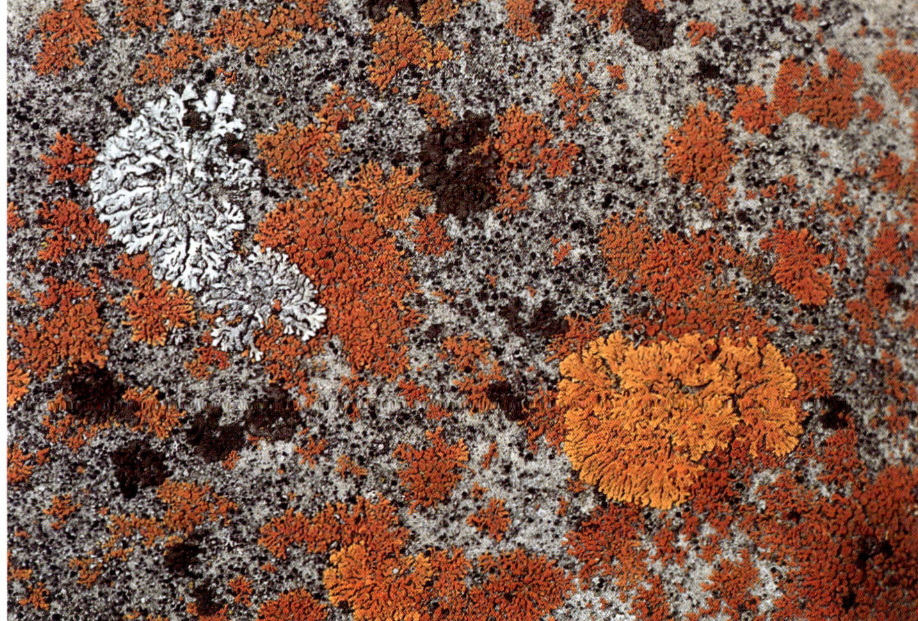

Above: A gold reflector evened out shadows cast by the sunlight falling on this close-up orange/yellow spike of *Kniphofia* 'Royal Castle'.

**Minolta Dynax 700si, 90mm macro lens, 81B filter, gold reflector. f/22 on Velvia**

## Case study 3: WISLEY GLASSHOUSE, SOUTH-EAST ENGLAND

**Shortly before the deadline for this book, I was asked by GardenWorld Images to take pictures of house and conservatory plants. A source of subject matter immediately available to me is contained in the glasshouse complex at RHS Wisley. I made three visits in quick succession and obtained a number of images for GardenWorld, from which I selected a few for this book.**

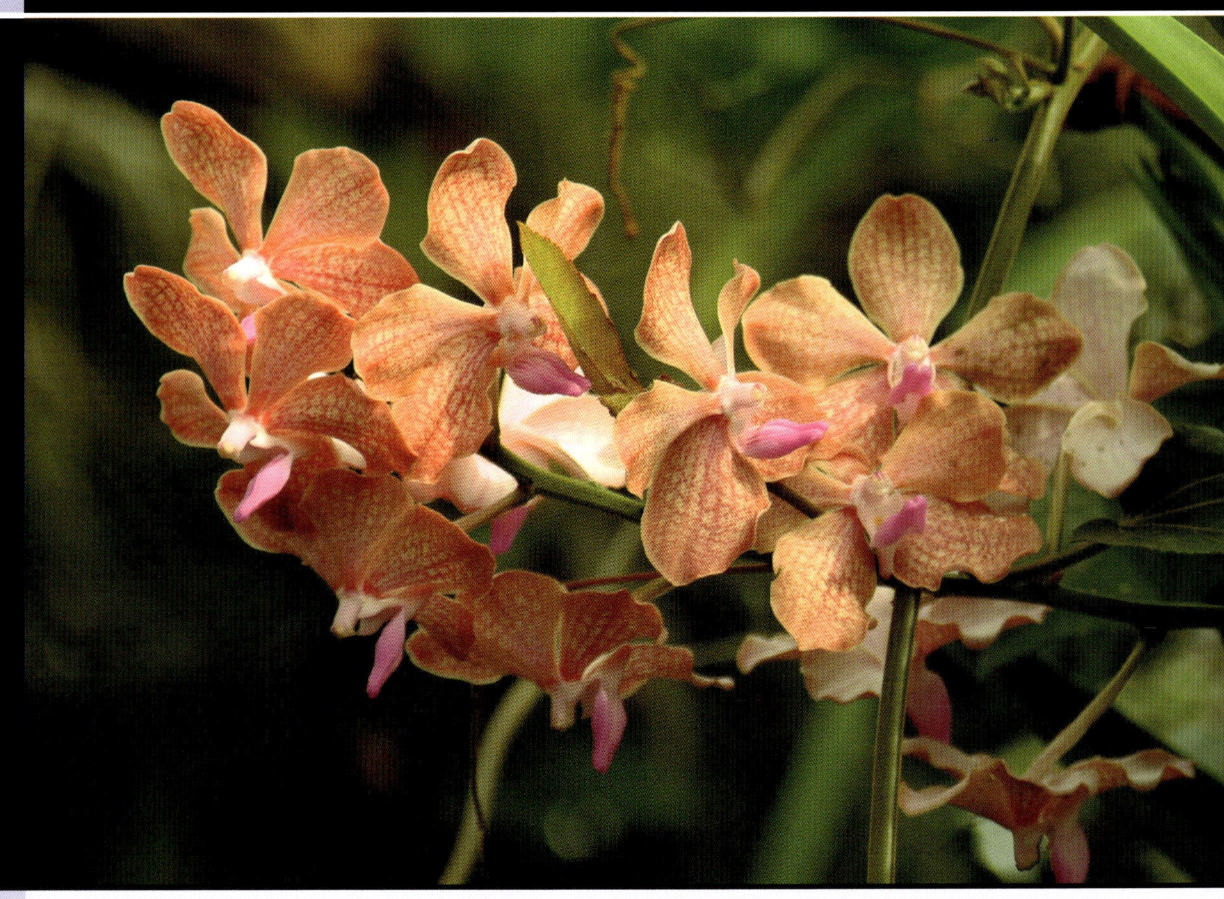

**Cameras: Fuji FinePix S2 Pro, Minolta Dynax 7**

**Film: Fujichrome Velvia 100F**

**Lenses: Nikkor AF-D 28–105mm zoom, Tamron 90mm macro**

**Filter: 81A warm-up**

**Notes: Diffuser for subjects in strong/contrasty light**

Photography in a location such as RHS Wisley's glasshouse complex presents a few minor problems.

On a busy day (and most days seem to be at Wisley) one has to be careful not to get in the way of visitors. Fortunately, the glasshouse is fairly spacious and I did not lose many pictures because of lack of space. Another way around this problem was to get there early, which has the additional benefit of allowing photography before the lighting becomes too overhead and contrasty (for more on lighting, see Chapter 5, page 68).

Above: These shaded flowers of *x Ascocenda* 'Flambeau' were growing over water in the orchid section of the Wisley glasshouse. The reach of the lens, when used at 105mm on my digital SLR (on which it equates to 150mm), was sufficient to capture a large image of the flower cluster. The main problem was finding a secure and dry footing for the tripod, while not causing an obstruction to visitors.

**FinePix S2 Pro, 28–105mm lens, tripod. f/5.6 at ISO sensitivity 100 and white balance 'Shade', TIFF 17.5MB**

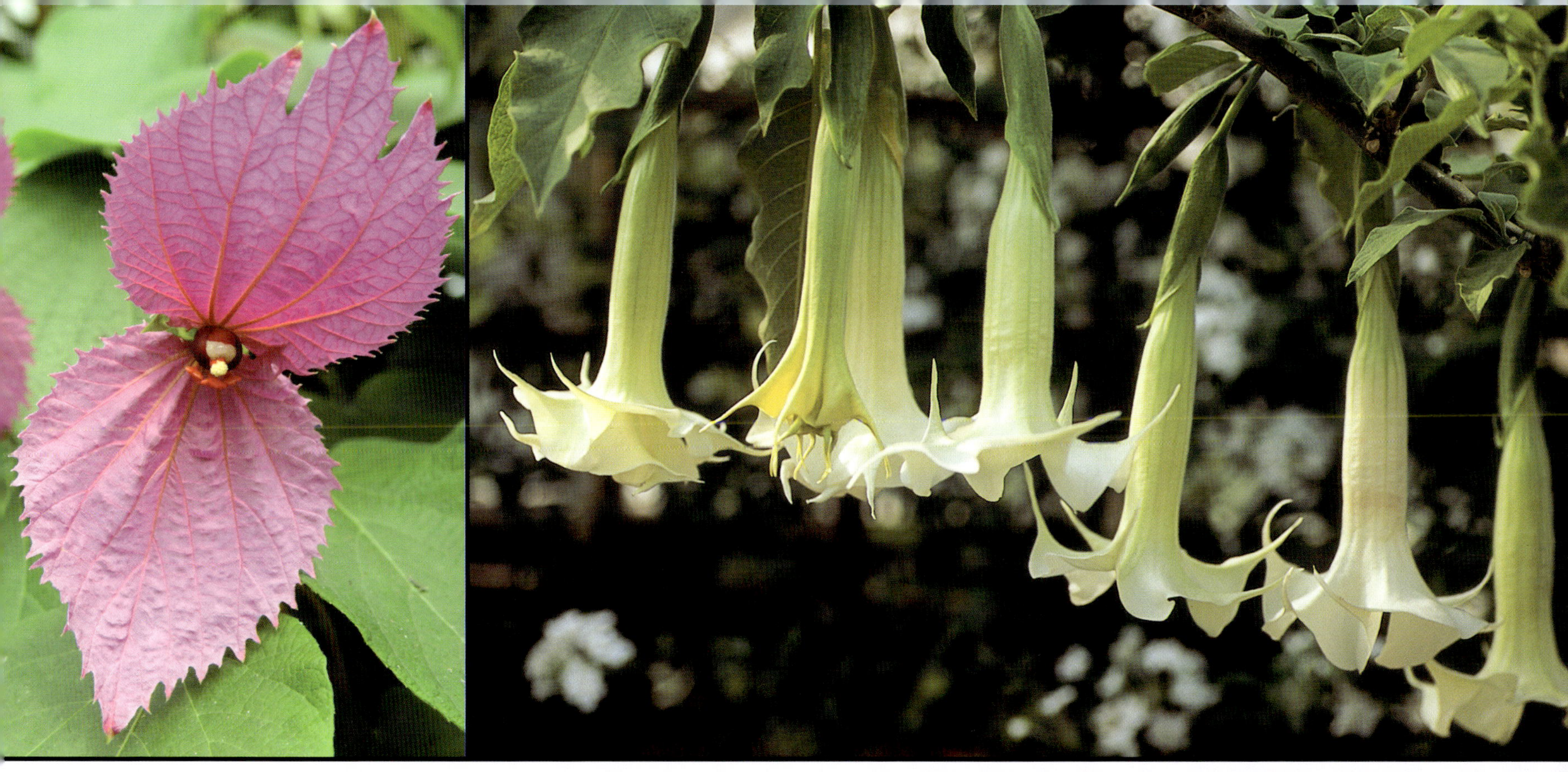

Above: A diffuser was used as a weak white reflector to obtain even illumination of the flower of the attractive *Dalechampia arisolochiaefolia*.

**FinePix S2 Pro, 28–105mm lens, tripod. f/11 at ISO sensitivity 100, white balance 'Auto', TIFF 17.5MB**

Above Right: Weak sunlight illuminated these trumpet flowers of *Brugmansia* x *insignis*.

**Minolta Dynax 7, 90mm macro lens, 81A filter, tripod. f/5.6 on Velvia 100F**

Condensation on the lens is another problem encountered in glasshouses, especially when the weather is cold outside and a cold camera is brought into contact with the warm and humid atmosphere inside. This can be a particular problem in a multi-section complex such as Wisley's, which has a number of different areas. These range from the unheated Cool House, to the hot and humid Stove House.

Common sense dictates that the best way to counter this problem is simply to be patient: let the camera and lens warm up gradually, and to refrain from entering the warmest and most humid sections straight away.

A third problem can be contrasty light on a sunny day. This problem was present on two of my three visits, and I dealt with it either by choosing subjects in shade or by using a diffuser (see page 27). I also used a diffuser to mitigate the problem of unwanted reflections in the water caused by the glasshouse's roof struts. These were particularly apparent when photographing some tropical waterlilies, such as the one shown overleaf.

Singling out flowers for photography involves consideration of both the individual bloom and the background. It was not difficult to find a flawless specimen in the Orchid House because the flowers look good for ages, but avoiding highlights caused by sunlight coming through the glass can be a problem. Again, where this was the case, I generally used a diffuser to shade the plant and adjusted the setting by plus one stop to obtain a correct exposure.

I knew that GardenWorld would be content to receive either transparencies or the 17MB TIFF files output from my digital SLR. I therefore used my Tamron 90mm macro lens on one of my Minolta SLRs and the FinePix S2 digital SLR with a 28–105mm Nikkor zoom, which has a macro capability. An additional advantage of using the digital SLR is that the focal length of the 28–105mm lens equates to about one and a half times that when used on a 35mm film camera (for an explanation of this see Chapter 2, page 36). This proved particularly useful when shooting the orchids shown on page 104.

I tended to use the digital camera more because of the ease with which I could keep an ongoing check on the results. As I write this, the deadline for this book has now passed, but my project for the picture library continues and I shall now switch the emphasis onto obtaining images of houseplants, both as straight portrait records and *in situ*.

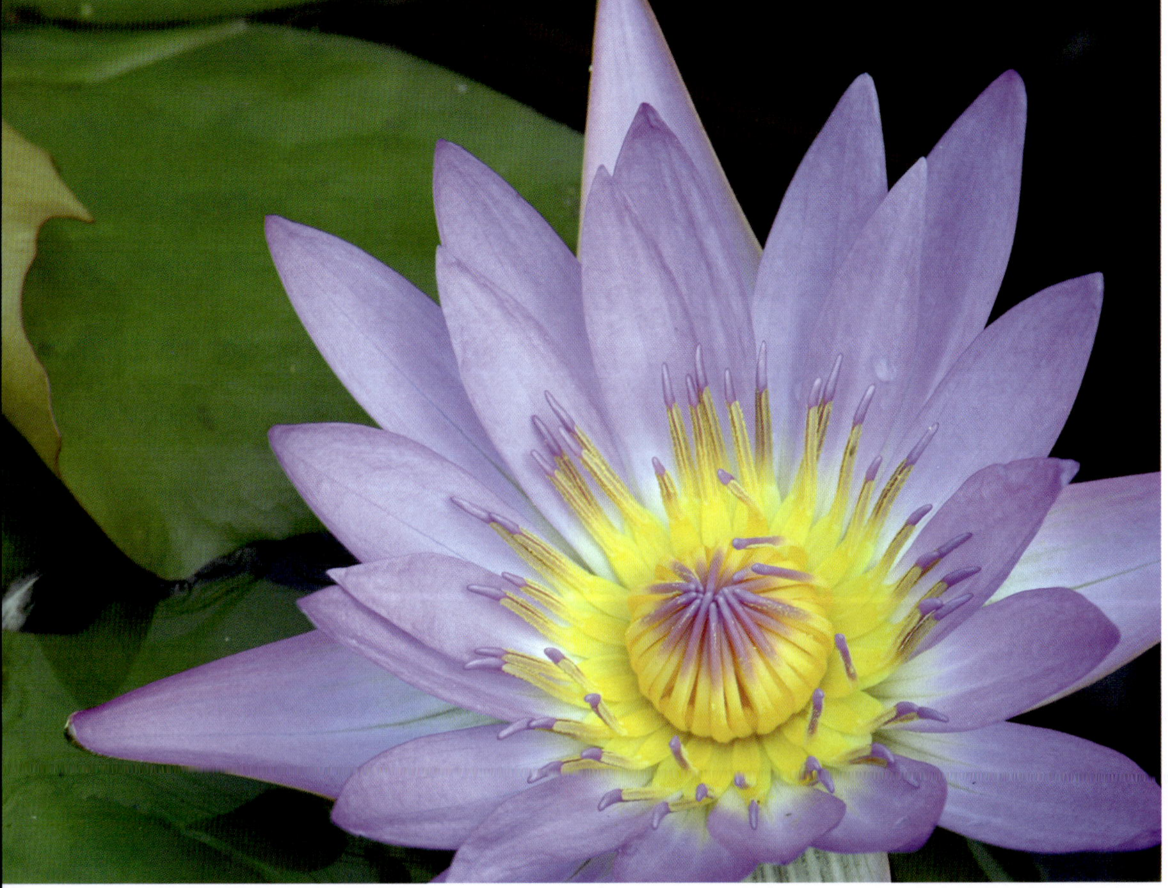

Reflections of the strut framework of the glasshouse roof dictated that the bloom of *Nymphaea* 'Tina' filled most of the frame. A smaller image of the flower would have allowed reflections to creep in, and these were difficult to subdue with the small diffuser I had with me.

**FinePix S2 Pro, 28–105mm lens, tripod. f/16 at ISO sensitivity 100 with one-stop extra exposure, white balance 'Auto', TIFF 17.5MB.**

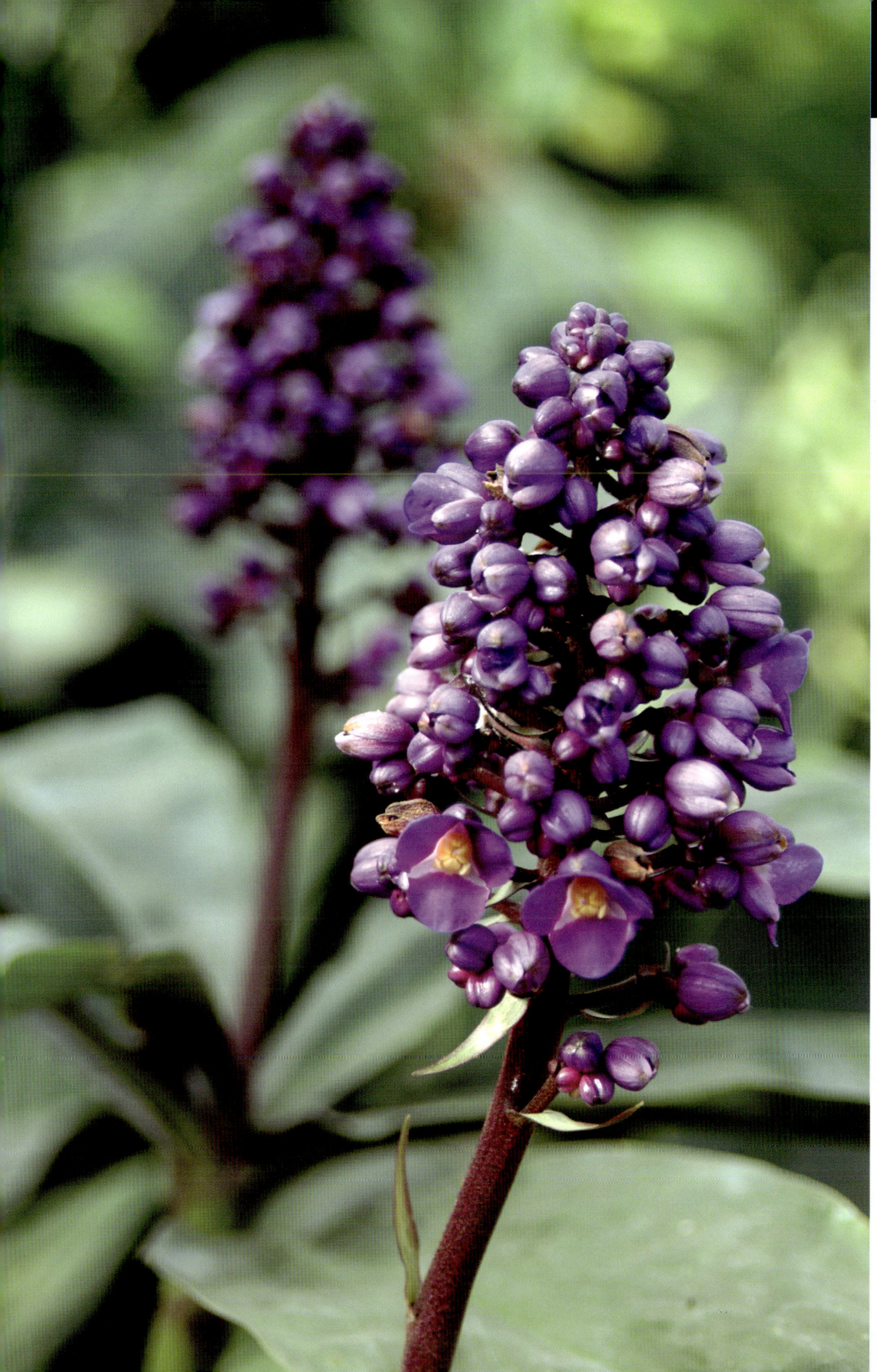

This *Dichorisandra thyrsiflora* from Brazil was growing in the Stove House – the warmest and most humid section of the glasshouse at Wisley. The flower spikes were illuminated by weak sunlight and I deliberately focused on the nearer one, placing it off-centre and using the one farther away to mirror the main subject and balance the picture.

**FinePix S2 Pro, 28–105mm lens, tripod. f/5.6 at ISO sensitivity 100, white balance 'Auto', TIFF 17.5MB**

# 8

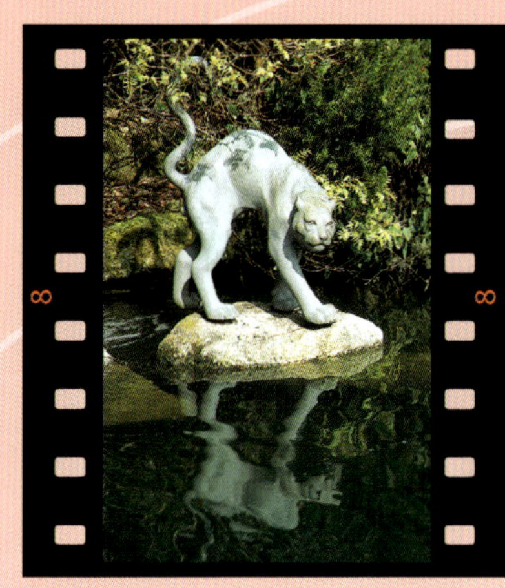

# Garden **Buildings** and **Ornaments**

**An enormous range of buildings and artefacts can be found in gardens. Included, in myriad shapes, sizes and ages, are smallish objects like pots and urns, statues and sundials, on up to pergolas, bridges, temples, ruins and even the house itself.**

Buildings and ornaments provide a wealth of subjects for the camera, as well as giving a feeling of solidity, scale and, at times, a strong sense of place to the garden scene.

Backgrounds, as ever, should be studied carefully to ensure that the shooting position, besides giving favourable lighting to the subject, deals satisfactorily with what is behind the subject. Check for intrusive objects or unwelcome highlights – leaves and branches have an uncanny knack of producing these at times. It is worth bearing in mind that a subject is often improved by making it stand out from a background thrown well out of focus by differential focusing (see pages 47–9). It is better still if the background is of a suitable tone or colour.

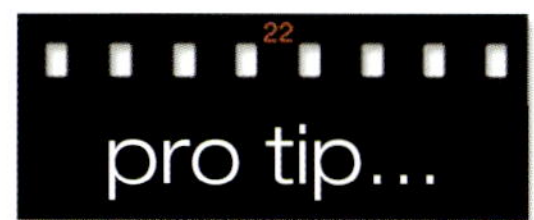

**The seasons**

Photographing most garden structures is less dependent on the time of year than plant photography is.

## Lighting Buildings and Ornaments

Lighting is so often crucial to achieving a successful image. Sunny conditions help to give an object a three-dimensional feel and create shadows that can

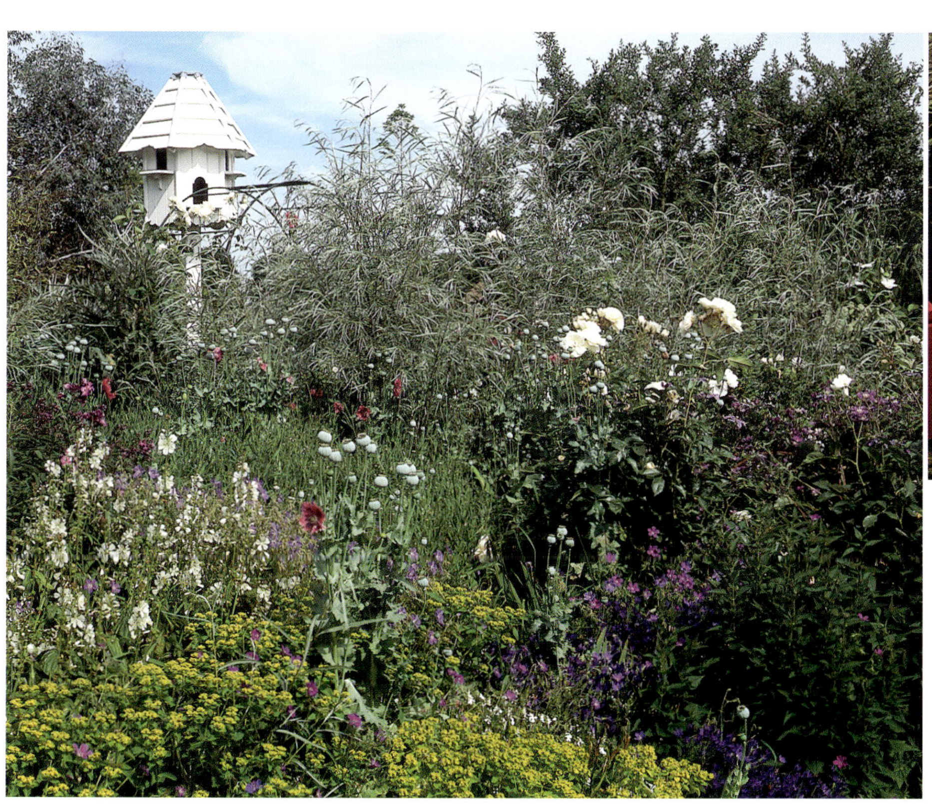

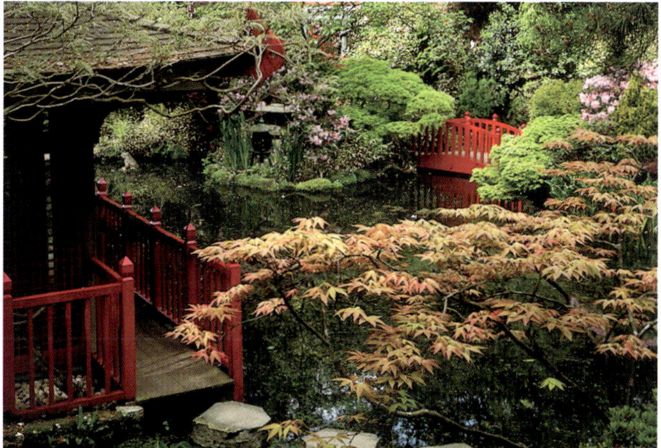

Left: The dovecote provides a focal point to this scene at Merriments Gardens.

**Mamiya 645 Super, 80mm lens, 81A filter, tripod. 1/8sec at f/22 on Velvia**

Above: Compton Acres is full of authentic Japanese structures.

**Fuji GW670III, 81B filter, tripod. 1/2sec at f/27 on Velvia**

perhaps be incorporated into the composition. It is often vital to photograph at the optimum time of day when the direction of light is just right for the subject.

### Photographing Stone

When a statue is made from a warm-toned stone, a little enhancement to underline the fact is, I feel, justified, perhaps with an 81B filter. I know that the rock in my own small rock garden looks more attractive when shot using an 81A or 81B.

Stone can also look better wet than dry, particularly as the colours may be stronger and textures more pronounced, so in some instances it is advantageous to photograph it after a shower.

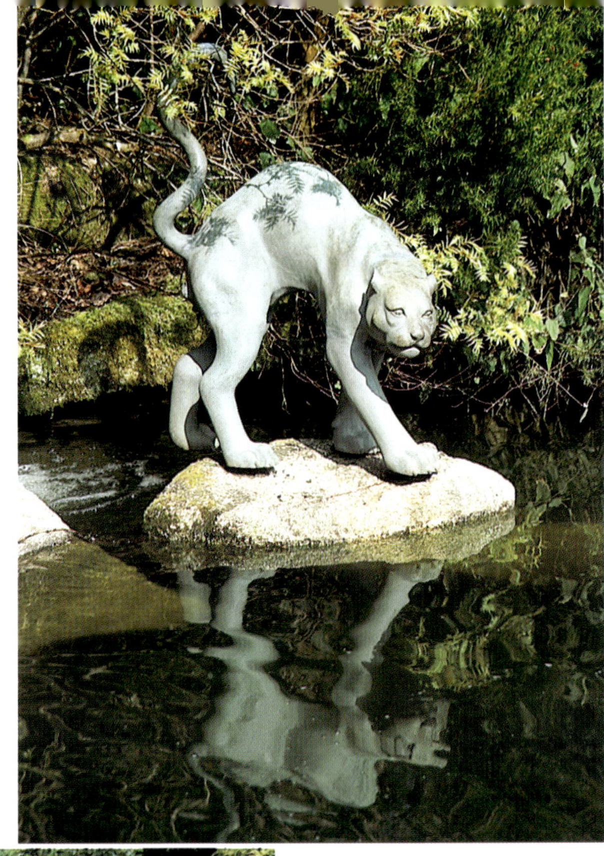

Right: A puma at the edge of the koi pond at Pine Lodge in Cornwall. The lens was zoomed to include the puma's reflection and an 81A filter warmed up Provia 100F a trifle.

**Minolta Dynax 7, 28–135mm lens, 81A filter, tripod. f/8 on Provia 100F**

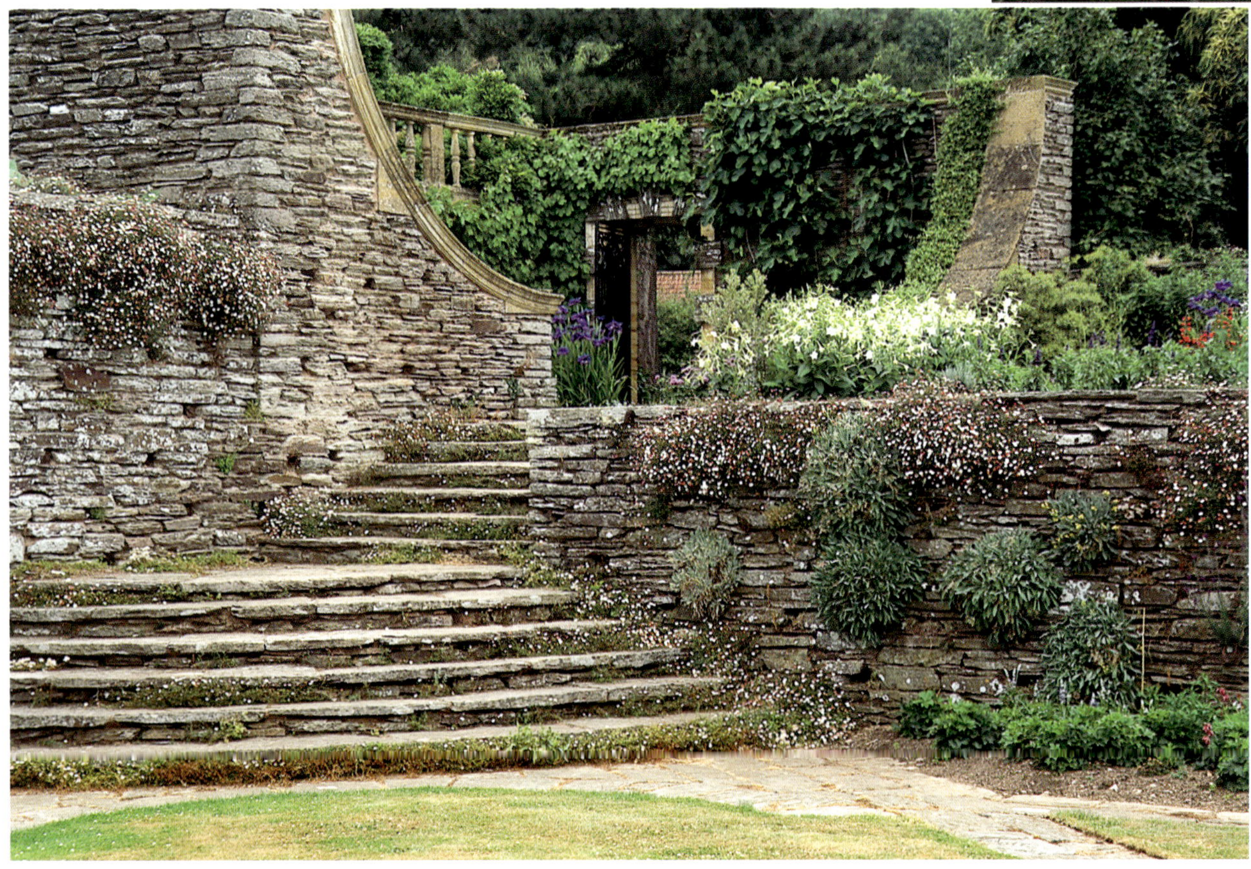

The Edwardian garden at Hestercombe is an intricate arrangement of space on varying levels. Steps lead down onto a large sunken parterre, known as the Great Plat, at its four corners and one of the flights is shown. Use of an 81B filter was necessary because of the overcast light and this has helped to give the stonework a warm feel.

**Minolta Dynax 700si, 28–135mm lens, 81B filter, tripod. f/16 on Velvia**

## Technique: **Converging Verticals**

When buildings or a house are included in a picture, great care should be taken to ensure that converging verticals (which give the appearance that a building is falling backwards, and are caused by tilting the camera upwards) are avoided. This can be achieved by keeping the film plane parallel to the building's walls, although this may mean that the whole building cannot be accommodated in the picture area, even if one retreats to a more distant shooting position.

It is possible that a short telephoto lens used from the new position might retrieve the situation, but the probability is that, barring being able to use a much higher viewpoint (or a large-format camera), only a perspective-control or 'shift' lens will resolve the matter satisfactorily.

Another way to deal with converging verticals is to scan the transparency and then manipulate the digital file with image-editing software.

Below: This 'ruined abbey' at Painshill Landscape Garden, in Surrey, was shot from across the lake using a 70–300mm zoom lens, thus avoiding converging verticals on the building.

**Minolta Dynax 700si, 70–300mm lens, tripod. f/22 on Ektachrome 100G**

## Equipment: **PC Lenses**

Perspective-control (PC) or 'shift' lenses, which are expensive items, are often used by specialists in architectural photography. The front lens element is adjusted to include the top of the building, which in turn shifts the optical axis of the lens and prevents converging verticals.

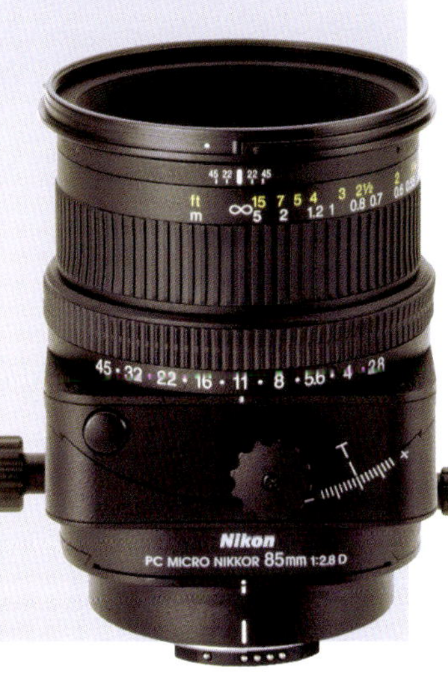


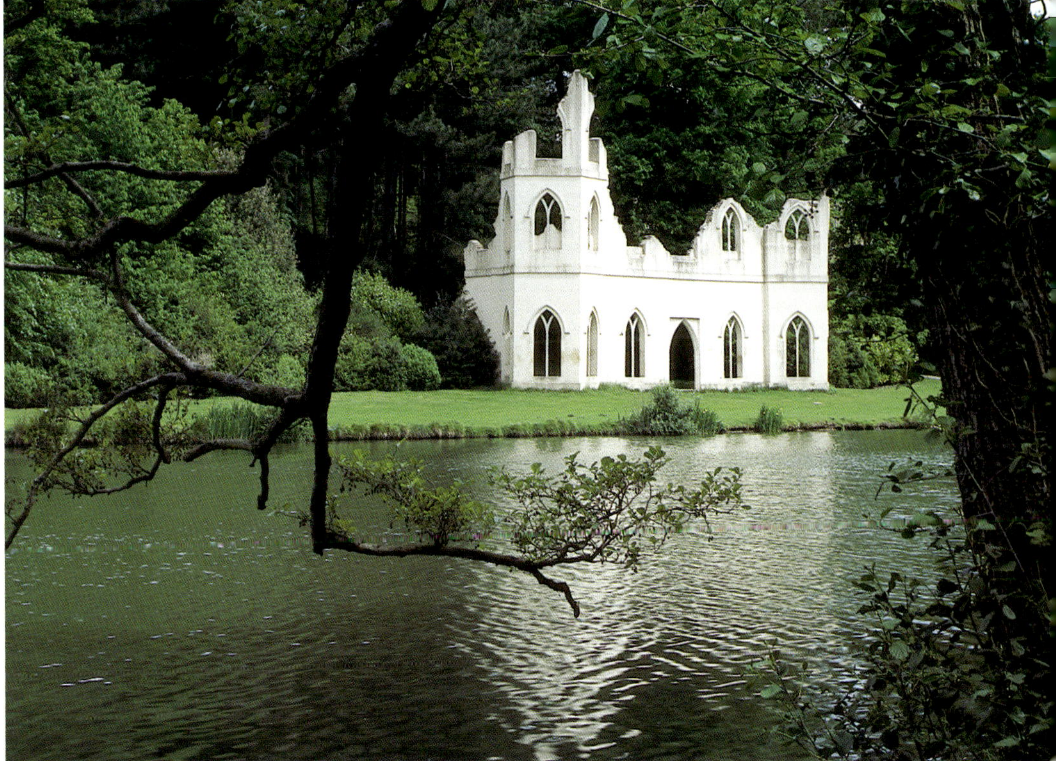

# Case study 4: BODNANT GARDEN, NORTH WALES

**Bodnant Garden in North Wales is laid out on the grand scale with a series of inspired terraces around the house, each different but with a strong Italian feeling. There are also lovely views to the Snowdon Mountains. Away from the house, and behind the terraces, lies an altogether different area: a magical woodland of spring colour known as 'the Dell'. This diverse combination of subject matter makes it an ideal – if challanging – location for the garden photographer.**

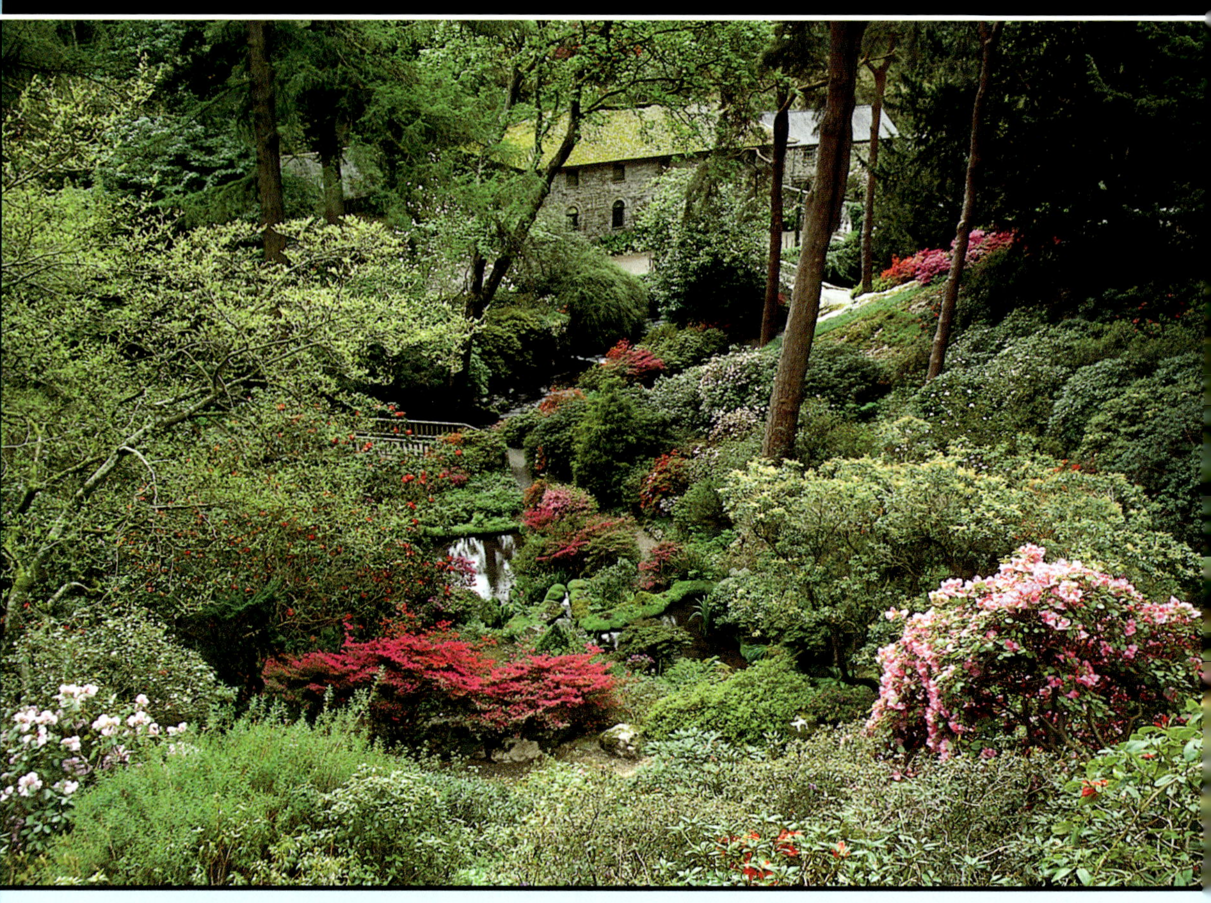

A view down to the valley floor of the Dell. This was a straightforward shot once a cloud had eliminated high levels of contrast and harsh shadows from the scene.

**Minolta Dynax 700si, 28–135mm lens, 81B filter, tripod. 1/6sec at f/11 on Velvia**

**Cameras: Fuji GW670III, Minolta Dynax 700si and Minolta Dynax 7**

**Film: Velvia**

**Lens: Sigma 28–135mm zoom and Tamron 90mm macro**

**Filter: 81A–C warm-ups**

**Notes: Permission to use a tripod was gained in advance**

### 14.00

I decided to make the trip to Bodnant in North Wales immediately after photographing the Japanese Garden at Tatton Park (see Case study 2, page 64–7), a journey of around 70 miles (110km). It was raining at Tatton and my wife and I hoped that the rain might have eased by the time we reached Bodnant. Some months previously I had sought and received permission from the general manager to photograph there. This included permission to use a tripod – something that should always be cleared in advance.

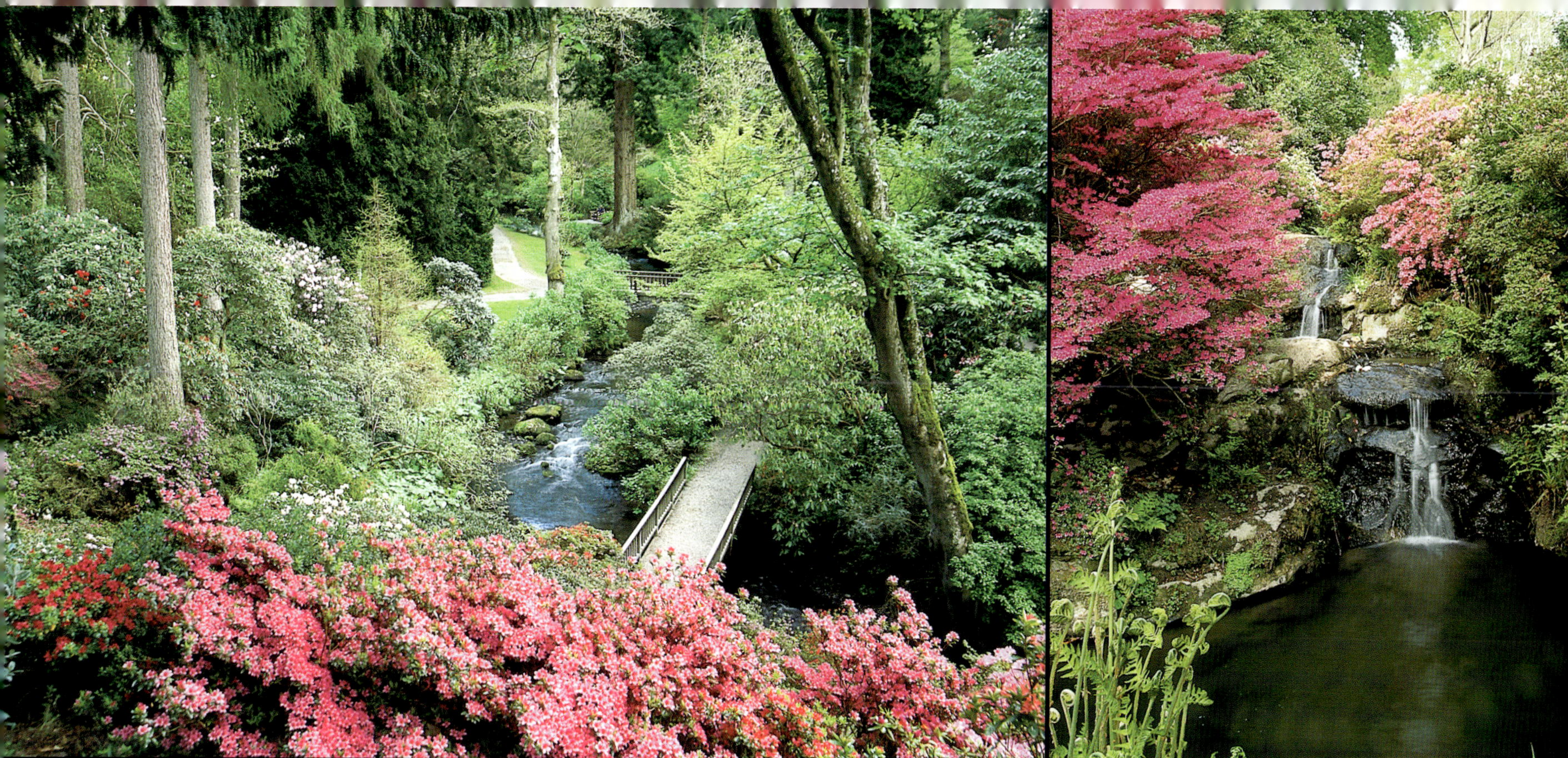

A view along the valley down which flows a tributary of the River Conwy. Again, it was necessary to wait for a cloud to obscure the sun before taking this shot.

**Minolta Dynax 7, 28–135mm lens, 81B filter, tripod. 1/6sec at f/11 on Velvia**

A stream in the Dell, the pool flanked by an azalea in full bloom. A long exposure was given so as to highlight the water flowing over the waterfalls.

**Minolta Dynax 700si, 28–135mm lens, 81B filter, tripod. 1sec at f/22 on Velvia**

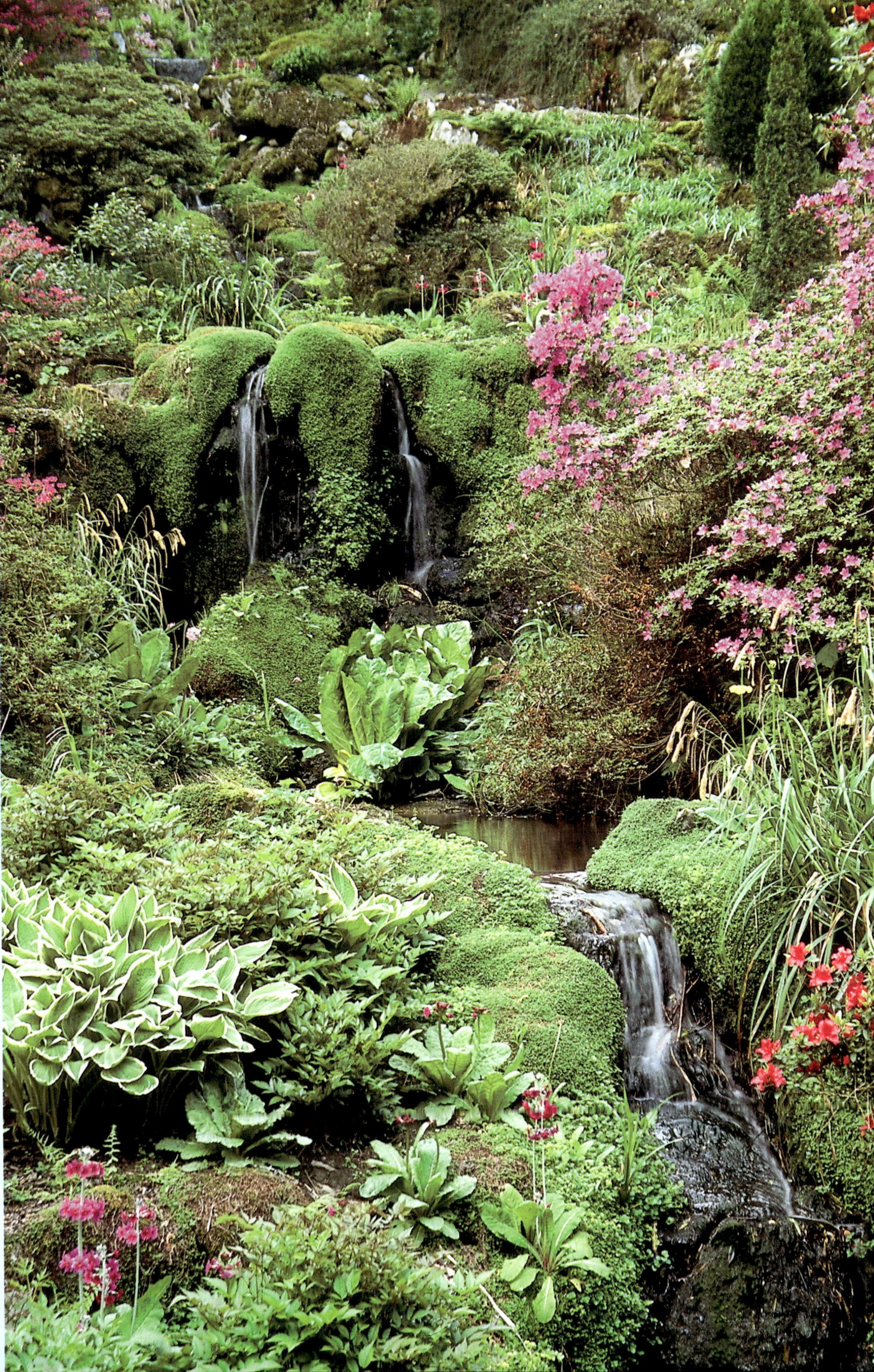

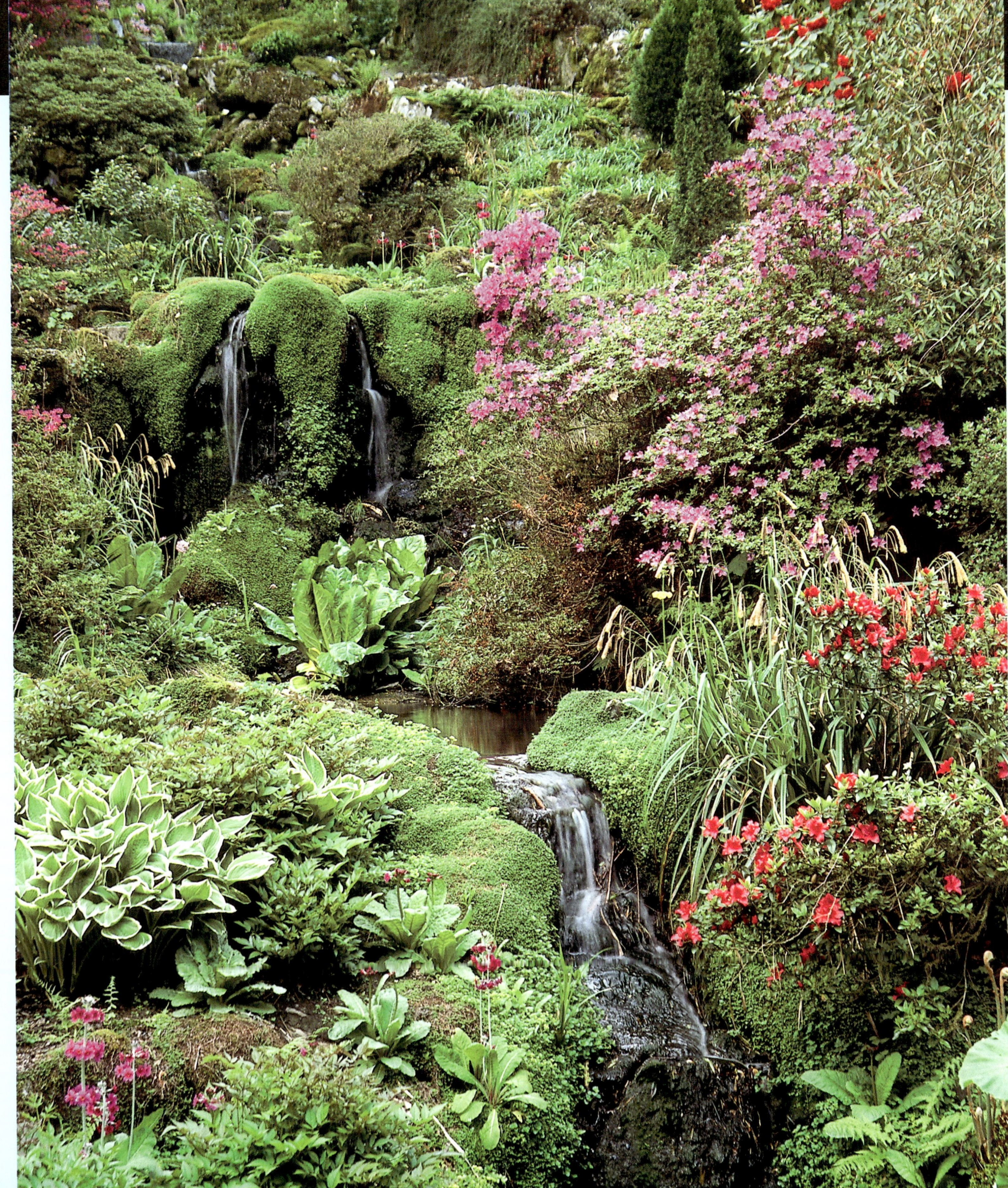

Left: According to the dictionary, a 'dell' is a small hollow or valley, usually with tree-clad sides. The one at Bodnant is actually rather large and, as can be seen from this photo, almost ravine-like. Its sides are covered with a prolific variety of tree and plant life, with rhododendrons, azaleas, camellias and many impressive conifers. At the foot of the valley, a tributary of the River Conwy flows strongly to the sea not far away.

**Minolta Dynax 7, 28–135mm lens, 81B filter, tripod. 1/3sec at f/11 on Velvia**

My hopes for better conditions were realized as we reached our destination, the last raindrops falling as we drove into the car park. The recent rain gave the plants a pleasant luminance, but unfortunately the sun had come out, creating strongly contrasting light conditions similar to those later experienced at Wakehurst Place (see Case study 1, page 50).

### 16.00

I particularly wanted to secure some images of the Dell, which is famous for its magnificent woodland garden. No time was lost in getting to the section of the garden where the Dell is situated, and we followed a winding path down the valley, photographing on the way. The late afternoon sunlight would have created ruinous shadows on any pictures; it was a matter, therefore, of waiting for stray clouds to dampen down the contrast.

I did in fact experiment with a shot or two on my medium-format camera while waiting for the conditions to improve. However, as I feared, the high contrast of sunlight and shadow rendered them fit only for the bin. Far more sucessful were the shots taken on 35mm SLRs where I had waited for cloud to even things out, as illustrated by the selection of images shown here.

### 17.00

Our time at Bodnant went all too quickly and at five o'clock a handbell signalled the closure of the garden for the day. On the trek back uphill to the entrance, further scenes of magic cried out to be photographed, particularly as the lower sunlight had now reduced the level of contrast, but most of these had to be reluctantly ignored if we were not to be locked in for the night.

# 9

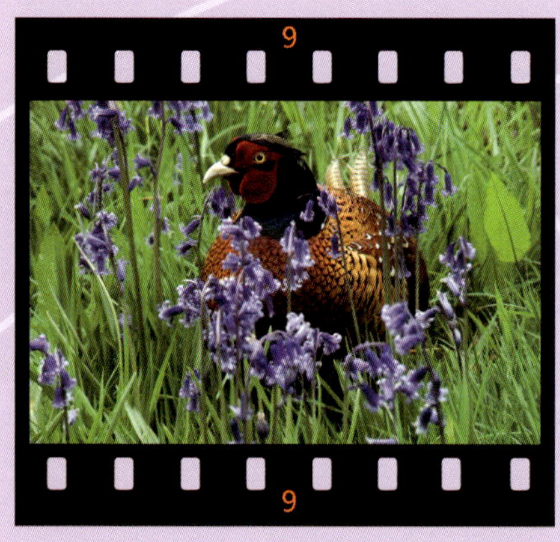

# Wildlife in the Garden

**One of the great pleasures of gardens is the wildlife that they attract, and, generally speaking, the more mini-habitats a garden contains, the greater variety of species it will support. The presence of birds, insects, amphibians and mammals adds variety and fresh challenges for the garden photographer.**

Establishing the garden as a miniature nature reserve will help to create picture-taking opportunities. The steps that you can take to enhance your chances will depend largely on your location and the indigenous wildlife. In temperate regions like the UK, a garden pond, nectar-producing flowers, and, for nesting sites, hedges of thorn and yew will all help. In drier regions, such as California, sugar-solution feeders will help to attract hummingbirds.

It can pay dividends not to let tidy-gardener instincts get the better of your photographer/naturalist side. By leaving seed heads on perennials over the winter, finches are attracted into the garden. Last winter, the seeds on a clump of *Rudbeckia fulgida* var. *sullivantii* 'Goldsturm' in my garden were visited regularly by goldfinches, and to have them feeding for up to a quarter of an hour not 15ft (5m) from the kitchen window was a great opportunity.

## Birds

Birds are the most obvious wild creatures we see in the garden, but they are not easy to photograph well and some thought has to be employed to capture them on film. As with all wildlife photography, it really does help if you have a good knowledge of your subject. I would urge careful consideration before attempting photography of birds at the nest. This has been done many times in the past and it is only too easy to stress the nesting pair, with desertion a possible outcome. The stages of nest photography involve the erection of a hide or 'blind' at a distance away from the nest, and its gradual movement forward to within shooting range. This process calls for experience and has to be carried out over a period

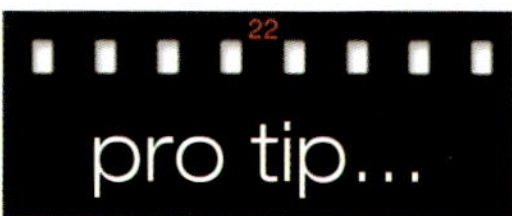


### Combining elements

I try, whenever possible, to obtain a shot of the wildlife subject combined with another ingredient that would make a picture in its own right. For example, a dragonfly with flowers of a marginal plant or a robin in the snow.

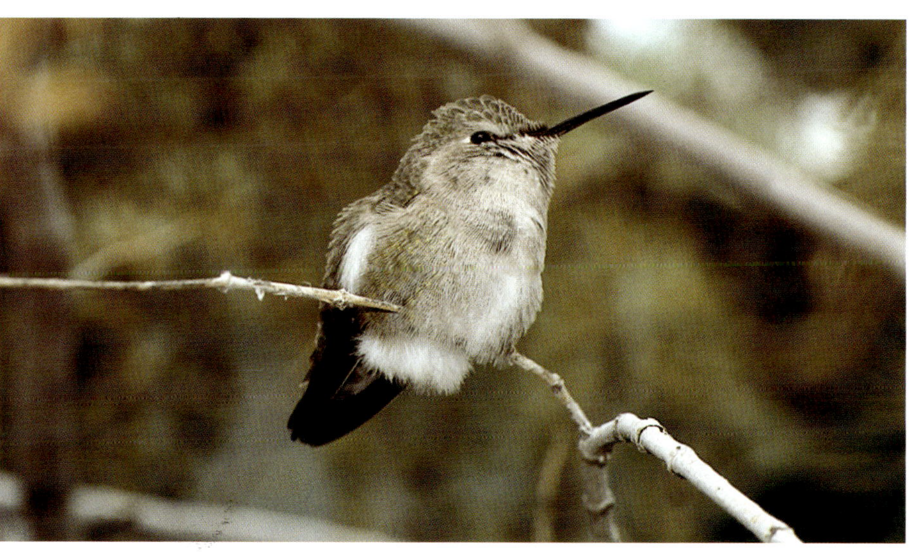

This tiny hummingbird was resting in a desert shrub at Moortens Botanical Garden in Palm Springs. I shot three frames, of which this is the last, and used a 1.4x teleconverter on a 90mm macro lens, combined with manual focusing and fill-in flash.

**Minolta Dynax 700si, 90mm macro lens with 1.4x teleconverter, 81A filter, fill-in flash, tripod. f/4.5 on Agfa RSXII up-rated to 200 ISO**

## Equipment: **Bird Photography**

An SLR is the ideal camera for bird photography in the garden. Firm support from a tripod or beanbag is necessary because the lens will be focused on a precise spot for a considerable length of time.

Lenses of between 200mm and 500mm that are capable of fairly close focusing (or used with extension rings or a teleconverter) will be required; zoom lenses are excellent in that adjustments can easily be made for varying sizes of subject.

In winter sunlight, film with an ISO of 100 gives an exposure of around 1/125 at f/5.6. This may not deal adequately with the constant movement of some smaller subjects, in which case a 100 ISO film up-rated by one stop could provide the answer.

When light does not provide a highlight in the bird's eye, a touch of fill-in flash will enhance the subject and bring a picture to life.

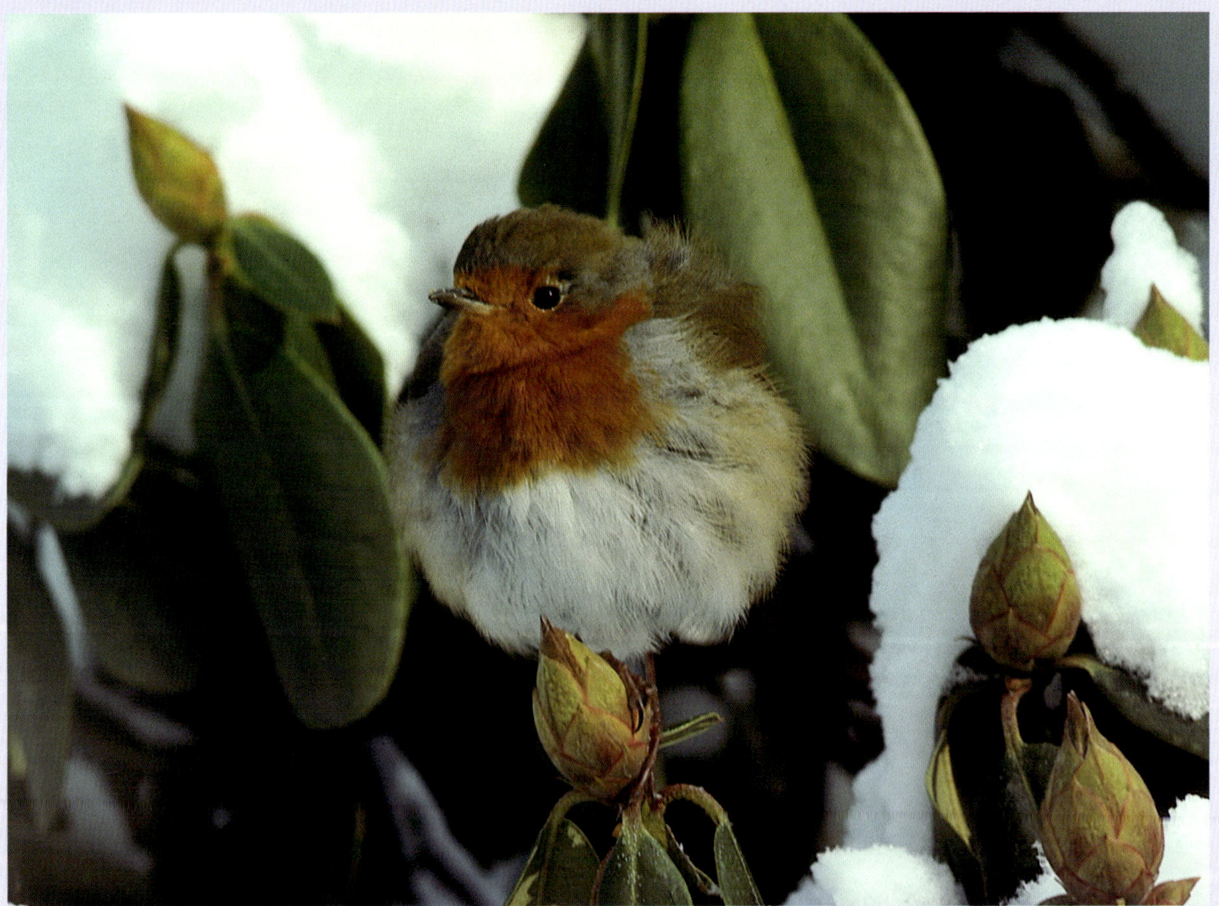

Robin *Erithacus rubecula*. An exception to my policy of always using a tripod, this hand-held shot was taken one biting-cold winter morning using a shutter speed of about 1/30sec. One stop of extra exposure was given to adjust for the light in the snowy conditions. (See pages 92–3 for more on photographing snow.)

**Praktica VLC2, 135mm lens. f/5.6 on Kodachrome 64**

of some days, with the obligation to abandon the project immediately if the nesting pair appears at any stage not to accept the situation.

It is preferable to photograph garden birds when they are concerned with other activities, perhaps feeding, singing or bathing. If you are lucky, you can work without a place of concealment, especially if you are using a long lens, but generally a surer way to success is to use some form of hide.

**Using a hide** A hide is simply a structure that enables you to view the subject from a concealed position. It can be constructed from branches and vegetation, from scrap wood or from canvas like a tent. Purpose-built hides are available commercially (advertised in wildlife and photographic magazines) or a conveniently situated outbuilding, such as a garden shed, can be used as a makeshift hide. In the latter case, open the window and fix a cloth – with a hole cut in it to accommodate the camera – across the window space. On occasion a ground floor room can be pressed into service as a hide, with the camera lens poking out of an open window and drawn curtains keeping you hidden from your subjects.

**Using a feeding station** In the winter and early spring a well-provisioned feeding station should provide many opportunities. For a natural feel to the pictures it is preferable not to include the bird table or the seed/peanut container in the picture. Instead, train the camera on a suitable perch that can be used by the birds on their way to and from the food. Care will have to be given to siting the perch in a position with an unobtrusive background (mid-toned preferably) and receiving favourable light at those hours of the day when you want to use the hide.

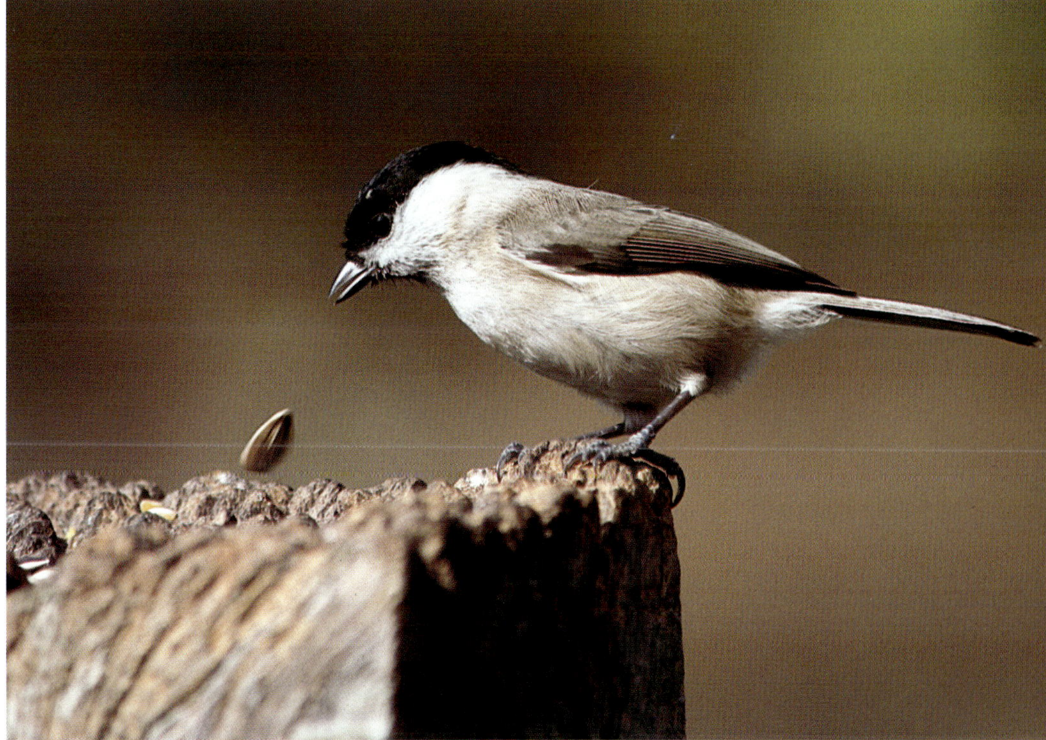

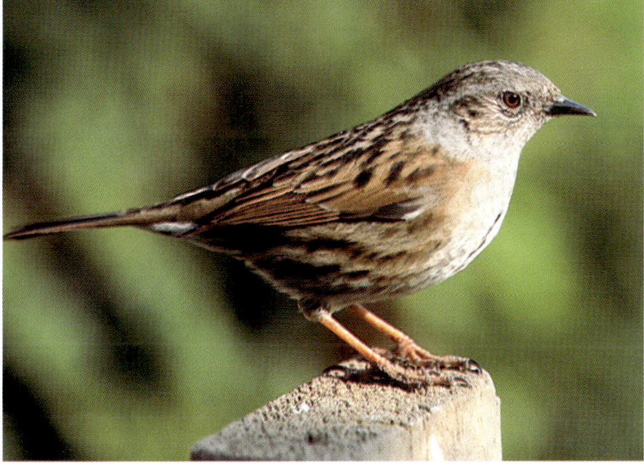

Above: Dunnock *Prunella modularis*. This is a winter picture taken from my garden shed, which was used as a hide. Black cloth (with a hole cut in it to accommodate the lens) was used to cover the window frame.

**Minolta 7000i, 70–210mm lens (used at 200mm). f/5.6 on Fujichrome 100**

Above: No hide was used for capturing this early-spring image of a Marsh Tit *Parus palustris*. It was simply a matter of putting some wild birdseed on the wooden post and waiting quietly in an area of the garden at Wakehurst Place, where the birds are used to people.

**Minolta Dynax 700si, 70–210mm lens (used at 210mm), tripod. f/8 on Agfa CT100i**

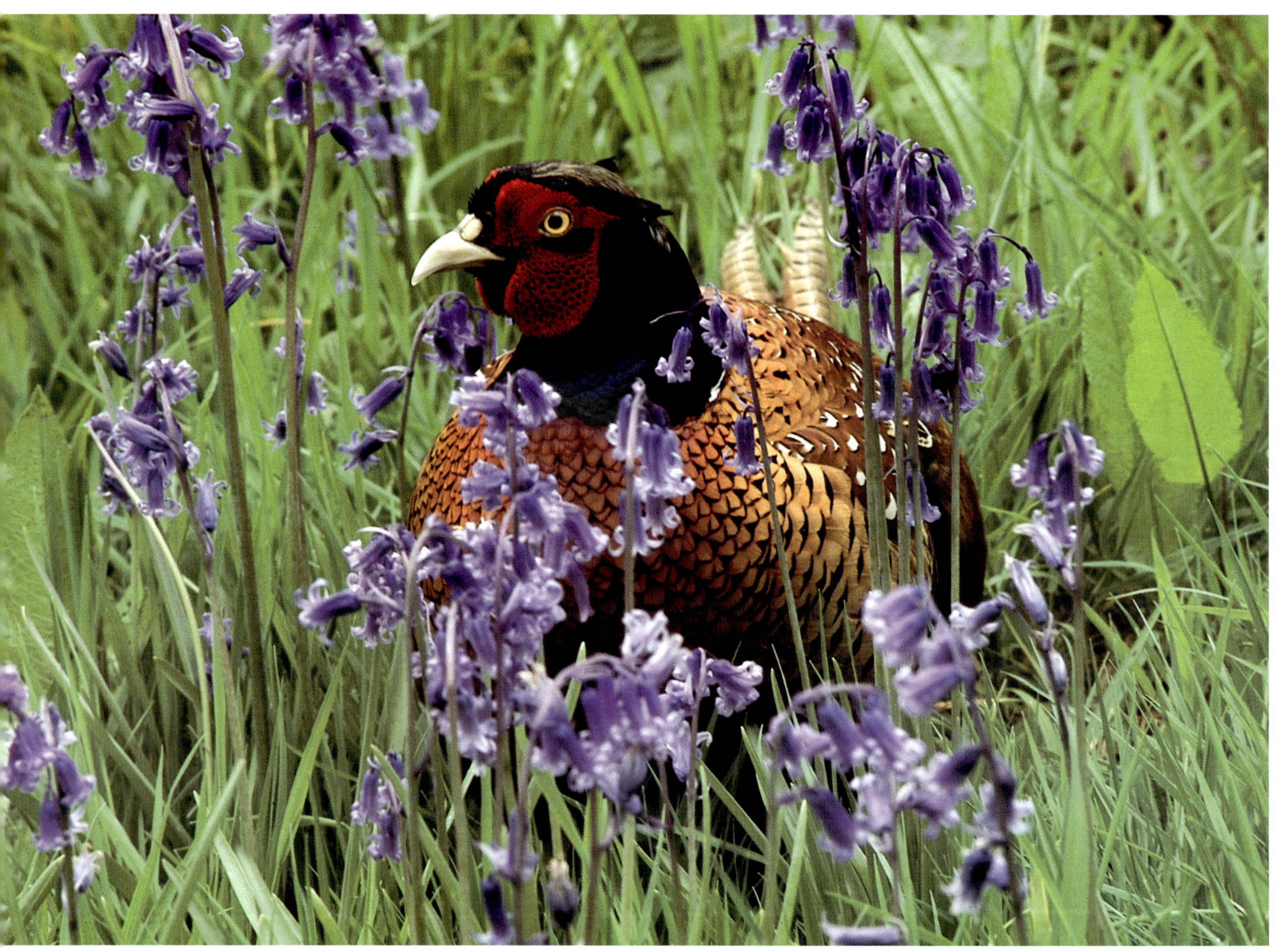

Pheasant *Phasianus colchicus*. For this spring scene, at Wakehurst Place, the cock pheasant was enticed within camera range among the bluebells by a pinch of grain.

**Minolta 7000i, 70–210mm lens (used at 210mm), tripod. f/8 on Fujichrome 100**

Camera-to-perch distance is critical and depends on how large you want your subject to appear in the frame. As a guide, when using a 200mm lens and 35mm film a sparrow-sized bird side-on to a camera fills about three-quarters of the frame at a distance of just over 3ft (1m). At this distance, most of the frame will be filled when using a 300mm lens. Once everything is set up, all that is required is a bit of luck and a lot of patience!

## Pond Life

Frogs soon find the garden pond and use it for spawning. This normally takes place in late winter or early spring and is dependent on water temperature. A polarizing filter will cut out sheen from the water and reveal the whole scene, but try some shots unfiltered with just the frogs' heads and eyes showing above water. The secret is to shoot from a low angle, as near the waterline as possible. A macro lens of 180mm or 200mm, or a 70–210mm zoom lens with a close-focusing facility, is ideal for this situation. Any sudden movement on the part of the photographer will send these subjects below water and it is necessary to position tripod and camera slowly and deliberately, taking advantage of the extra shooting distance afforded by longer lenses.

In my own garden, both frogs and toads spawn in the pond and this sometimes enables both the beadlike frogspawn and the long laces of toadspawn to be pictured together.

A pond also attracts dragonflies and there are chances to photograph them either resting between forays or egg-laying on floating vegetation. Dragonflies are very alert and I have found that more frequent success comes from using a 300mm lens (possibly with extension rings or a teleconverter) used at a

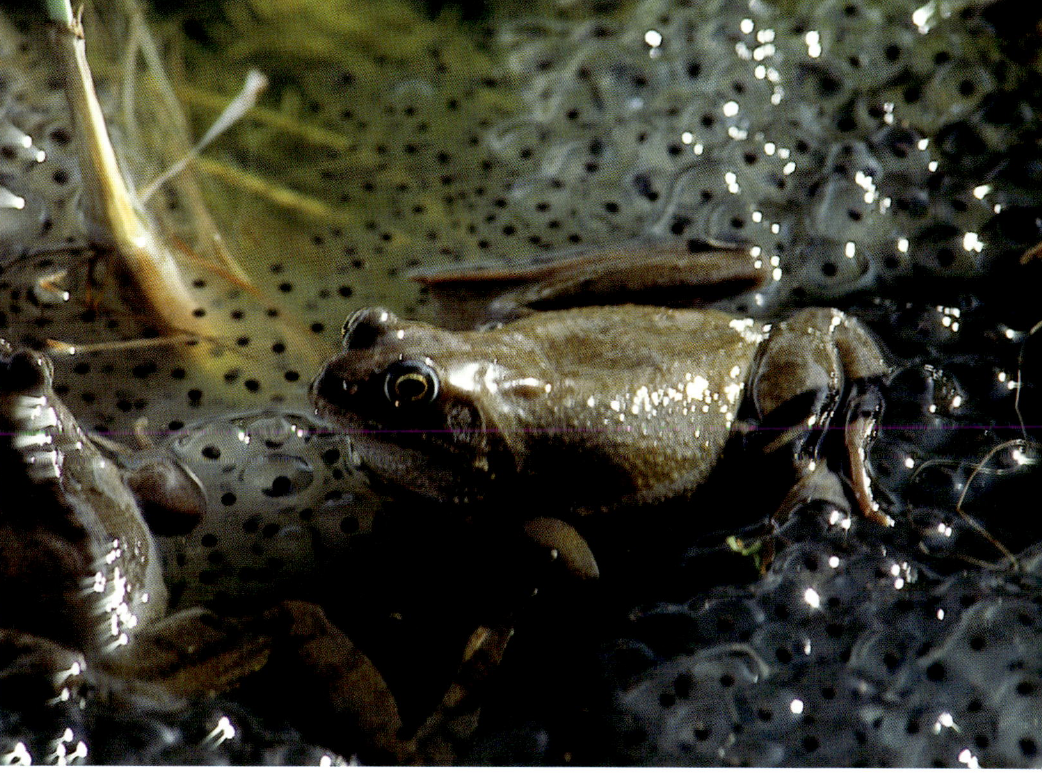

Frogs *(Rana temporaria)* spawning. Stealth was required in order to avoid disturbing this noisy, bustling early-spring scene. A low camera position and a polarizing filter were selected to cut out the glare so that the spawn was clearly visible.

**Minolta 7000i, 70–210mm lens, polarizing filter, tripod. f/11 on Fujichrome 100**

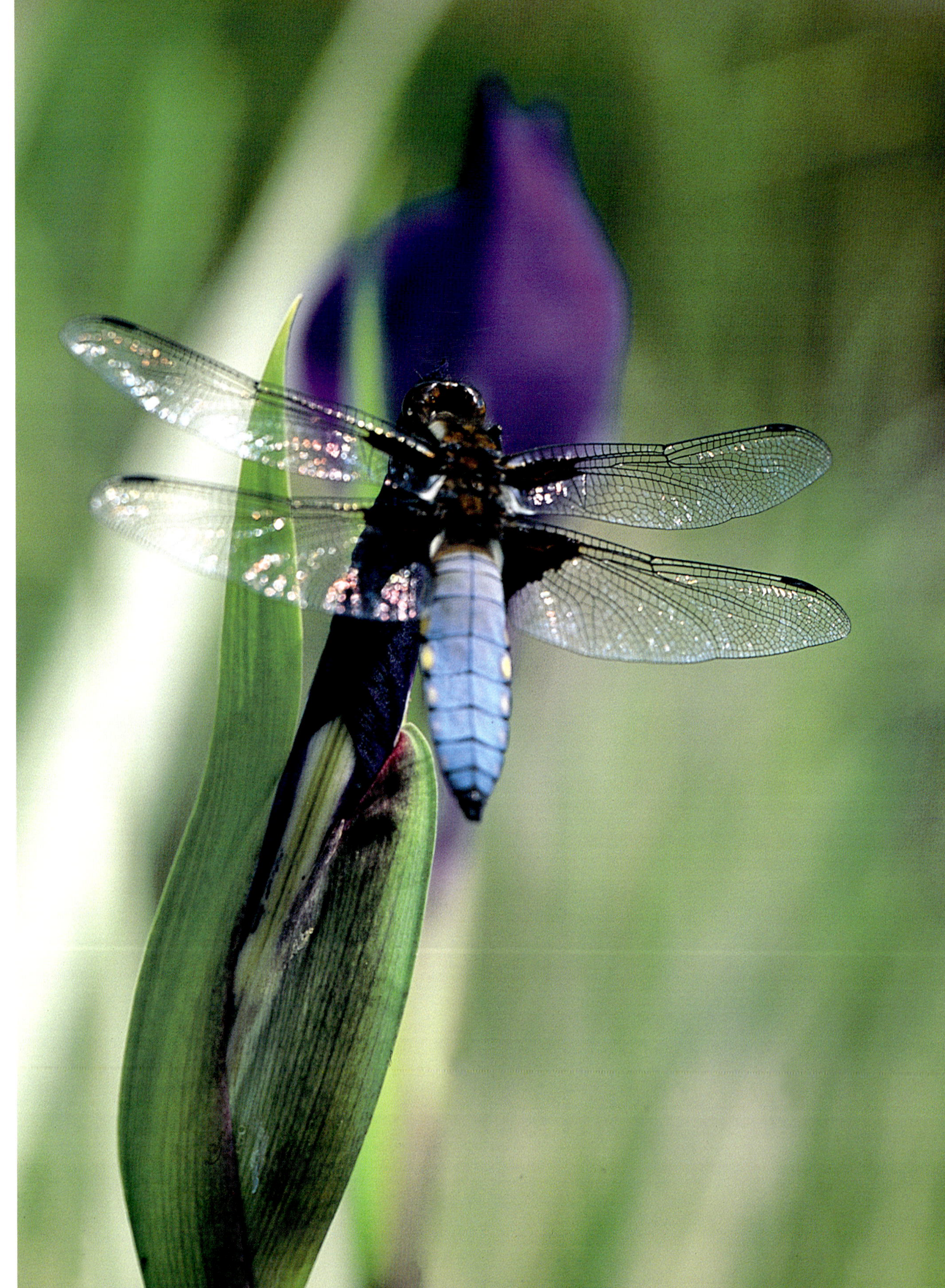

Broad-bodied *Libellula Libellula depressa*. This is a late-spring image of a male dragonfly, with *Iris laevigata* 'Colchesterii' adding context and additional interest.

**Minolta Dynax 7000i, 180mm macro lens, tripod. f/6.7 on Velvia**

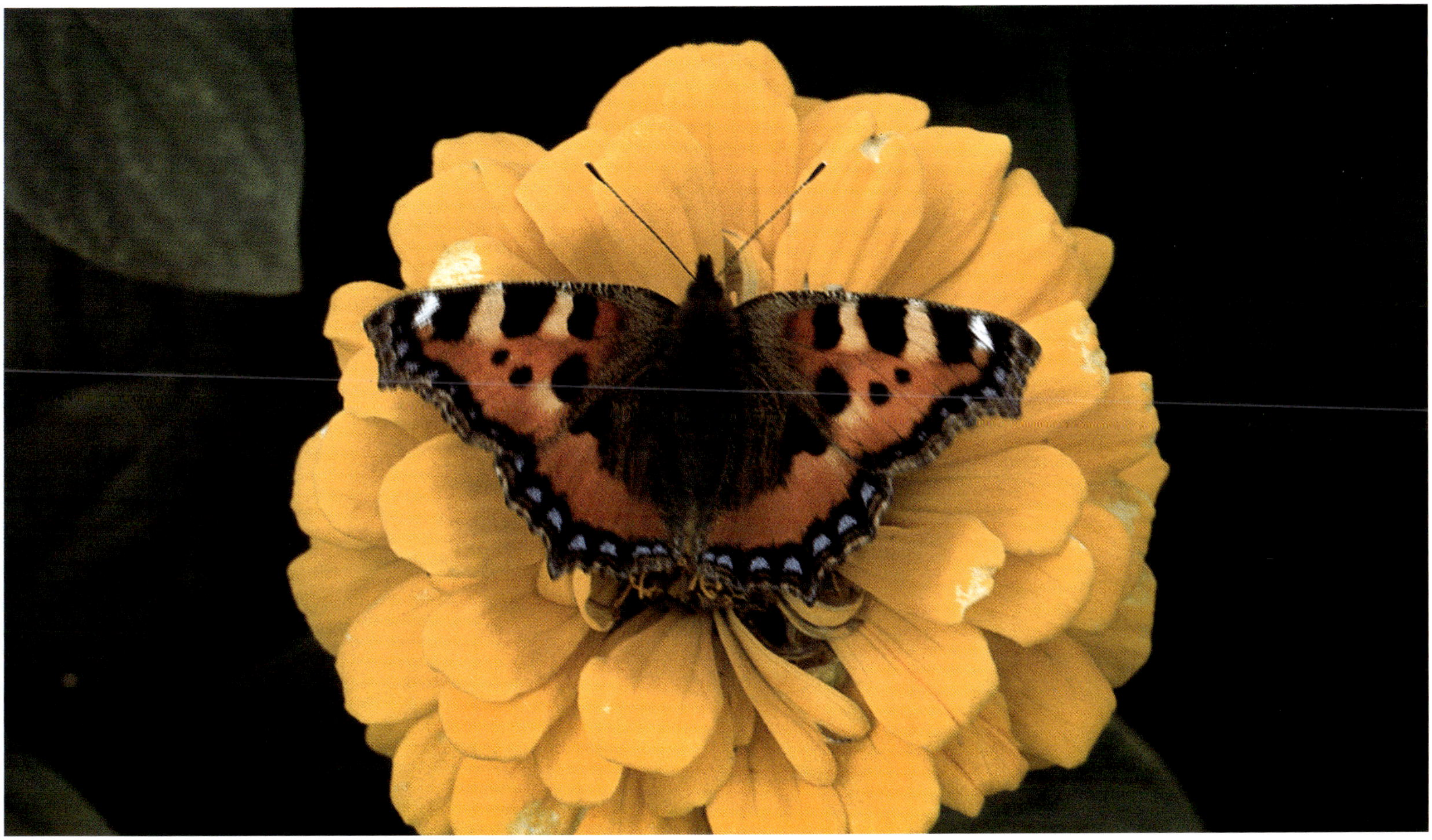

shooting distance of 3ft (1m) or so, rather than trying to get closer with a 180mm macro lens. If you can catch sunlight shimmering on the insect's wings, so much the better.

Small Tortoiseshell butterfly *Aglais urticae* resting on a zinnia on a sunny day. I waited until a passing cloud obscured the sun, thus reducing unwanted shadows.

**Minolta XG-M, 90mm macro lens, tripod. f/16 on Agfachrome 100**

### Insects

Butterflies make beautiful and challenging subjects, and their photography is a specialization in its own right. Gardens containing a good variety of nectar-producing plants are happy hunting grounds for the photographer wishing to capture the commoner species on film, with summer and early autumn being the most productive times. Butterflies are often around while one is busily engaged in photographing plants, and sometimes the right camera/lens combination is to hand. Ideally this is an SLR with a macro lens of between 90mm and 200mm, and a dedicated flash gun to give a touch of fill-in flash to reduce shadow contrast on sunny days or enliven a picture on a cloudy day. A longer lens with extension

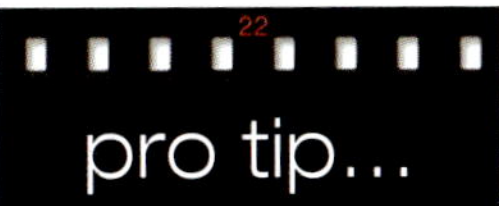


**Butterflies**

Keep your camera's film plane parallel to the butterfly's wings to maximize depth of field.

tubes is an alternative to a macro lens. As always, better results will be obtained if a tripod is used and manual focus is best employed to ensure that the eyes of the insect are sharp. A fine-grained film of 100 ISO should suffice, although this can be pushed one stop to 200 ISO to provide more options.

## Mammals

Wild mammal species in English gardens are somewhat limited in number. Grey squirrels are a possibility in some areas and a certainty in others. Hedgehogs are likely, too, along with fieldmice and maybe foxes, rabbits and deer (although, purely as a gardener, you may consider the latter undesirable). Some gardens have resident breeding foxes or foxes that visit regularly on their daily or nightly rounds. They can become quite tame where encouraged, as was the case with the fox shown below.

**Squirrels** Grey squirrels are very partial to peanuts and are attracted to bird tables and feeders. It is relatively simple to attract them to within photographic range without the need for a hide. Squirrel-proof bird feeders give rise, initially at any rate, to incredible contortions as the squirrels attempt unsuccessfully to snatch a snack from them.

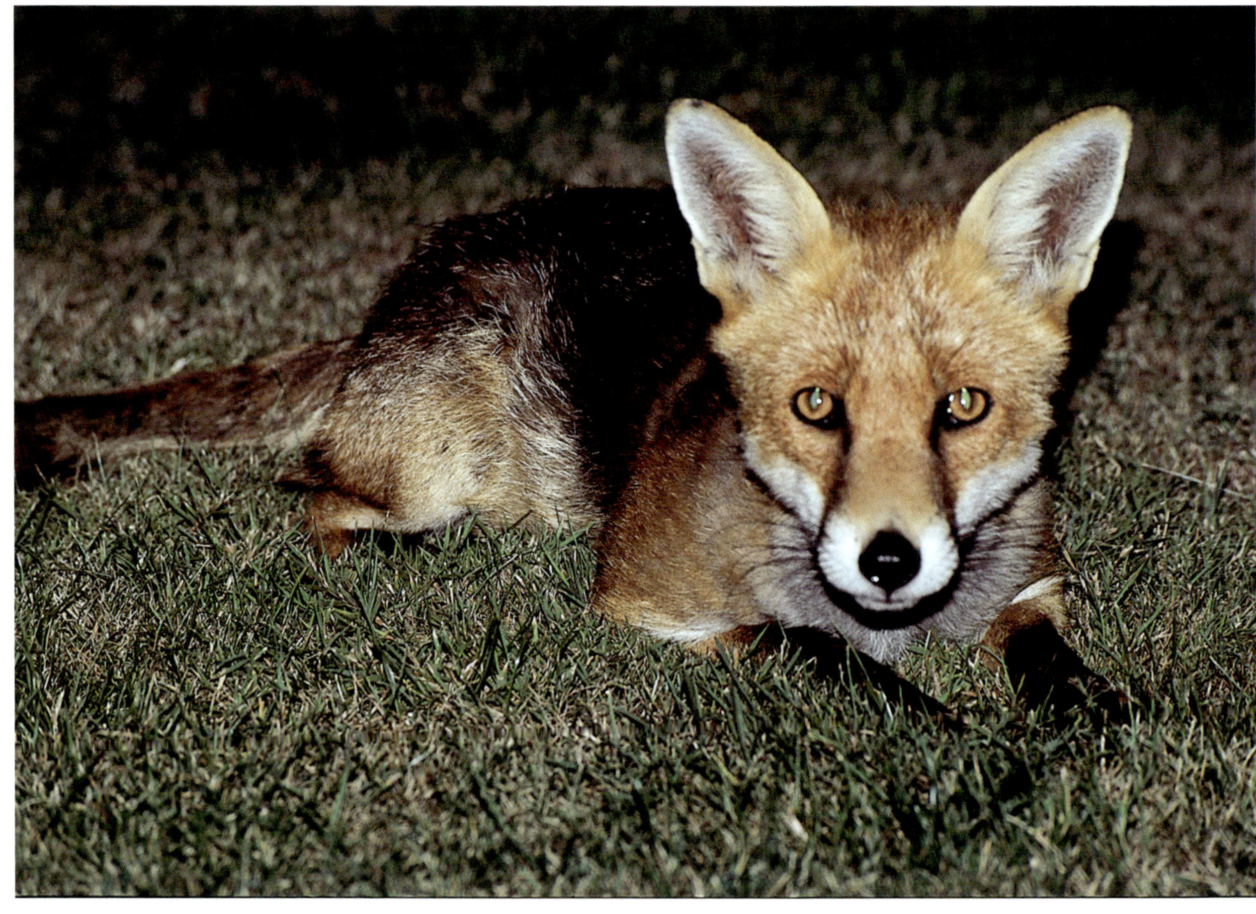

Fox *Vulpes vulpes*. A dog fox photographed in a suburban garden just south of London, where it was befriended over a period of time. On the evening the picture was taken the fox was quite unfazed by a group of us chatting in the gathering dusk. The tripod was set at a low height from the ground.

**Minolta Dynax 700si, 70–300mm lens, tripod, flash. f/8 on Ektachrome 100VS**

Grey Squirrel *Sciurus carolinensis*. Some squirrels (this one was in the garden of friends in Kent) take a little time to accept that squirrel-proof bird feeders are indeed squirrel proof.

**Minolta Dynax 7000i, 70–300mm lens, tripod, remote shutter release. F/8 on Provia 400**

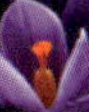

## Attracting Wildlife

- ✓ Try to establish the garden as a miniature nature reserve
- ✓ Create as many different habitats as possible in order to encourage a greater variety of wildlife
- ✓ Put up nesting boxes and plant hedges of thorn and yew to act as nesting sites
- ✓ Keep feeding stations well stocked with seed and peanuts to attract birds and also small mammals such as squirrels
- ✓ Add sugar-solution feeders in habitats with hummingbirds
- ✓ Ponds attract not just amphibians, but also insects such as dragonflies
- ✓ Nectar-producing flowers encourage many species of butterfly

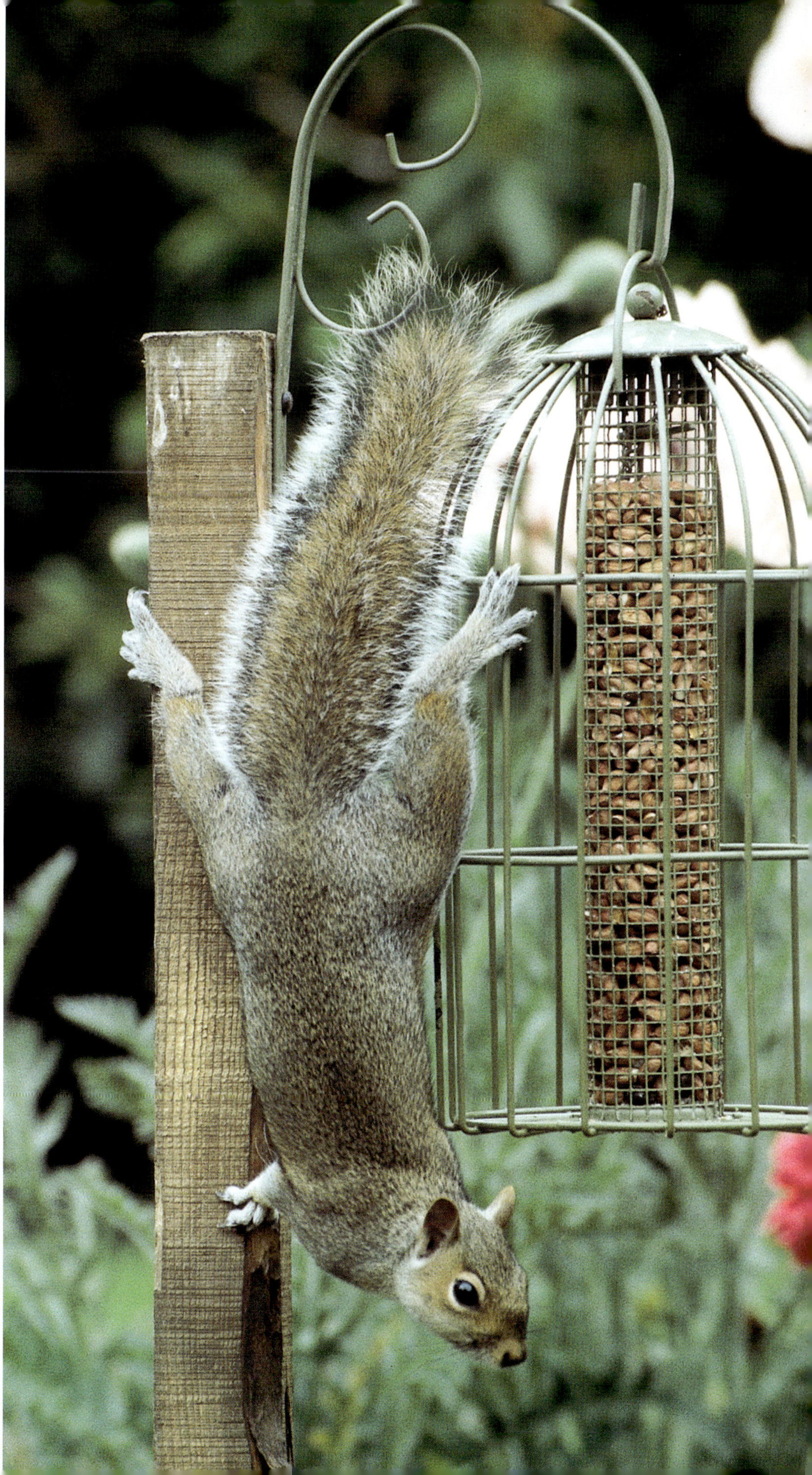

On location:

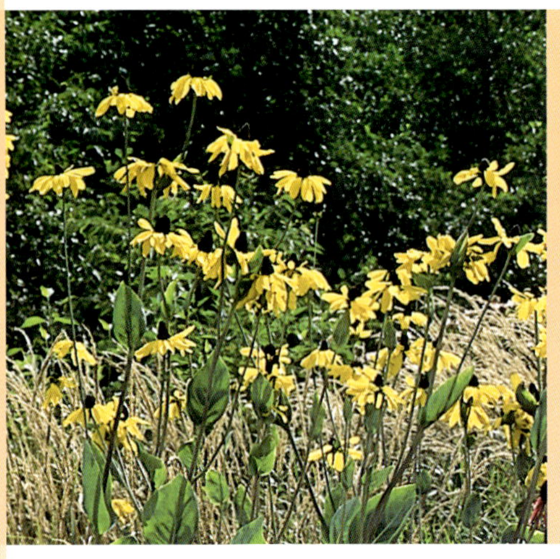

# Wild and Natural Gardens

**Garden photographers should always try to remain aware of developments in horticulture, and this should be reflected in their choice of subject matter. Recently there has been a rise in the popularity of gardens with a wild feel. This is primarily linked to gardens using herbaceous plants and grasses, but trees and shrubs can also be included and here this `modern' movement becomes blurred with long-established gardens – woodland gardens, for example – which have always striven to reproduce a natural look.**

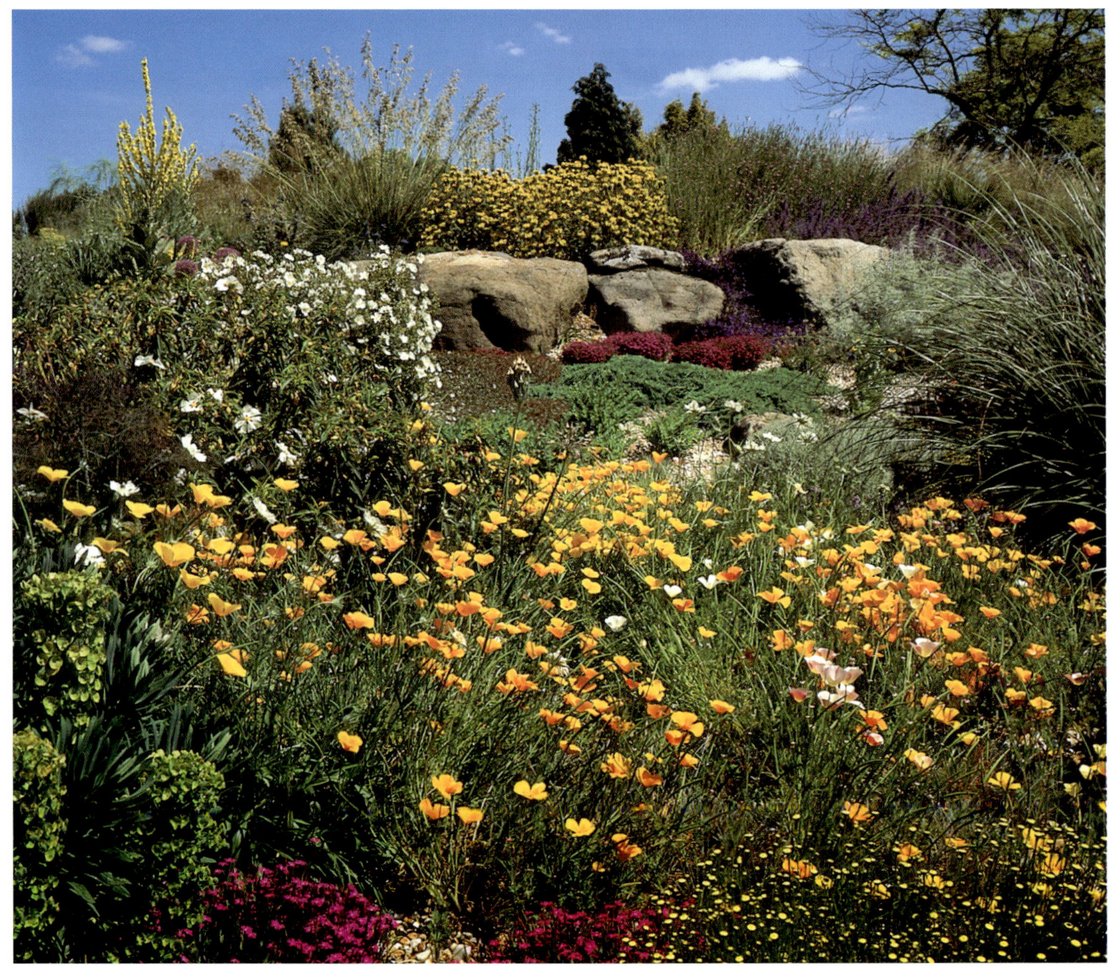

Dry Garden, RHS Garden Hyde Hall, Rettendon, Essex. Dry and gravel gardens have assumed added importance in these times of ecological awareness, and that completed in 2001 at Hyde Hall is a fine example of its kind. In this garden, plants that thrive in areas of low rainfall provide a most attractive and colourful show from spring through to late autumn and demonstrate what can be achieved with no watering and a good helping of expertise at the planning stage. The garden fends for itself; it's a case of no fertilizers, no spraying and no staking.

**Fuji GW670III, 81B filter, tripod. 1/8sec at f/27 on Velvia**

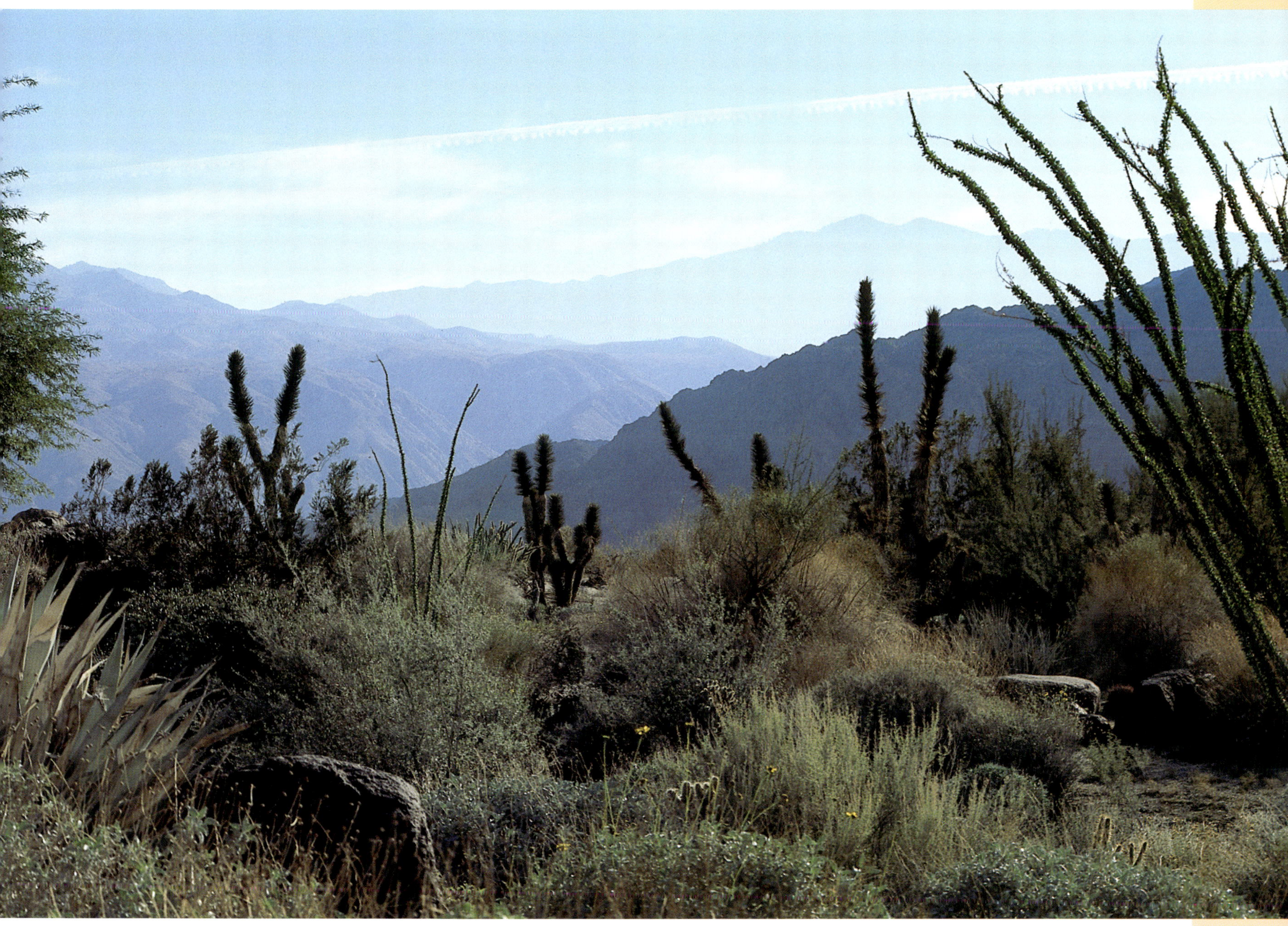

To wild and free-roaming desert wildlife, the botanical and wildlife park at The Living Desert, Palm Desert, California, is a home from home, with greater roadrunners, cactus wrens, hummingbirds and many desert species common. Dedicated to conservation and education, it contains both animals and plants from desert regions. The animals have generous enclosures and American desert plants are grouped in botanical garden eco-zones. A late afternoon scene in the fall is shown here, with the Santa Rosa Mountains in the background.

---

**Minolta Dynax 700si, 70–210mm lens, tripod. f/22 on Velvia**

Right and below: Two 450ft (147m) long borders at Wisley contain a carefully selected mix of perennials and ornamental grasses. This style of gardening, generally included under the heading of prairie planting, was developed on the continent of Europe and in America with the aim of reducing maintenance to a minimum. Watering is minimal and, except for the removal of perennial weeds in the early years and some winter tidying up, the plants are left to develop naturally. These borders were designed by Piet Oudolf, the Dutch plantsman, 'to capture the feel of a summer meadow'.

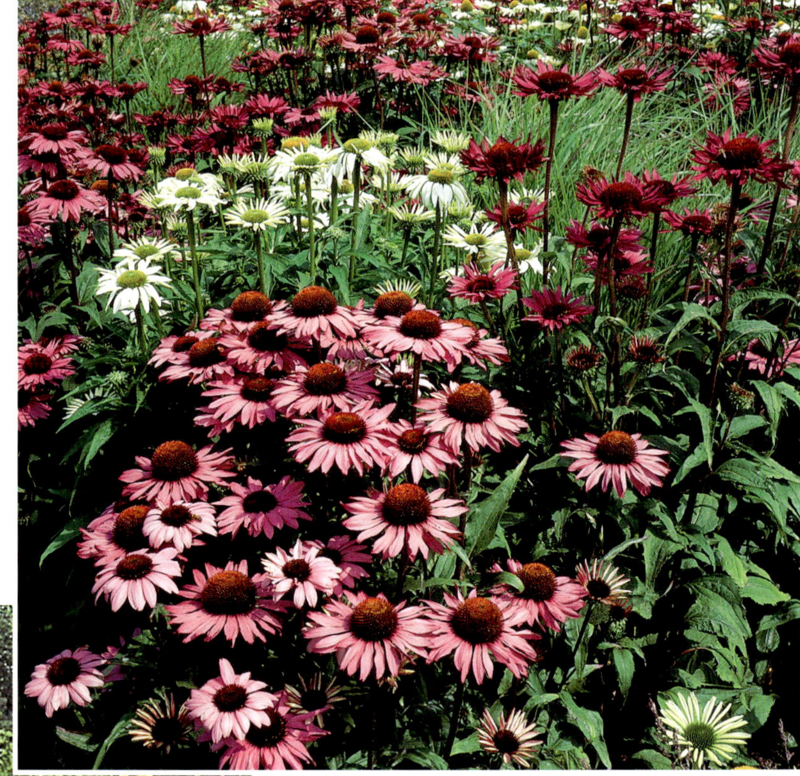

Above: A detail of purple and white echinacea in the border. The origins of this style of natural planting can be traced back to Dutch garden design of the 1920s.

**Fuji GW670III, 81B filter, tripod. f/22 on Velvia**

Left: Using backlighting against a dark background has helped to accentuate the yellow flower heads in this border from the same garden.

**Minolta Dynax 700si, 90mm macro lens, 81A filter, tripod. f/9.5 on Provia 100F**

Tropical Rainforest Garden: Quail Botanical Gardens, Encinitas, California. Anyone looking at this picture could be forgiven for wondering whether there had been a mix-up – this tropical rainforest does not look typical of dry and sunny Southern California. But not only is the location correct, this is out in the fresh air, not in a glasshouse. A thundering torrent (Mildred MacPherson's waterfall, discernible in the top right) rushes downhill through dripping tropical vegetation and the atmosphere is humid. Epiphytes grow in the trees and one half expects to see some stealthy jungle cat stalking through the undergrowth. I found it a fascinating piece of garden magic.

---

**Minolta Dynax 7, 28–135mm lens, tripod. f/16 on Velvia**

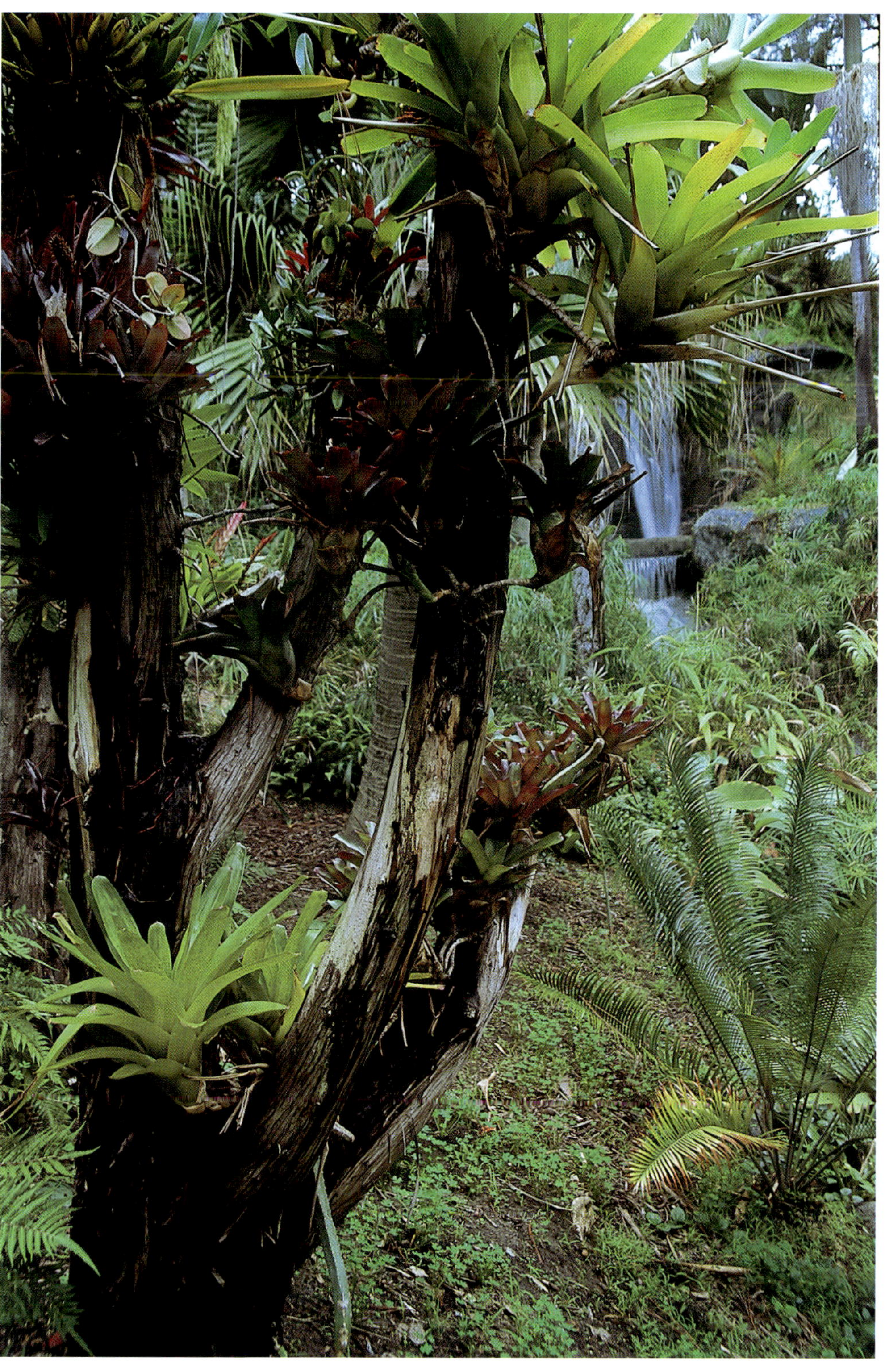

10

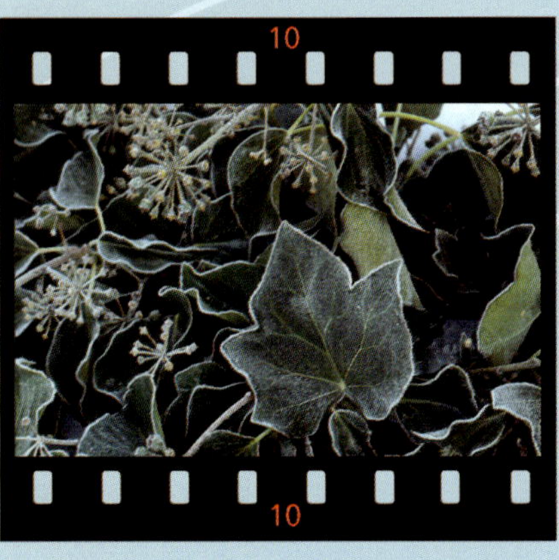

# **Making** Your Pictures **Pay**

**Over time, a committed garden photographer will build up a substantial body of work. Rather than leave this collection to languish in slide boxes, many consider the possibility of selling their work, perhaps to a magazine or through a library, and recovering a little of photography's considerable expenses.**

Dedication to selling your work, especially if you decide to approach picture buyers direct, must equal the dedication put into the work in the first place. If you do not wish to engage in the business of selling, or do not have the time available, your best course would be to approach a photo library with a view to reproduction rights for your pictures being sold on your behalf. Thoughts on choosing a photo library are set out later in the chapter (see page 138). However, it would be well to point out that, as an interim step, a worthwhile option to consider is that of taking a course on selling your pictures, such as that run as a correspondence course by the Bureau of Freelance Photographers in the UK. Advertisements for these courses are often to be found in photography magazines of the relevant country.

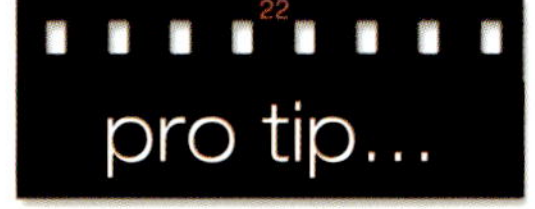


**Composition**

When composing a picture it is often worthwhile taking additional shots, in both landscape and portrait formats, so that you are not limiting the end use of the photograph.

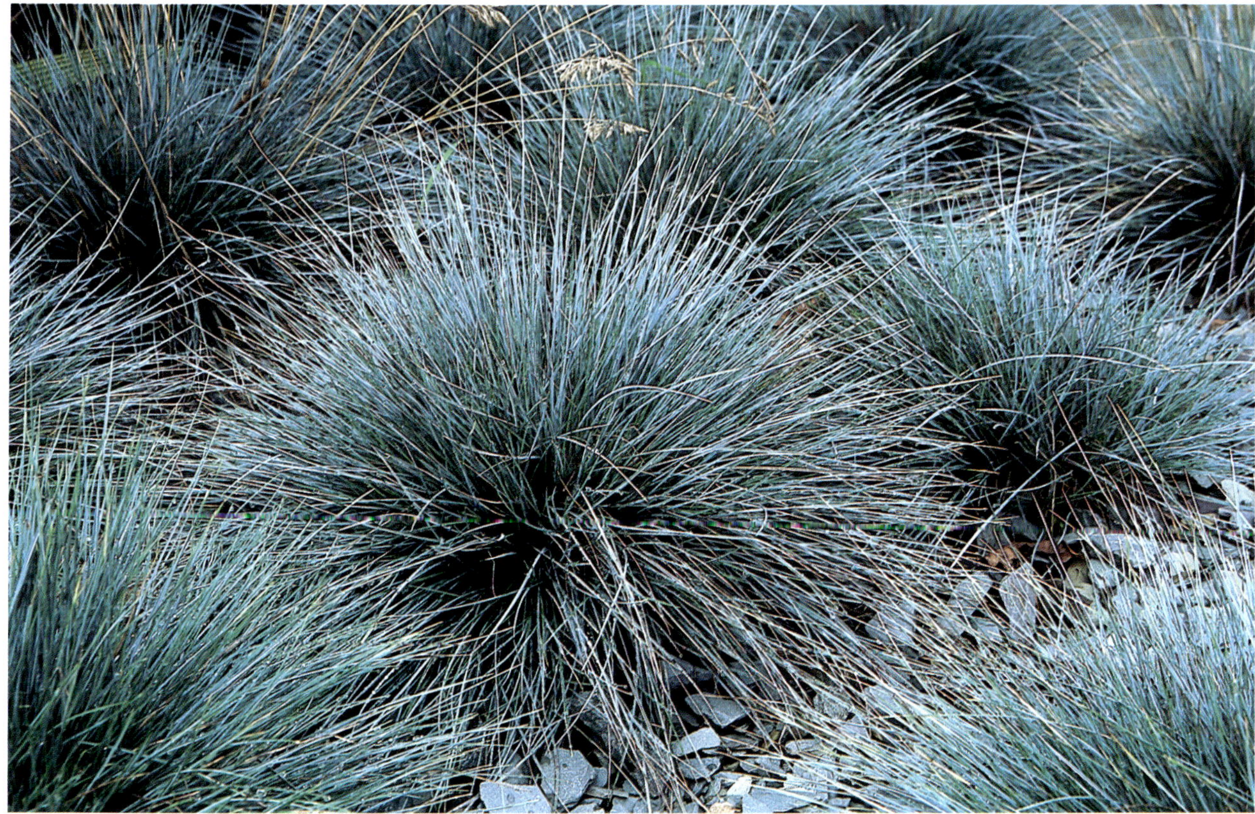

This image has been reproduced several times. Although this shot was easy to take, its selling power lies in the fact that it depicts a popular cultivar of *Festuca glauca* – i.e. 'Elijah Blue'.

**Minolta Dynax 7, 28–135mm lens, tripod. f/16 on Velvia**

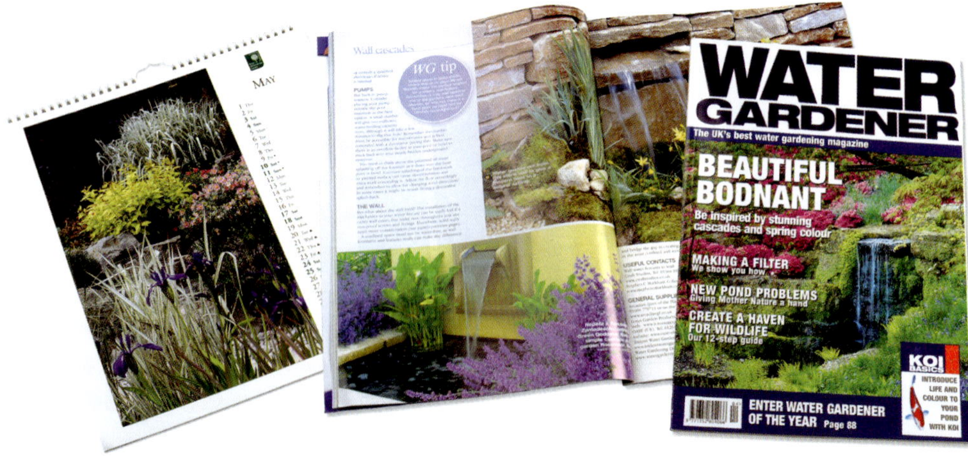


Magazines, books and calendars are just some of the publications that commission good garden photography from freelancers.

## Saleable Photography

Let us assume though that you wish to plunge straight ahead in trying your hand at selling. We will start by considering what makes a saleable picture, although I hope that reading the rest of this book and looking over the photographs will give you a good idea, and most of the requirements are common sense.

### Creating Saleable Photographs

- ✓ Check in the media and watch gardening programmes to find out what is popular in terms of subject matter and style
- ✓ Transparencies can be either 35mm or medium format
- ✗ Prints (i.e. negative film) are generally unacceptable, apart from good quality black-and-white prints
- ✓ Images can be digitally originated if of sufficient file size and quality
- ✓ Images must be correctly exposed, well composed and pin-sharp
- ✓ The subject should be in peak condition
- ✓ Composition should include extra space to allow for text
- ✓ Slight underexposure of a third of a stop is fine, half a stop at most
- ✗ Overexposure is normally unacceptable, unless the mood of the picture demands it

It goes without saying that to be suitable for publication an image must be pin-sharp, well lit and nicely composed. One further point to stress is that the subject of the picture – whether it is a single bloom, a full herbaceous border or masses of roses on a pergola – must be in peak condition or captured perhaps just before its peak, but not afterwards.

A point to bear in mind when composing a picture is that it is often worthwhile taking additional shots with extra space around the subject. This will leave room for different elements, such as a masthead (title text) in the case of a magazine cover, to be added.

## Choosing Film Types

In an ideal world an image should be on roll (or sheet) film, as the larger transparancy contains more visual information and will give higher-quality results when reproduced, especially if a considerable enlargement is required. However, 35mm images are generally acceptable, particularly for close-ups where the entire frame area will be used uncropped. Garden scenes that might be reproduced full-page or on a double-page spread, or in a calendar, are more acceptable on roll film, but 35mm shots of garden scenes are not ruled out. For example, a horizontal (landscape) 35mm transparency of mine has been reproduced in a calendar, having been cropped to a vertical format and then enlarged to A4 size.

## Submitting Your Work

Where to place your work is the next problem to be tackled. Firstly, a study of the market is imperative, and this can be undertaken in various ways. Study copies of magazines to which you feel you would be able to contribute pictures, or, better still, a package of pictures and words in the form of an article. Study the

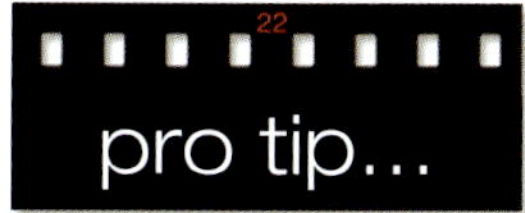


**Giving credit where its due**

In professionally designed gardens you may be asked to credit the landscape designer as well as the location when you sell your photographs. At garden shows and events, you may also be expected to credit the event. Always ask the event's organisers before taking any photos professionally and mark your work clearly if you are planning to submit it for publication.

style of the publication. For example, are the articles predominantly descriptions of gardens or are they step-by-step 'how to' articles? Have they been written 'in house' or does the editor accept freelance contributions? Normally there is an indication at the front of the magazine on the contents page as to whether articles and pictures are welcomed.

Let's assume you have the outline of an article in mind and want to illustrate it with a selection of a dozen rigorously edited transparencies. A sensible first step is to telephone the editor of the magazine you have pinpointed to enquire whether or not he or she is interested. Assuming that interest is shown, draft a covering letter for the article and transparencies, stating in the letter how many transparencies you are enclosing, and send them off with a stamped, addressed envelope for their return in due course. It is essential that this return envelope is adequately stamped. To keep your images secure, send packages by recorded or special delivery where possible.

## Legal Issues

Models If you plan to submit any photographs of people – such as the owners of a private garden forming the subject of your article – for publication, a standard model-release form should be obtained from them beforehand.

Gardens You should also, of course, in the first place have obtained the owners' permission to photograph their garden for the purposes of your article. This is vital, especially if the garden is being photographed 'commercially'. Normally those who own or are in charge of gardens are very accommodating in this respect, but sometimes a charge is made and very occasionally any commercial photography is refused.

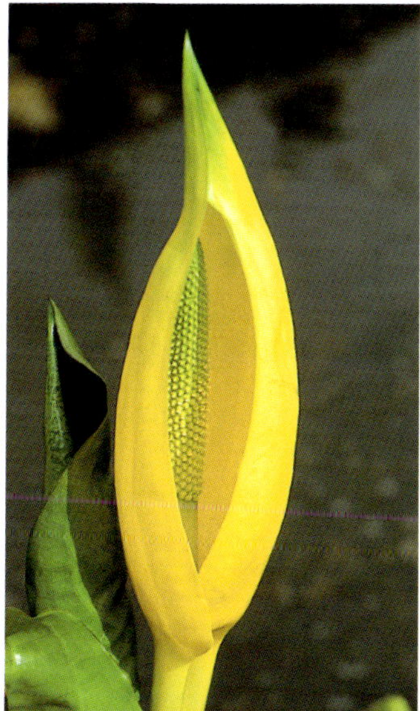

This image featured in two magazines. Water gardening has become very popular and it is worth considering future trends when planning photos.

**Minolta Dynax 700si, 180mm macro lens, 81A filter, tripod. f/6.7 on Velvia**

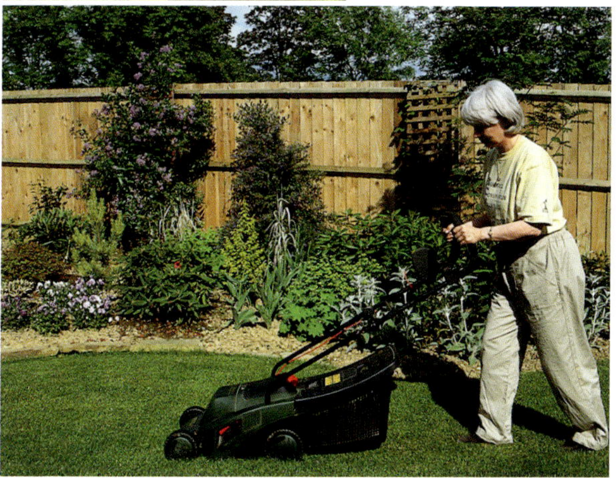

Picture libraries receive frequent requests for activity and 'how to' pictures. These can be either single shots or a series showing the various steps involved in garden tasks. Remember to obtain a model release form before submitting pictures with people in for publication. This image was used in a magazine.

**Minolta Dynax 700si, 35–70mm lens, tripod. f/11 on Velvia**

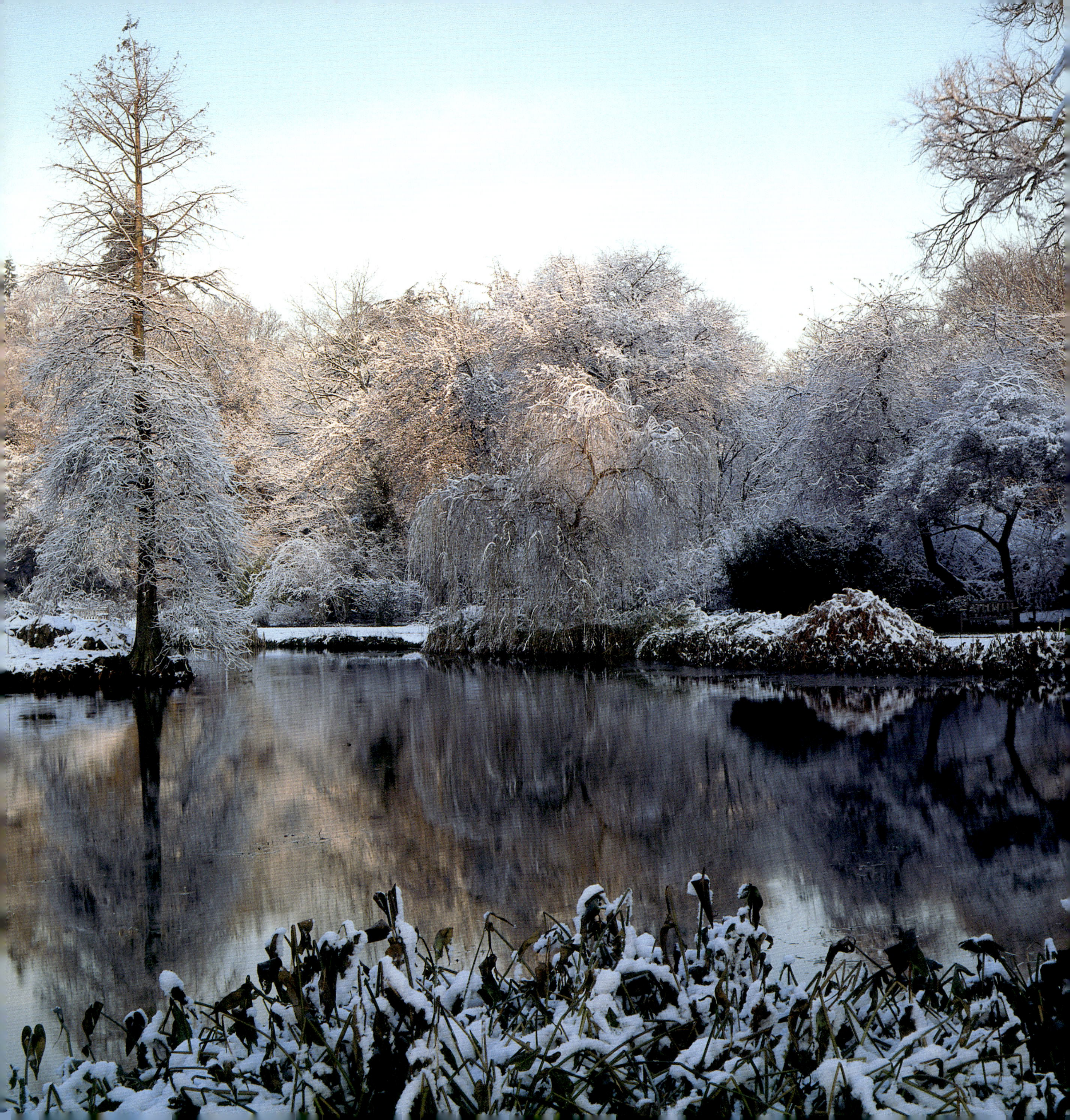

**Tripod usage** When seeking permission to take photographs in a garden, always obtain clearance before using a tripod. A tripod fee is chargeable in some gardens. For instance, in the UK an annual fee is payable to the Royal Horticultural Society for the use of a tripod in their gardens. The fee covers tripod photography in all four gardens for a year from the date of payment.

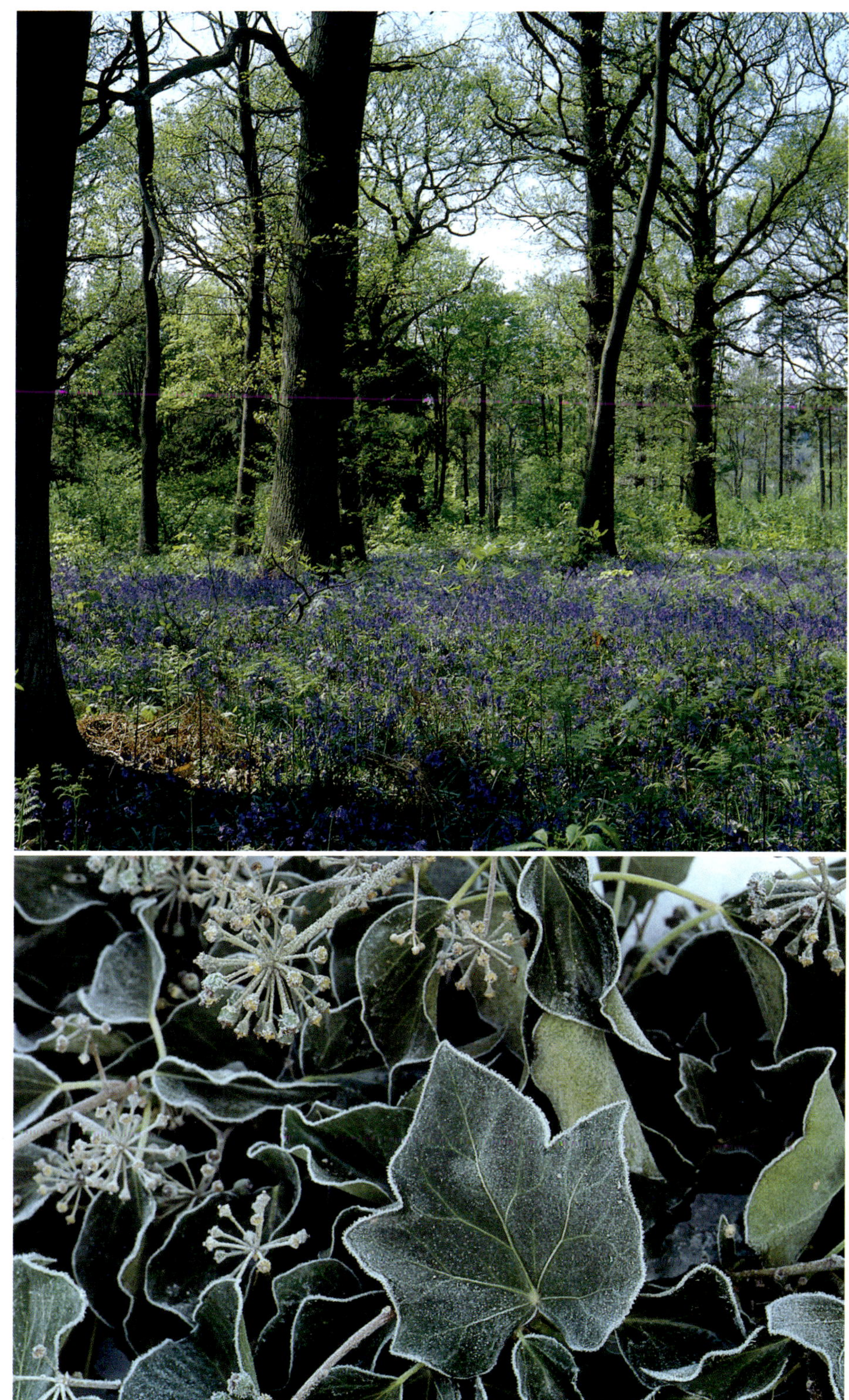

Left: Adverse weather conditions shouldn't discourage garden photography – this scene, lit by the rays of a setting winter sun, has been used in a calendar and as a Christmas card.

**Mamiya C330f, 80mm lens, tripod. f/32 on Ektachrome 64**

Above right: Bluebells with the canopy of the wood coming to life. This may seem a hackneyed subject, but it is irresistible nevertheless and this image was reproduced on the cover of a magazine.

**Mamiya C330f, 80mm lens, tripod. f/32 on Ektachrome 64**

Right: This almost monochrome picture of frost outlining the edges of ivy leaves was used in a calendar.

**Minolta XG-M, 90mm macro lens, tripod. f/32 on Ektachrome 100**

## Technique: **Cataloguing Your Photographs**

Before beginning the process of contributing to photo libraries, it is necessary to organize the documentation backing up your photography properly. In order to clarify how to go about this, I will give a brief outline of my own system.

First and foremost it is essential to jot down complete details of plants photographed at the time the picture is taken. Note the full Latin name because this information could be of crucial importance if the picture is to be published at any time in the future. For example, a shot of one of the black-eyed Susan cultivars would be written in my notebook as *Rudbeckia fulgida* var. *sullivantii* 'Goldsturm', this name being composed of:

| | |
|---|---|
| *Rudbeckia* | the genus |
| *fulgida* | the specific epithet (the species) |
| *sullivantii* | the varietas (variety) |
| 'Goldsturm' | the cultivar (the cultivated variety) |

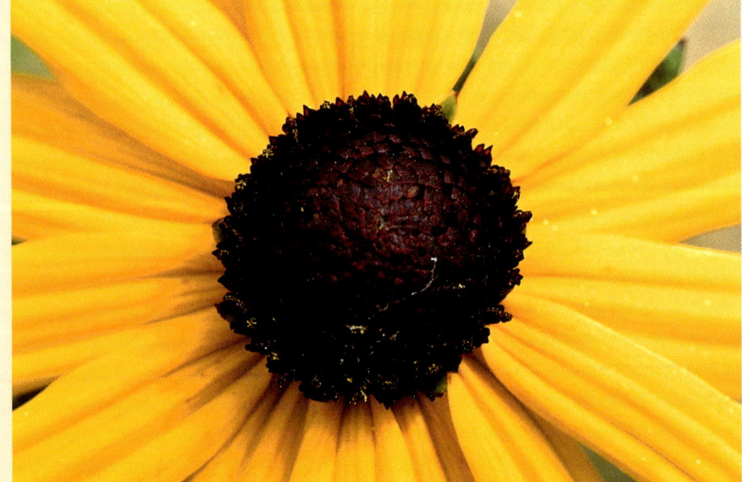

Once the film is back from the processing laboratory, the pictures need to be referenced. I reference 35mm transparencies on the back of the mounts, and medium-format transparencies on a label attached to the back of the plastic sleeves into which I put the transparencies when guillotined. Each picture is examined on a light box and, if up to standard, is labelled. In addition to the identifying information, the location and the month during which the picture was taken are included, together with my name. The picture details are then inputted into a computer register. I should point out that inputting could be undertaken prior to labelling and, using the relevant software, the details then printed onto labels.

Although it might seem that the recording of all this data would be onerous, the input is in fact quickly accomplished, particularly if much on each line of the spreadsheet is identical to the line above it. I do not normally record exposure details, although I have for many of the pictures taken for this book.

Once details have been entered in the register, work on the transparencies is complete and they are filed in pocketed transparent pages prior to being despatched to an image library or direct to picture buyers.

Details of digital files are recorded in a separate register that includes details of format (TIFF or JPEG) and file size. The files themselves are then resized to 300dpi.

Left: *Rudbeckia fulgida* var. *sullivantii* 'Goldsturm'

**Minnolta Dynax 700si, 90mm macro lens, 81A filter, tripod. f/5.6 on Velvia**

As an example, the register details for the picture of *Primula vialii* on page 47 are shown below:

| 1 | 2 | 3 | 4 | 5 | 6 | 7 | 8 | 9 | 10 | 11 | 12 | 13 |
|---|---|---|---|---|---|---|---|---|---|---|---|---|
| DYX | J | 32 | 310502 | *Primula vialii*, Wisley | – | FVP | 90 | T2 | – | 81A | – | P |

1 = My code for my Minolta Dynax 7000I camera

2 = Running alphabetic code for each film to make it easier to pinpoint on the register an individual image at a later date

3 = The frame number of the image on the roll of film

4 = The date photographed

5 = The subject and location

6 = Details (written in later) of recipient of transparency and date of posting

7 = Code for film used, in this instance Velvia

8 = Code for lens used, in this instance Tamron 90mm f/2.8 macro

9 = Code for tripod used, in this instance my lighter Manfrotto

10 = Space for flash details if used – e.g. FIF for fill-in flash

11 = Code for filter used, in this instance an 81A warm-up

12 = Space for reflector/diffuser details if used – e.g. WR for white reflector

13 = Code for whether image was taken in landscape or portrait format

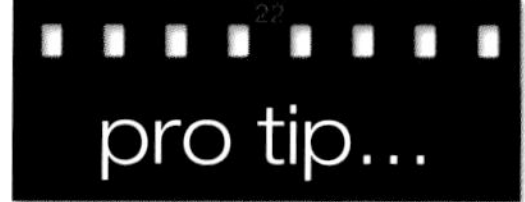


**Picture requests**

The majority of requests to picture libraries are for straightforward images showing specific plants, fruits and so on.

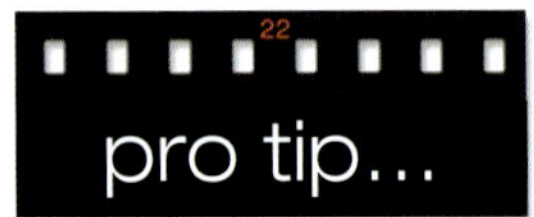


**Contracts**

Find out when your picture library accounts to its contributors for sales. Are payments made promptly at set periods, perhaps quarterly? A contract should set this out. Obviously the draft contract must be studied with care and steps should be taken to change anything with which you are not entirely content.

## Image Libraries

Contributing to a photo library has many advantages, especially if you have neither the time nor the desire to market your pictures yourself, but careful thought should be given to the matter before any decision on the choice of library (or libraries) is made.

Libraries sell reproduction rights, not copyright (this remains with you), and normally deduct a 50% commission on the sales they make on your behalf. This may seem high, but a library concentrates on selling pictures full time; it knows the fiercely competitive market inside out and has many more clients than an individual photographer could hope to aquire. Taking the pictures into the library, indexing and filing them, sending them to clients, dealing with the pictures on their return, chasing up payments for sales and so on is expensive. Taking all of this into account, 50% does not appear excessive.

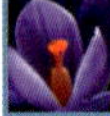

### Submitting Work to a Library

- Libraries differ in their minimum initial submission requirements. Normally this requirement is about 50 to 100 high-quality images, but sometimes it is much higher.

- Once accepted onto their books, contributors are expected to submit a regular supply of images. This could be around 500 images a year, although the library will want to know how many you can realistically send each year. In other words, they will look for a commitment from you.

- By the very nature of things in publishing it can be some time before the library is paid for, say, a picture in a book that takes many months to prepare, print and release. With good images and a dash of good fortune, though, results will come in time.

A library also has to keep up to date with market developments. The major development at present is the switch to selling pictures online. Once the high initial costs have been met, the hope is that cost savings will accrue. For example, handling expenses relating to the assembly and despatch of transparencies, and filing them on their return, should be obviated. However, while many clients may buy an image online, some still require the original transparency (likewise, if the image in question is digitally originated, a CD containing a high-resolution version may have to be dispatched).

**Approaching an image library** Let's say that in the quest for a picture library to take your work, your list of possibles has been whittled down to two specializing in horticultural images. Ideally, at this stage you should go and talk to those you have short-listed. This is important: you can then make a judgement on the sort of operation they run and their future potential. Have they installed up-to-date technology and have they sufficient staff to keep on top of things?

Do not forget you will be entering into a business relationship. You will put in many hours' work obtaining the images you are committing to the library's care and you want to ensure that the library is up to the job of selling your pictures in an efficient and effective manner. Once you have signed up, have patience and don't expect immediate results.

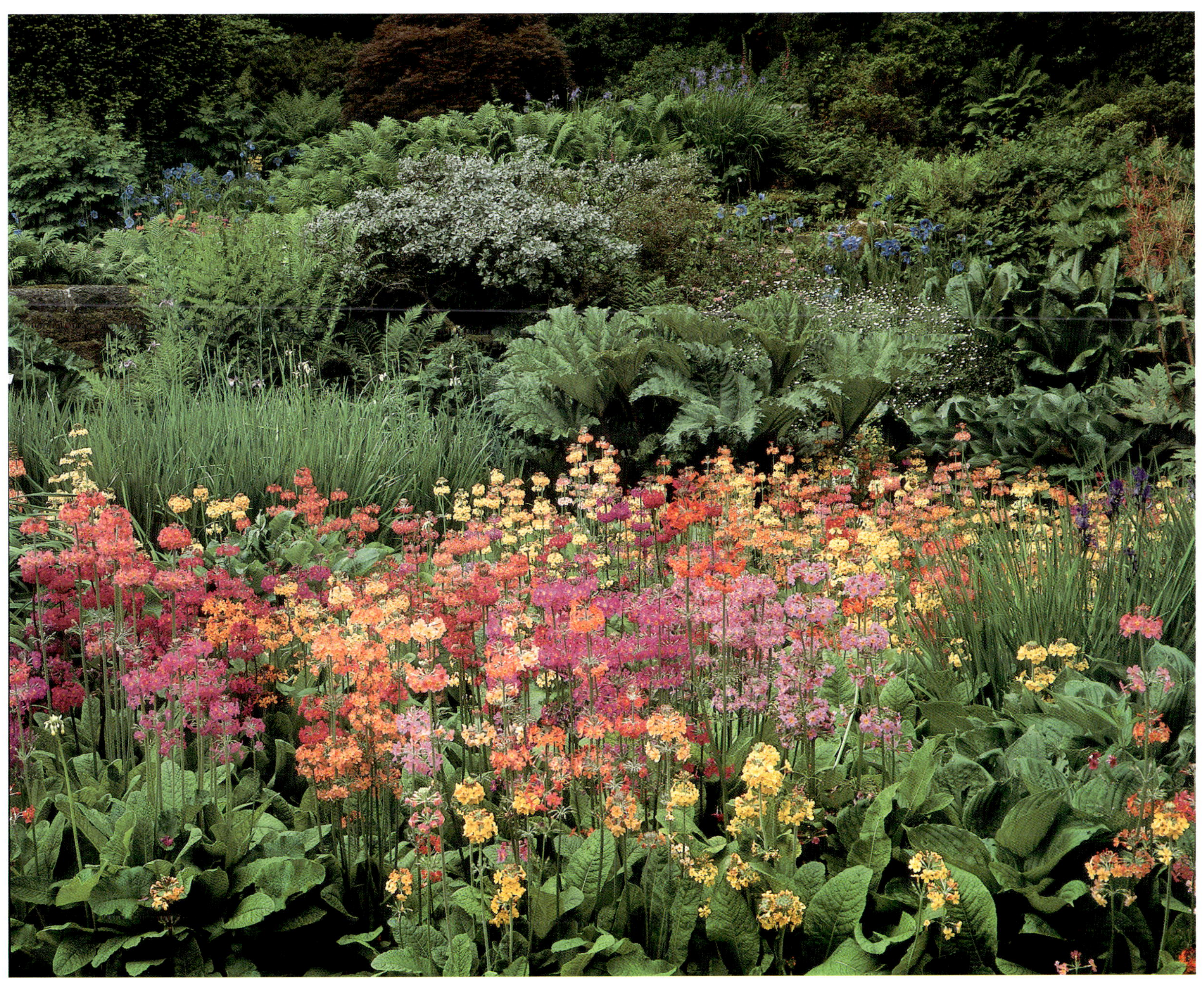

Some of the requirements of a calendar picture are to be seen in this medium format shot taken at RHS Harlow Carr in Yorkshire. It is colourful, razor-sharp and was shot in the low-contrast light that is perfect for garden photography.

**Fuji GW670III, 81B filter, tripod. 1/2sec at f/32 on Velvia**

# Appendix: Locations

**The following is a list of gardens featured in the book. All are open to the public but as many are not open throughout the year opening times should be checked before travelling. Entrance fees are payable for all the gardens listed except Crystal Palace Park in south London and Clyne Gardens near Swansea.**

## United Kingdom

### Cheshire

Tatton Park
Knutsford WA16 6QN
Tel: 01625 534400
www.tattonpark.org.uk tatton@cheshire.gov.uk

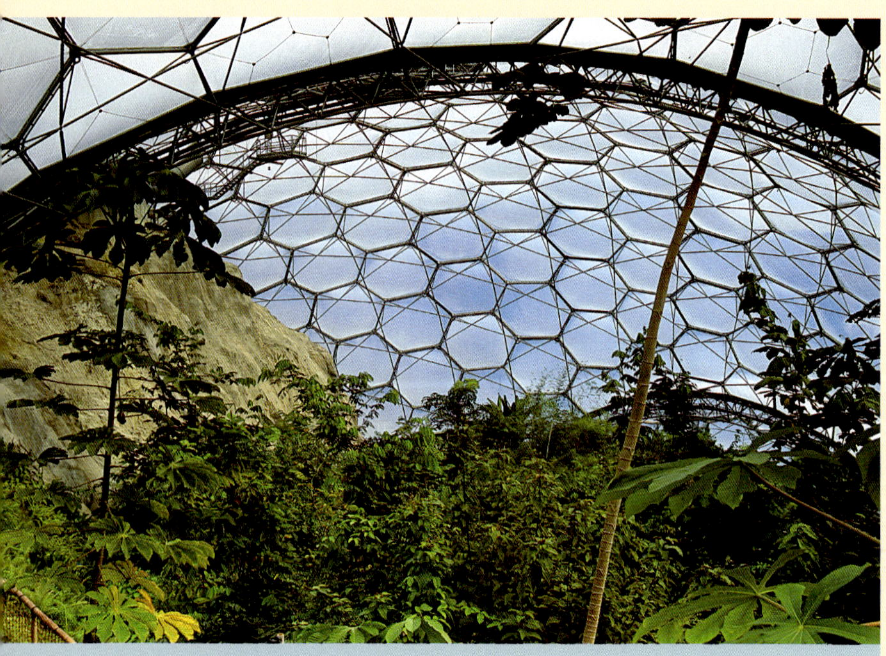

**Eden Project, Cornwall, UK**

### Cornwall

Eden Project
Bodelva,
St Austell PL24 2SG
Tel: 01726 811911
www.edenproject.com

The Lost Gardens of Heligan
Pentewan,
St Austell PL26 6EN
Tel: 01726 845100
www.heligan.com info@heligan.com

Pine Lodge Gardens
Holmbush,
St Austell PL25 3RQ
Tel: 01726 73500
www.pine-lodge.co.uk garden@pine-lodge.com

Trebah
Mawnan Smith,
Falmouth TR11 5JZ
Tel: 01326 250448
www.trebah-garden.co.uk mail@trebah-garden.co.uk

### Cumbria

Levens Hall

Kendal LA8 0PD

Tel: 01539 560321

www.levenshall.co.uk   email@levenshall.fsnet.co.uk

### Devon

RHS Garden Rosemoor

Great Torrington EX38 8PH

Tel: 01805 624067

www.rhs.org.uk

### Dorset

Athelhampton House and Athelhampton Gardens,

Puddletown, Dorchester DT2 7LG

Tel: 01305 848363

www.athelhampton.co.uk   office@athelhampton.co.uk

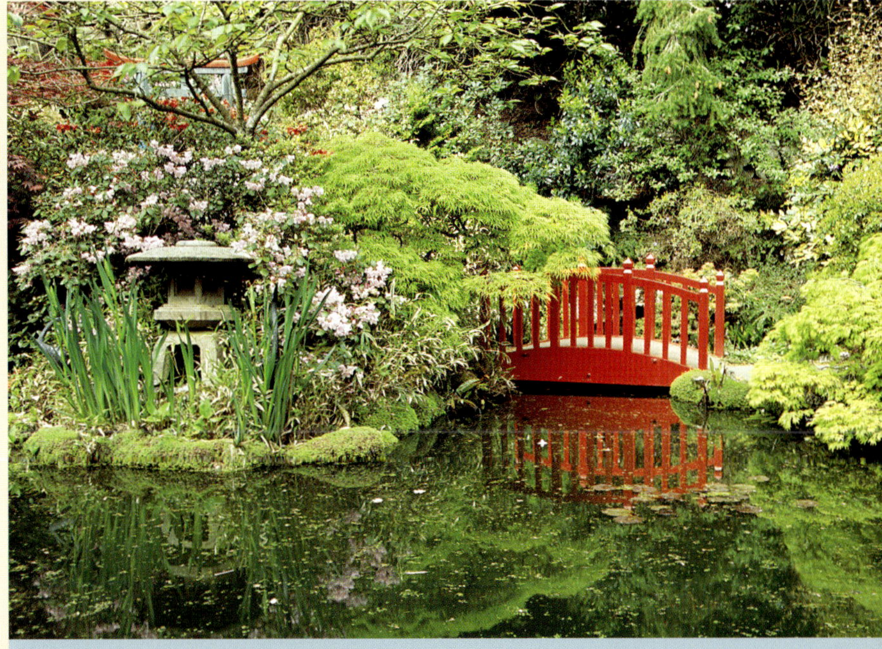

**Compton Acres, Poole, UK**

**Levens Hall, Cumbria, UK**

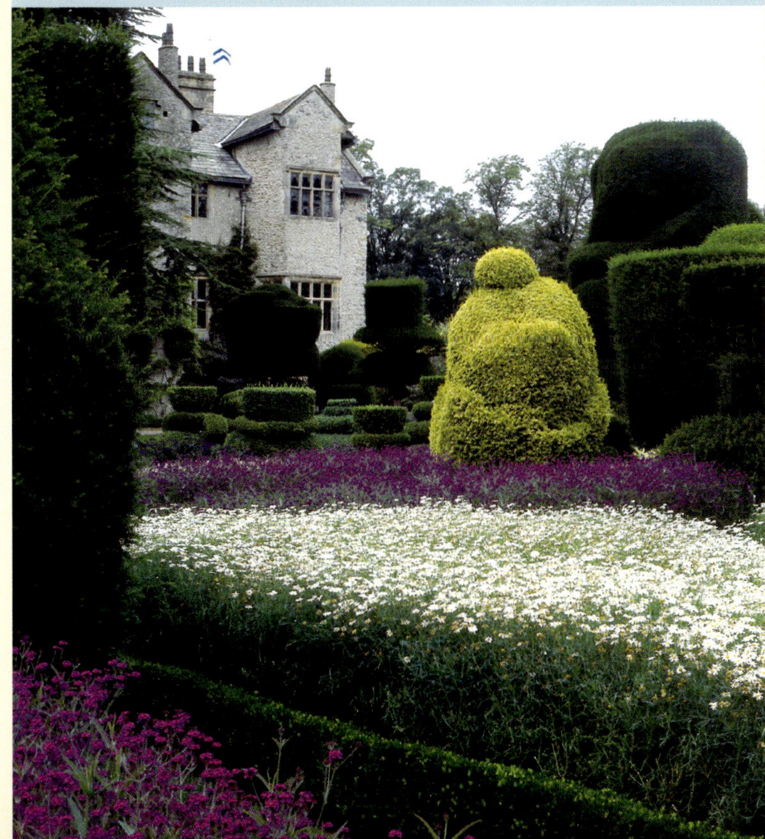

Compton Acres

164 Canford Cliffs Road,

Poole BH13 7ES

Tel: 01202 700778

www.comptonacres.co.uk   sales@comptonacres.co.uk

### Essex

RHS Garden Hyde Hall

Rettendon, Chelmsford CM3 8ET

Tel: 01245 400256

www.rhs.org.uk   hydehall@rhs.org.uk

### Hertfordshire

Benington Lordship

Benington, Stevenage SG2 7BS

Tel: 01438 869668

www.beningtonlordship.co.uk

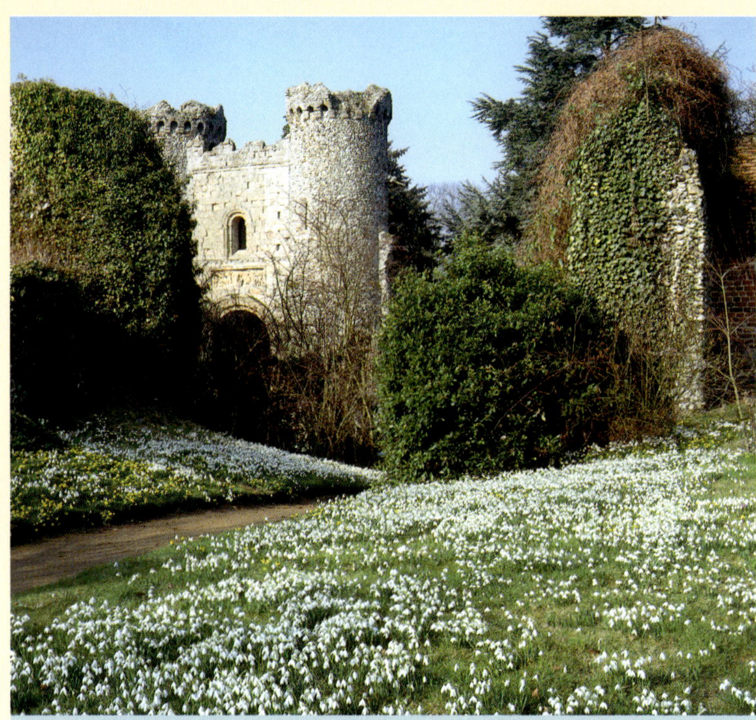

Benington Lordship, Hertfordshire, UK

## London Area

Crystal Palace Park

London Borough of Bromley, South London

Tel: 02087 789496 (info)

The Wetland Centre

Queen Elizabeth's Walk, Barnes,

London SW13 9WT

Tel: 020 8409 4400

www.wetlandcentre.org.uk info@wetlandcentre.org.uk

## Somerset

Hestercombe Gardens

Cheddon Fitzpaine, Taunton TA2 8LG

Tel: 01823 413923

## Kent

Great Comp Garden

Comp Lane, Platt,

Sevenoaks TN15 8QS

Tel: 01732 886154

www.greatcomp.co.uk greatcompgarden@aol.com

Hever Castle

Hever, Edenbridge TN8 7NG

Tel: 01732 865224

www.hevercastle.co.uk

Scotney Castle Garden

Lamberhurst, Tunbridge Wells TN3 8JN

Tel: 01892 891081

www.nationaltrust.org.uk scotneycastle@nationaltrust.org.uk

Crystal Palace Park, London, UK

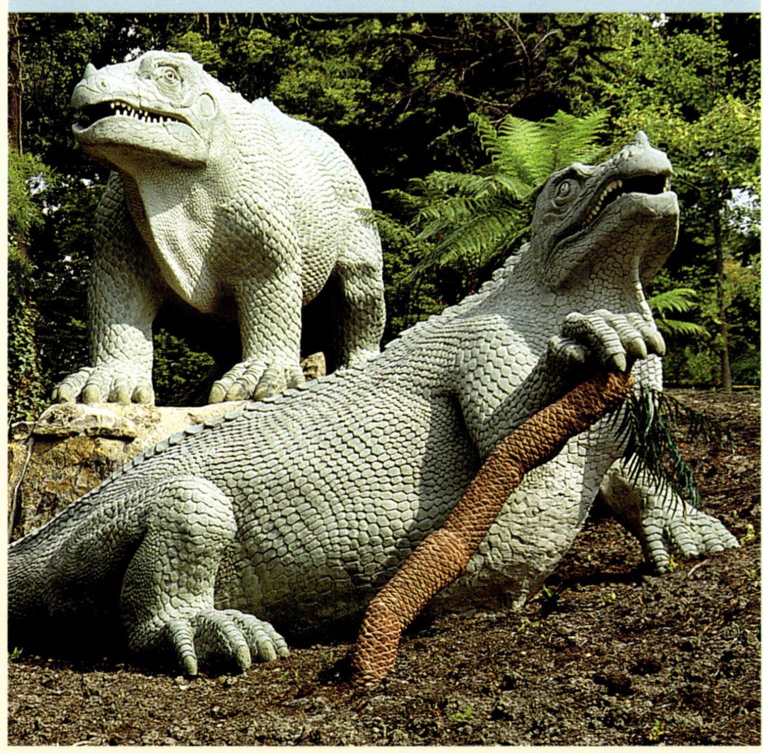

## Surrey

Painshill Landscape Garden
Portsmouth Road, Cobham KT11 1JE
Tel: 01932 868113(info) Tel: 01932 864674 (opening times)
www.brainsys.com/cobham/painshill
enquiries@painshill.fsbusiness.co.uk

RHS Garden Wisley
Wisley, Woking GU23 6QB
Tel: 01483 224234
www.rhs.org.uk

## Sussex, East

Merriments Gardens
Hawkhurst Road, Hurst Green TN19 7RA
Tel: 01580 860666
www.merriments.co.uk info@merriments.co.uk

Sheffield Park Garden
Sheffield Park TN22 3QX
Tel: 01825 790231
www.nationaltrust.org.uk sheffieldpark@nationaltrust.org.uk

## Sussex, West

Nymans
Handcross, Haywards Heath RH17 6EB
Tel: 01444 400321
www.nationaltrust.org.uk nymans@nationaltrust.org.uk

Wakehurst Place
Ardingly, Haywards Heath RH17 6TN
Tel: 01444 894066
www.kew.org wakehurst@kew.org

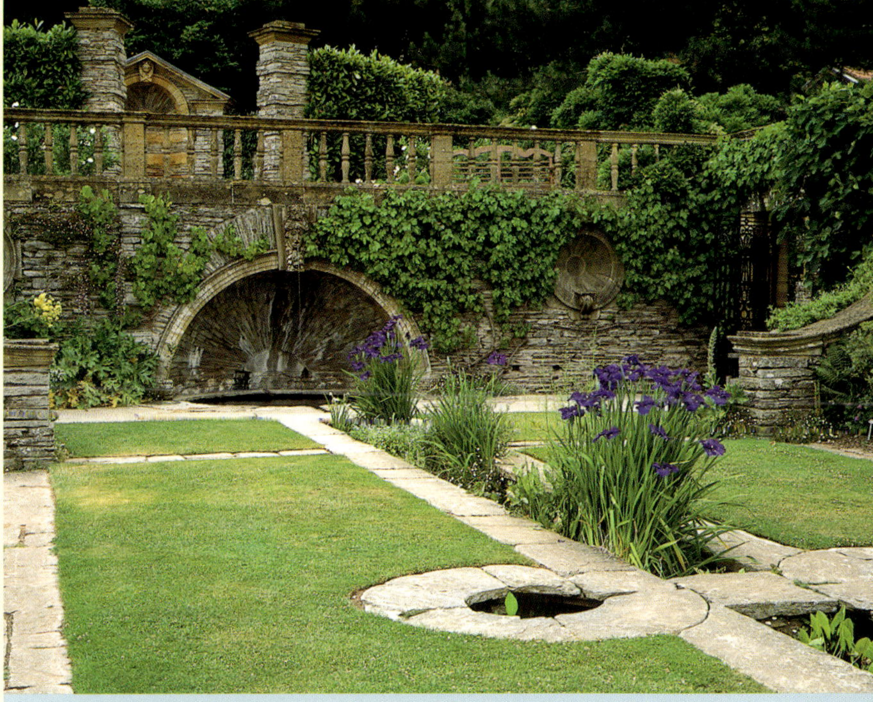

**Hestercombe Gardens, Somerset, UK**

West Dean Gardens
West Dean, Chichester PO18 0QZ
Tel: 01243 818210
www.westdean.org.uk gardens@westdean.org.uk

## Wiltshire

Abbey House Gardens
Malmesbury SN16 9AS
Tel: 01666 822212
www.abbeyhousegardens.co.uk
info@abbeyhousegardens.co.uk

Heale House Garden
Middle Woodford, Salisbury SP4 6NT
Tel: 01722 782504

### North Yorkshire

RHS Garden Harlow Carr
Crag Lane, Harrogate HG3 1QB
Tel: 01423 565418
www.rhs.org.uk  admin-harlowcarr@rhs.org.uk

### Wales

Clyne Gardens
Blackpill, Swansea, West Glamorgan SA3 5AR
Tel: 01792 401737
www.swansea.gov.uk

Bodnant Garden
Tal-y-Cafn, Colwyn Bay,
Conwy LL28 5RE
Tel: 01492 650460
www.nationaltrust.org.uk

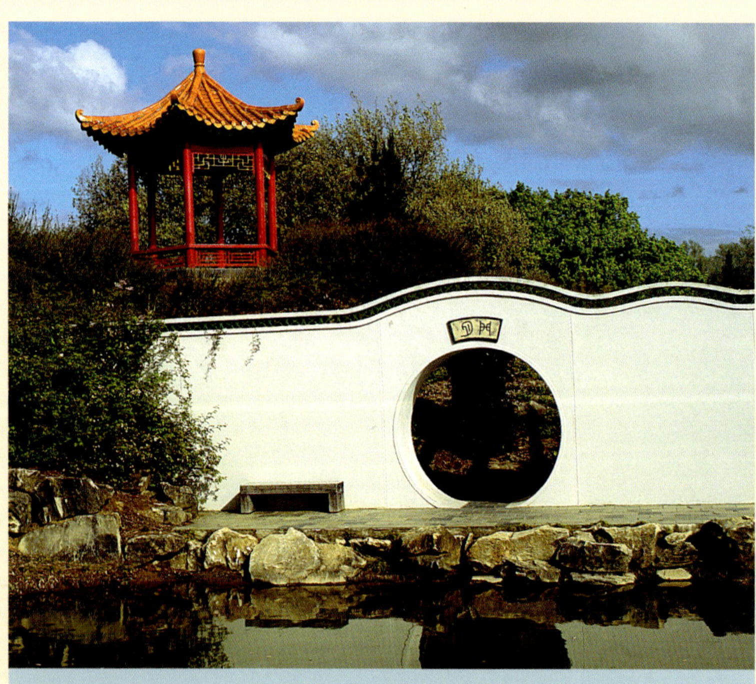

**Hamilton Gardens, New Zealand**

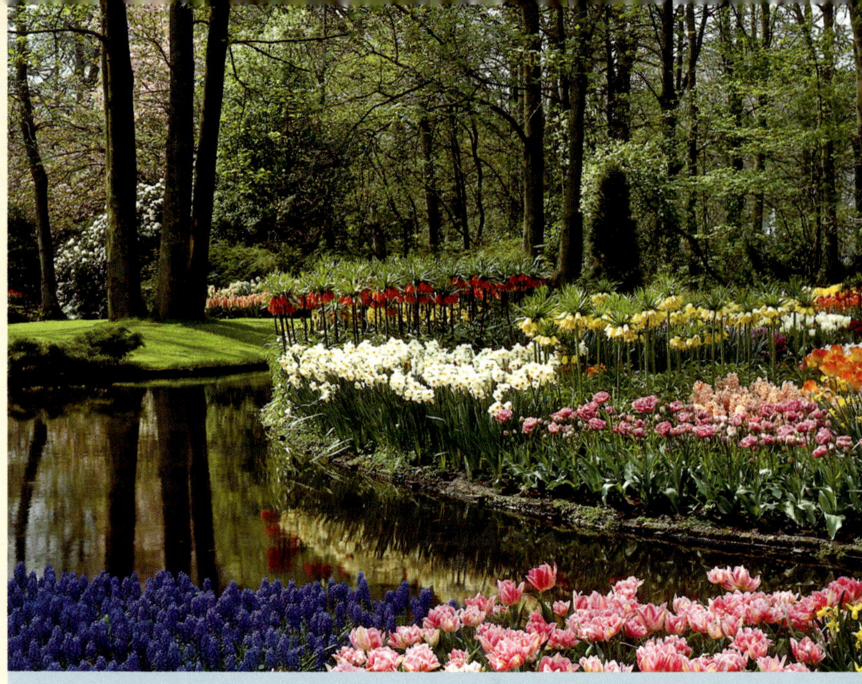

**Keukenhof, Netherlands**

National Botanic Garden of Wales
Llanarthne, Carmarthen,
Carmarthenshire SA32 8HG
Tel: 01558 668768
www.gardenofwales.org.uk  info@gardenofwales.org.uk

### Netherlands

Keukenhof
Stationsweg 166A, Postbus 66,
2160 AB Lisse
www.keukenhof.nl  info@keukenhof.nl

### New Zealand

Hamilton Gardens (Chinese Scholar's Garden)
Hamilton, North Island
Tel: (07) 856 3200
www.hamiltongardens.co.nz  hamilton.gardens@hcc.govt.nz

## United States of America

The Living Desert Zoo and Gardens
47-900 Portola Avenue, Palm Desert,
California 92260
Tel: (760) 346 5694
www.livingdesert.org   information@livingdesert.org

Quail Botanical Gardens
230 Quail Gardens Drive, Encinitas,
California 92024
Tel: (760) 436 3036
www.qbgardens.com   QBGardens@aol.com

Moorten Botanical Garden
1701 South Palm Canyon Drive, Palm Springs,
California 92264
Tel: (760) 327 6555

Joshua Tree National Park
74485 National Park Drive, Twentynine Palms
California 92277
Tel: (760) 367 5500
www.nps.gov/jotr   JOTR_Info@nps.gov

## Canada

Jasper Natioanal Park
Alberta
Canada
www.jaspernationalpark.com

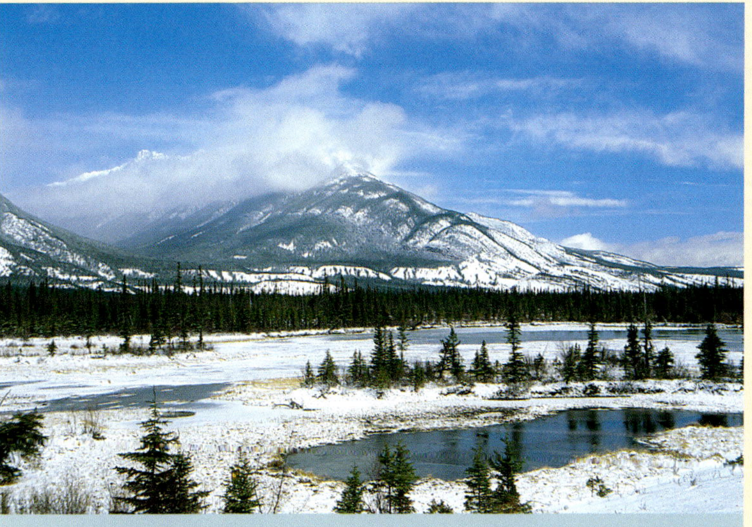

**Jasper National Park, Alberta, Canada**

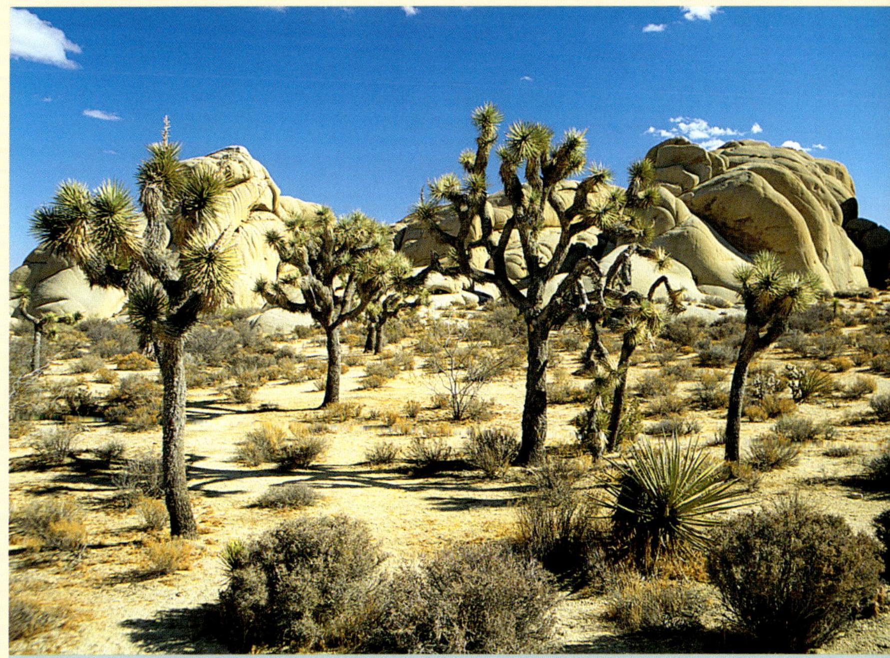

**Joshua Tree National Park, California, USA**

# Glossary

### Ambient light
The light available, whether natural or artificial, to the photographer (not including flash).

### Aperture
A lens's adjustable diaphragm, which controls the amount of light reaching the film emulsion or CCD. The aperture is calibrated in f-numbers known as stops. A low number denotes a large aperture and vice versa. For example, f/22 is a small aperture; f/2 a large one.

### Artificial-light film
Colour film manufactured for use with tungsten light.

### Autoexposure
Camera setting that automatically selects the combination of aperture and shutter speed to be used.

### Autofocus
An electronic system that focuses the lens automatically.

### Ball and socket
A type of head for a tripod, which allows flowing movement in all directions. See also 'Pan and tilt'.

### Bit
A binary digit, the smallest unit of computer data.

### Bracketing
Used in difficult lighting conditions, bracketing involves taking a series of exposures of the same subject from the same camera position. Each exposure is varied by, for example, a third of a stop in the expectation that one will give the optimum result.

### Bus
Electronic pathway for sending data within a computer or between a computer and an external device.

### Byte
Unit of digital data made up of eight bits.

### C-41
Process used to develop colour negative film, and some black-and-white negative films.

### Cable release
Flexible cable that is attached to the camera and allows the shutter to be fired remotely. Cable releases are used to ensure that camera shake is kept to a minimum. See also 'Remote release'.

### Camera shake
Blurring of an image caused by camera movement during exposure.

### CCD
(Charge Coupled Device.) A light-sensitive chip that converts light from the lens into an electrical signal. In-camera processing turns this into a digital image.

### CD-R
Compact disc used for the storage of up to 700MB of digital data.

### Colour cast
A bias towards a particular colour, which appears on transparencies or prints when the picture is taken in light having a colour temperature differing from that for which the film was manufactured. In digital cameras the bias is caused when the camera's white-balance setting does not match the light source.

### Contrast
The range of tones in an image from dark to light.

### Contre jour
A term for photographing into or against the light.

### Cropping
Discarding a portion (or portions) of the edge(s) of an image in order to improve composition or, when being reproduced, to fit to specific dimensions.

### Depth of field
The range of acceptably sharp focus extending in front of and behind the plane of critical focus. Depth of field can be increased by stopping the lens down to a smaller aperture or by increasing camera-to-subject distance.

### Diaphragm
Adjustable lens aperture that controls the amount of light passing through a lens to the film emulsion or CCD.

### Differential focus
Separation of a sharply focused subject from an unfocused background by the selection of a wide aperture.

### dpi
(Dots per inch.) A measure of printer or scanner resolution. The more dots per inch, the higher the quality.

### E6
Process used to develop colour-reversal (transparency) film.

### Emulsion
Layer sensitive to light on photographic film and papers.

### Exposure
Amount of light falling onto the film or the CCD (in a digital camera).

### Exposure compensation
A feature offered by some cameras that allows a specified increase or decrease in the exposure settings indicated by the camera's exposure system.

**f-stop** See 'Stop (f-number)'.

### Fill-in flash
Easily employed with dedicated flash units to lighten shadows in high-contrast conditions. The camera controls the flash intensity so that it is balanced with ambient light levels and black backgrounds are avoided. Can also be used to put a 'catchlight' in the eye, to add a little brightness to a dull close-up scene or to soften shadows cast by another flash unit.

### Filter factor
The increase in exposure required with the filter in use. A factor of two, for example, will require an extra stop of exposure and a factor of four will require an increase of two stops.

### Focal length
The distance between the centre of the lens and the film when the lens is focused on infinity.

### Focal-plane shutter
Shutter type used in SLR cameras.

### Focus
Adjustment of the lens to make the subject of the picture sharp.

### Grazed lighting
Obliquely angled lighting used to emphasize texture.

### Guide number
Denotes the power of a flash gun according to film speed and is used in calculating the aperture required for the flash-to-subject distance.

### Hard disk/hard drive
Computer disc that provides memory to store software and files. External hard drives can be held separately outside the computer linked by a bus.

### Hardware
Physical components of a computer and peripheral devices.

### Hyperfocal distance
The closest distance at which an object will be rendered acceptably sharp when the lens at a given aperture is focused on infinity. When the lens is then focused at that distance, details nearer the camera than the hyperfocal distance will also be rendered sharp, thus ensuring the maximum depth of field.

**Hyperfocal focusing**
See 'Hyperfocal distance'.

**Image manipulation**
Changes to an image carried out by software once the digital image has been transferred on to the computer.

**Incident light reading**
An exposure reading made with a hand-held meter measuring light falling on the subject rather than that reflected from it.

**ISO rating**
(International Standards Organization.) Standard by which film speeds are measured. The most common ratings range between 25 and 3200 ISO; the higher the number, the 'faster' the film.

**JPEG (pronounced 'Jay-peg')**
(Joint Photographic Experts Group.) A file format in which digitized data is compressed to make a smaller file size.

**LCD**
(Liquid Crystal Display.) Flat-screen display on digital cameras used to preview the image or to review the image(s) taken.

**Long focal-length lens**
Lens having a focal length greater than the standard (i.e. 50mm) lens.

**Macro lens**
A lens that is specifically designed to focus at distances close to the subject in order to yield an image of up to life size in the frame.

**Manual override**
The ability to override the automatic exposure and focusing functions of a camera by altering the aperture, the shutter speed and the focusing.

**MB**
(Megabyte.) Approx. one million bytes. The standard unit to measure storage space in computer files and memory.

**Megapixel**
One megapixel equals one million pixels. A measure of image resolution, especially for digital cameras.

**Mirror lock**
A feature on an SLR that enables the mirror to be flipped up out of position before the shutter is fired. This procedure reduces vibration and is useful in close-up work or when using lenses of long focal length.

**Overexposure**
Caused by too much light reaching the film emulsion, resulting in an image that is too pale on a transparency and too dark on a negative.

**Pan and tilt**
Type of tripod head by means of which the camera's position is controlled by separate horizontal, vertical and levelling movements. See also 'Ball and socket'.

**Parallax error**
Caused by the different positions of the lens and the viewfinder on non-SLR cameras. The image shown in the viewfinder is not exactly that recorded by the camera, the discrepancy being most noticeable with close-ups.

**PC socket**
A socket on the camera that accepts a flash sync cable.

**Pixel (PICture ELement)**
The smallest unit in a matrix that makes up a digital image. A pixel is a minute square dot of light of a specific tone and colour. See also 'Megapixel'.

**Prime lens**
A lens of fixed focal length.

**Pulling**
A method of decreasing the speed of a film (ISO rating) by adjusting the development time.

**Pushing**
A method of increasing the speed of a film (ISO rating) by adjusting the development time.

### Remote release
Electronic shutter release employed to minimize camera shake.

### Slow shutter sync
Fill-in flash balanced with the level of ambient light.

### Software
The programs that enable a computer to perform tasks.

### Spot metering
A method of measuring exposure from a very small area of the image.

### Stop (f-number)
Aperture of a lens's diaphragm, which, in combination with the shutter speed, controls the amount of light reaching the film emulsion or CCD.

### Stopping down
Altering the lens aperture to make it smaller. Stopping down has the effect of increasing the depth of field.

### Teleconverter
Normally available in a magnification of 1.4x or 2x, this optical device is fitted between the camera and (normally) a telephoto lens, and has the effect of multiplying the focal length of the lens by the strength of the teleconverter.

### Telephoto lens
A compact, long focal-length lens.

### TIFF
(Tagged Image File Format.) A file format that is the most widely used standard for high-resolution digital images (especially in publishing).

### TLR
(Twin-lens reflex.) Reflex camera with separate lenses for viewing the subject and taking the picture.

### TTL meter
(Through the lens.) Abbreviation for a camera's in-built exposure metering system.

### Underexposure
Caused by insufficient light reaching the film emulsion, resulting in an image that is too dark on a transparency and too pale on a negative.

### Up-rating
Exposing a complete film at a speed above the manufacturer's stated speed and then ensuring that the film is developed at the up-rated speed.

### USB
(Universal Serial Bus.) Links digital cameras and other devices to the computer to allow the transfer of information between them.

### Viewfinder
Optical system used for viewing the subject.

### Vignetting
Darkening at the corners of the frame.

### White balance
Refers to the determination of colour temperature by a digital camera to ensure that white areas in an image do not take on extreme colour casts. On some models white balance can be adjusted by the photographer.

### Wide-angle lens
Short focal-length lens having a wider angle of view than a standard lens, which has an angle of view of just under 50°.

### Windows
Operating system developed by Microsoft for PCs.

### Working distance
Distance between the subject and the camera.

### Zoom lens
A lens that combines a continuously variable range of focal lengths.

# Bibliography

*A Camera in the Garden*
Heather Angel, Quiller Press, London 1984

*Better Picture Guide to Flower and Garden Photography*
Michael Busselle, RotoVision, Crans-Pres-Celigny, Switzerland 1988

*Flower and Garden Photography*
Derek Fell, Silver Pixel Press, New York 2000

*Photographing Plants and Flowers*
Paul Harcourt Davies, Collins & Brown, London 2002

*Photographing Plants & Gardens*
Clive Nichols, David & Charles, Newton Abbot 1994

*Photo Libraries and Agencies*
David Askham, BFP Books, London 2000

*The Freelance Photographer's Market Handbook*
Edited by John Tracy and Stewart Gibson, BFP Books, London

*Writers' and Artists' Yearbook*
A & C Black, London

# About the Author

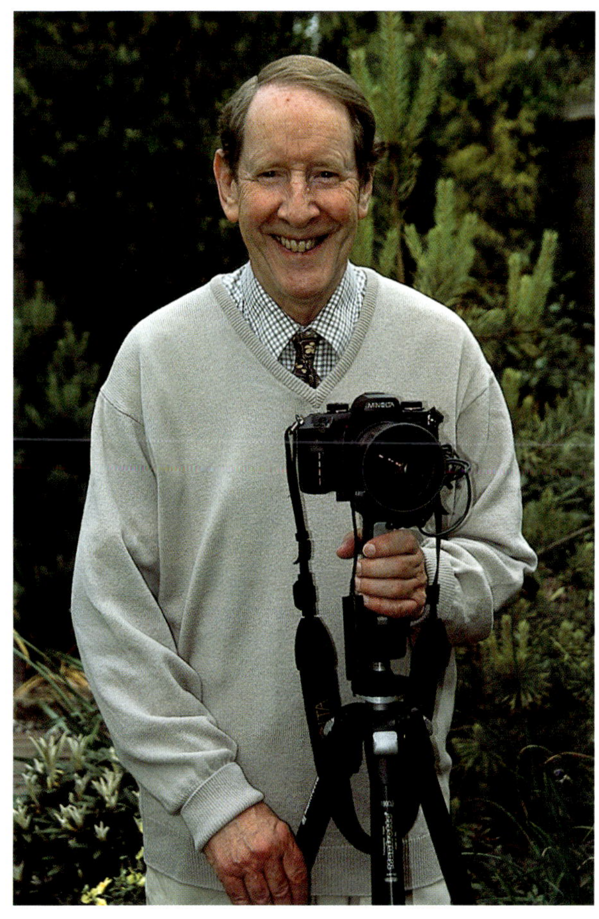


Tony Cooper lives in Surrey, UK. He is married and has two daughters and one granddaughter. A schoolboy interest in photography remained latent until the 1970s, when he purchased a Praktica SLR and started contributing to Aquila Wildlife Images, the natural history photo library. Always interested in gardens and gardening, horticultural subjects started to feature prominently in his photography from the 1980s, after he took early retirement from his career in the Bank of England. He then started sending work to the A–Z Botanical Collection, while the natural-history interest widened into environmental photography, for which the photo library, Ecoscene, became the outlet. In 2001, he started contributing to GardenWorld Images, and this library and the three already mentioned now hold many thousands of his images. Two years ago, Tony decided that it was about time he got to grips with the fast-developing world of digital photography and he now runs digital capture alongside film-based work.

## With thanks...

Sincere thanks are due to my family and many friends who have been of great help on this project. I particularly appreciate their patience when they have accompanied me in the field – an essential attribute, I suspect, for many a photographer's helper. Special thanks are also due to the staff at GardenWorld Images, especially Françoise Davis and Tyrone McGlinchey; always ready to guide one in the right direction, their advice has been particularly valuable in enabling me to tackle the digital revolution effectively. I also wish to put on record my appreciation of the skill and flair with which the team at PIP have put the book together from my manuscript and images; I must specifically mention James Evans and Gilda Pacitti, with whom it has been a pleasure to work. Finally, I am much indebted to all the garden owners and/or managers for their kind permission to photograph so many idyllic creations, and for their unfailing courtesy and enthusiasm for this project.

# Index of Plants

Page numbers in **bold** refer to photographs

# Index

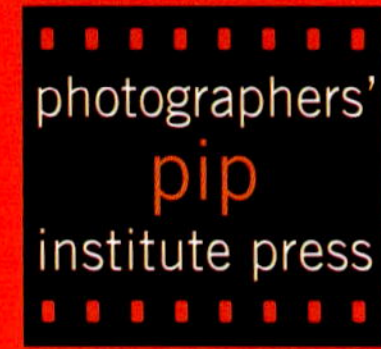


TITLES AVAILABLE FROM

# THE PHOTOGRAPHERS' INSTITUTE PRESS

*The Photographers' Institute Press, PIP, is an exciting name in photography publishing. When you see this name on the spine of a book, you will be sure that the author is an experienced photographer and the content is of the highest standard, both technically and visually. Formed as a mark of quality, the Photographers' Institute Press covers the full range of photographic interests, from expanded camera guides to exposure techniques and landscape.*

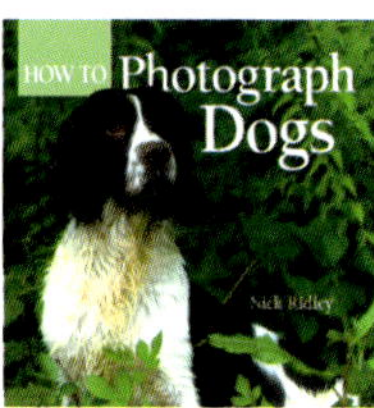


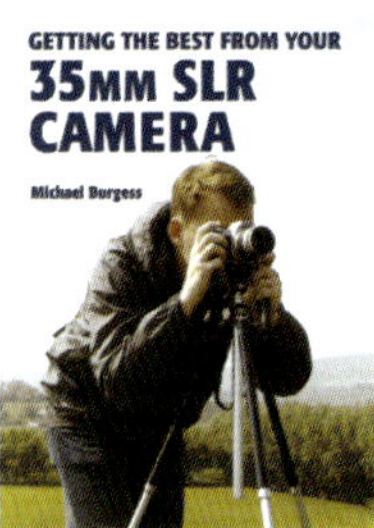


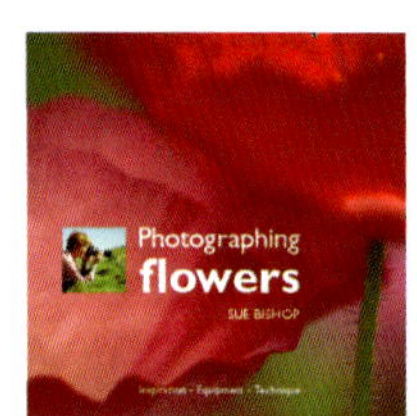


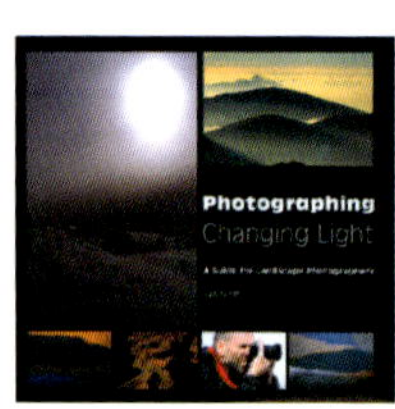


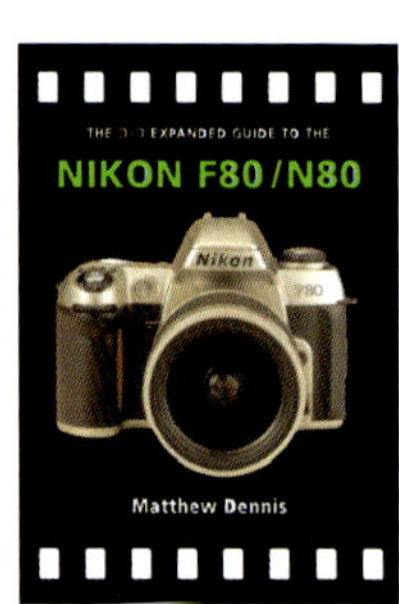


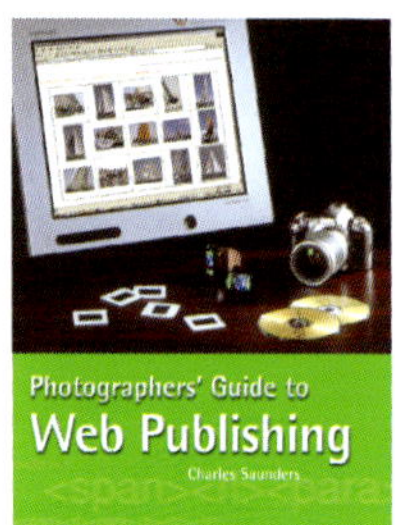


**Animal Photographs: A Practical Guide** Robert Maier
ISBN 1 86108 303 3

**Approaching Photography** Paul Hill
ISBN 1 86108 323 8

**Bird Photography: A Global Site Guide** David Tipling
ISBN 1 86108 302 5

**Digital SLR Masterclass** Andy Rouse
ISBN 1 86108 358 0

**Garden Photography: A Professional Guide** Tony Cooper
ISBN 1 86108 392 0

**Getting the Best from Your 35mm SLR Camera**
Michael Burgess
ISBN 1 86108 347 5

**Photographers' Guide to Web Publishing** Charles Saunders
ISBN 1 86108 352 1

**Photographing Changing Light: A Guide for Landscape Photographers** Ken Scott
ISBN 1 86108 380 7

**Photographing Flowers** Sue Bishop
ISBN 1 86108 366 1

**Photographing People** Roderick Macmillan
ISBN 1 86108 313 0

**Photographing Water in the Landscape** David Tarn
ISBN 1 86108 396 3

**The Photographic Guide to Exposure** Chris Weston
ISBN 1 86108 387 4

**The PIP Expanded Guide to the: Nikon F5** Chris Weston
ISBN 1 86108 382 3

**The PIP Expanded Guide to the: Nikon F80/N80**
Matthew Dennis
ISBN 1 86108 348 3

**The PIP Expanded Guide to the: Canon EOS 300/Rebel 2000** Matthew Dennis
ISBN 1 86108 338 6

The list represents a selection of titles currently published or scheduled to be published.

All are available direct from the Publishers or through bookshops and specialist retailers.

To place an order, or to obtain a complete catalogue, contact:

**Photographers' Institute Press,**
**Castle Place,**
**166 High Street, Lewes,**
**East Sussex BN7 1XU**
**United Kingdom**

**Tel: 01273 488005**
**Fax: 01273 402866**
**E-mail: pubs@thegmcgroup.com**

Orders by credit card are accepted